Mary

# The Oresteia

# AESCHYLUS: ORESTEIA

# AGAMEMNON

Translated with notes by

## HUGH LLOYD-JONES

## UNIVERSITY OF CALIFORNIA PRESS

Berkeley • Los Angeles

University of California Press
Berkeley and Los Angeles, California

© 1979 by Hugh Lloyd-Jones

Original Edition published by Prentice-Hall, 1970
First published in one volume by Duckworth, 1979

First California Paperback Printing 1993

Library of Congress Cataloging-in-Publication Data

Aeschylus.
[Oresteia. English]
Oresteia / Aeschylus ; translated with notes by Hugh Lloyd-Jones
p.   cm.
Includes bibliographical references.
Contents: Agamemnon—Choephoroe—Eumenides.
ISBN 0-520-08328-8 (alk. paper)
1. Orestes (Greek mythology)—Drama.   I. Lloyd-Jones, Hugh.
II. Title.
PA3827.A7L5   1993                                      93-15929
882'.01—dc20                                               CIP

Printed in the United States of America

9   8   7   6   5   4   3   2   1

# CONTENTS

# AESCHYLUS: ORESTEIA

# AGAMEMNON

# INTRODUCTION

The *Agamemnon* is perhaps the greatest of all Greek tragedies, and the most read. An introduction to it should therefore say something about tragedy in general; and since the *Agamemnon* serves as an introduction to the *Oresteia*, the trilogy of which it is the first play, an introduction to the *Agamemnon* must be to some degree an introduction to the *Oresteia* as a whole.

534 B.C. is the traditional date at which the festival of the god Dionysus observed annually in Athens at the end of March came to include a performance which later developed into what we know as tragedy. We are painfully ignorant of the early stages of its development; the earliest complete tragedy that survives is the *Persians* of Aeschylus, produced in 472 B.C., and of the tragedies earlier than that we have only a few small fragments. But fortunately it is less important to know the origins of tragedy than to understand the extant specimens. Tragedy was a solemn performance, enacted in the precinct of the god and forming part of his annual festival. In a certain sense it was a religious ritual; but it was a ritual of a religion very unlike modern Christianity, and since the expression carries Christian associations for most modern readers, its use has led to serious misunderstandings. A tragedy enacted a story from heroic myth; but since the early Greeks recognised no fixed boundaries between myth and history, a comparatively recent event might occasionally be the subject of a tragedy, if like the defeat of the Persian expedition against Greece in 480/79 B.C. it seemed to possess heroic magnitude.

The mythic subject was presented against the background furnished by Greek religion, which is not easy for a modern man to understand. Most moderns tend to assume unconsciously either that since the Greeks

3

had a religion it must have resembled the religion they know or that since Greek religion did not resemble the religion they know the Greeks cannot really have had a religion. The main outlines of their religion may be set out without much difficulty; but the imaginative sympathy which is necessary for proper understanding does not come so easily. An understanding of the nature of Greek religion is the main requirement for an understanding of Greek tragedy.

That religion contrasted the weakness and mortality of men with the power and immortality of the gods, to whom all that was splendid in the world was due. The gods granted men only limited favours; they governed the universe not in men's interest but in their own. The gods differed from one another in character; thus Aphrodite the love-goddess was far apart from the virgin goddesses Artemis and Athena, and though Athena and Ares were both gods of war, Ares with his brutal violence was far apart from Athena, the personification of intelligence. The gods took pleasure in receiving honour from men; they had certain special favourites among them, particularly among those descended from themselves, as the great heroes of myth were thought to have been. A man could hardly honour all gods equally; Hippolytus, who paid great honour to Artemis but none at all to Aphrodite, angered Aphrodite; when Aphrodite decided to destroy him, Artemis could not save him, though she could avenge him.

But the general course of events was determined by one god, Zeus. He maintained the order of the universe. It was Zeus who imparted to kings the principles by which they gave justice to their subjects; clearly it was from human kings that Zeus derived his attributes. Zeus was the protector of suppliants and strangers, and would punish any offence against them; it was socially desirable that those who found themselves in the midst of communities to which they did not belong should be able to claim the protection of the highest god. Zeus had granted to mortals the favour of ensuring that their crimes against each other should not go unpunished. Belief in the justice of Zeus, like belief in that of Jehovah, had to reckon with the observable fact that the wicked often flourish like green bay trees; so it was recognised that Zeus often moved slowly, and that punishment often fell not upon the actual transgressor but upon his descendants. In time the chain of crimes and punishments inevitably became complicated, so that for humans the justice of Zeus was proverbially difficult to understand. To men, said the fifth-century philosopher Heraclitus, some things seem just and some things unjust, but to the gods all things seem just. The justice of Zeus maintained the order of the universe; men were not always in a position to understand its working.

4

# INTRODUCTION

In legend men were not the creation of Zeus, nor of the gods in general; their special protector among the gods was the Titan Prometheus, a minor divinity belonging to the earlier generation that lost power when Zeus took the lordship of the universe from his father Kronos. Men knew that if they had been as powerful as the gods, they would have governed the world in their own interest and not in that of others, so that the Greeks seldom ventured to blame their gods for having accorded them only a modest amount of consideration. They knew that the gods sent them more pain than pleasure; but they were grateful to the gods for the benefits they received from them. Under Zeus they led a harder life than they had under his father Kronos; yet they were grateful to Zeus for ensuring that their crimes against each other would not in the last resort escape punishment. Greece is a poor country, whose inhabitants have to struggle to extract a living from the rough and mountainous land; early Greek religion is correspondingly a hard religion, whose believers were able to endure far more reality than those who have put their faith in oriental cults have usually been disposed to bear.

When the age of innocent belief is passed, a religion of this kind has certain advantages over religions which depend upon supernatural claims made on behalf of historical individuals. From the fifth century before Christ onwards, allegorical interpretation became popular among philosophers and soon spread to wider circles. But even before the prevalence of allegory, scepticism about the truth of stories about the gods was perfectly compatible with the acceptance of what those stories signified; the gods, after all, stood in the last resort for elements in the universe whose reality could not be denied. In Greek legend from Homer's time on the gods work for the most part through human passions; they derive their attributes from qualities observable in the world as we know it. So when a modern producer of a Greek tragedy explains to us, with insufferable condescension, that he has made the action more plausible by eliminating the gods, we have no reason to be grateful. When Wagner's *Ring* was first produced in England, people like this producer took it for granted that a drama about gods, giants, dwarfs and heroes must be tiresomely unrealistic; it was left to Bernard Shaw to point out that Wagner's work had a direct relevance to the central problems of modern industrial society lacking in most of the naturalistic drama of the time. If we are to learn anything from the modern preoccupation with the study of myth, we must cure ourselves of the kind of childishness exemplified by this producer's attitude.

We must also be on our guard against the kind of writer who tries desperately to show that many Greek tragedies were really tracts

5

for the times, designed to advocate particular causes, policies or philosophies. The absence of any tangible evidence has forced such people to assume that the advocacy in question was cryptic; if so, the disguise was so successful that we have to had wait till modern times before it could be penetrated. The tragedians liked to allude to cults and institutions, particularly those of Athens; we shall find a notable instance of such an allusion in the third play of the *Oresteia*, the *Eumenides*. But tragedy was concerned not with the local and ephemeral, but with the permanent and unchanging features of the human situation; that is why it has retained its power to move us. Above all it is concerned with the predicament of men, able to some degree to understand the thoughts and values of the immortals, but themselves restricted by the limitations imposed by their mortality. Great men, thought to be descended from divine ancestors, were held to be dangerously prone to overstep the limits to human action laid down by the gods. This was the religion whose general truths were illustrated by the myths which the tragedians presented.

At each tragic festival, each of three chosen poets produced three tragedies and one example of a lighter kind of entertainment called a satyr-play. A satyr-play dealt with heroic legend, but in semi-comic fashion; it had a chorus consisting of satyrs, the snub-nosed, horse-tailed, drunken and lascivious companions of the god Dionysus. Often, at least in the first half of the fifth century, a poet gave the plays of his tetralogy a continuous theme. The only such tetralogy of which more than one play survives is the *Oresteia*, the story of Agamemnon's son Orestes. We possess its three tragedies, *Agamemnon*, *Choephoroe* (=The Libation-Bearers) and *Eumenides* (= The Kindly Ones); the satyr-play *Proteus*, which dealt with the wanderings of Agamemnon's brother Menelaus on the voyage home after the siege of Troy, is lost. The *Oresteia* was produced in 458 B.C., two years before its author's death at nearly seventy.

The theatre of ancient Athens was most unlike a modern theatre, and the technique of its tragedians was naturally conditioned by its character. The plays were acted in the open air, on the south-eastern slope of the Athenian Acropolis; a great auditorium with ascending rows of seats was cut into the side of the hill, and the actors occupied a raised wooden stage with a building at its back having a large double-leaved door. Broad ramps on either side led up to a wide space between stage and audience which was occupied by the Chorus; this was known as the *orchestra*, a word meaning 'dancing floor' from which the modern term orchestra derives.

Until not long before the *Oresteia*, all the parts in a tragedy had been divided between two male actors; they were now divided between three.

# INTRODUCTION

The actors wore long robes, very unlike everyday clothing, and calf-length boots, and their faces were hidden by masks appropriate to the characters they represented; their solemn manner of delivery and the poetic language which they spoke further emphasised their remoteness from ordinary life. For the most part they spoke in the metres (iambic, or occasionally trochaic) thought appropriate to dialogue; but occasionally an actor might sing lyric verses, as Cassandra does in her first utterances in *Agamemnon*. Sometimes an actor conversed with another, or with the leader of the chorus, in a formal kind of dialogue (stichomythia) in which each of the speakers spoke one (or two) lines at a time, using a brief and pregnant but stiff and archaic mode of speech. Actors often delivered long speeches; many plays contained one or more characters called 'messengers', though 'reporter' would be a more accurate term, whose function was to describe actions not easily represented on the stage. Messengers no doubt used a declamatory style like that adopted by those who have the same office in seventeenth-century French tragedies.

In Aeschylus' time the Chorus probably consisted of twelve members; later the number was increased to fifteen. They represented a group of persons concerned with the action, and were normally present on the stage throughout the play. Their normal medium of utterance was lyric verse; but they (and sometimes an actor) might chant a kind of recitative in anapaestic metre that was thought of as intermediate between lyric verse and the verse of dialogue, and the leader of the Chorus (the Coryphaeus) might briefly speak in dialogue verse. An Aeschylean tragedy normally contains some four long lyric utterances by the Chorus, serving to mark off the different sections of the play; these were accompanied by music and dances which the poet himself composed. As a rule the same metrical and musical pattern was repeated in two successive stanzas; the first was then called the strophe and the second the antistrophe; sometimes, usually at the end of the ode, an isolated stanza (called the epode) might be found. With the music and dances we have lost an integral part of the performances; but the music depended on the pipe, being like modern oriental music but utterly unlike that of a modern polyphonic orchestra, and it was kept in strict subordination to the words. The Chorus might narrate past events relevant to the present situation, try to interpret that situation, or speculate about the future. It usually has in mind the gods, who in the end will decide what is to happen; often it gives expression to religious truths, but since it is hard for men to know the purposes of the gods, the application of these often turns out to be different from what the Chorus itself supposes. The chorus does not enjoy a status or authority superior to those of the actors, nor is it spokesman for the gods, or for the poet himself; everything it says must be interpreted in the light of its dramatic context.

Not only the Chorus but the actors also spoke a language altogether removed from that of everyday life. Aeschylus' diction abounds with words borrowed from epic or lyric poetry, and he himself freely coined high-sounding compound nouns and adjectives. The language of tragedy was powerfully influenced by that of religious ritual; its influence can be seen especially in hymns, prayers and laments, but also even in the spoken portions of early tragedy. Such language will have seemed archaic even to its original hearers, so that it cannot be faithfully rendered without some degree of archaism.

The style of Aeschylus is above all a grand style, designed, like his manner of production, to carry the audience far from the world of ordinary reality. Nouns are regularly adorned with resounding poetic adjectives; metaphors, often of startling boldness, are abundant; lofty periphrases are substituted for the ordinary names of things; descriptive passages are made rich with vivid imagery.

Yet this grandeur is combined with an archaic simplicity. Long, tenuous sentences, consisting of a row of clauses loosely juxtaposed, are common; but the clauses tend to be less closely knit together by subordination than they are in later tragedy. On occasion Aeschylus shows a striking power of brief and concise expression; the strength of his writing is not diminished but is actually increased by an element of archaic roughness, akin to that which so much distressed the 'classicists' when they first saw the pediment sculptures of Zeus' temple at Olympia, works more or less contemporary with the *Oresteia*.

Aeschylean syntax is often jagged and irregular; sometimes a sentence is begun and left hanging; often the construction changes midway through a sentence. These features of his style help to account for the marked preference shown by the ancients after his own time for the later tragic poets. The comparative neglect of Aeschylus continued after the Renaissance, at first chiefly because of the difficulty of understanding his difficult and corrupt text, but later because he displeased a classicistic taste. Only with the start of the Romantic period, coinciding with a marked improvement in the appreciation and understanding of Greek, did he receive just appreciation. But to modern taste the style of Aeschylus may well seem more effective as a vehicle of poetry than that of smoother and more published writers. The strong tendency to antithetical expression inherent in the Greek language gives the discourse unity. But in Aeschylus this never becomes so marked—as it did in later tragedy under the influence of rhetoric—as to make the audience feel that balance and neatness are being carried too far. Like most poets writing in an inflected language (in which case-endings can indicate grammatical relations between words, which an uninflected language must convey by means of a fixed word-order) Aeschylus often varies the order of his words so as to secure effects of emphasis or contrast. To give some notion of these effects, the translator sometimes has to strain the rules of word-order of his own language.

Aeschylus' style varies widely according to the subject-matter, or the character or mood of the speaker or singer. Heroic characters constantly speak high poetry, but high poetry may also be found on the lips of humble persons, like the Watchman or the Herald. Their speech has some distinctive characteristics of its own—the broken, sometimes almost incoherent, syntax of the Herald, the breathless chatter, mentioning even the humblest domestic task, of the Nurse in the *Choephoroe*, the repeated use by Aegisthus of trite proverbial expressions, marking him off from a true hero like Agamemnon.

The effect of ancient Greek metre based on quantity cannot adequately be reproduced in modern languages. Our metres depend on rhyme and on stress accent; ancient Greek metre made no use of rhyme, and depended on not stress accent but on quantity—long or short—belonging to each syllable. Modern verse in ancient metres has to use stress accent in place of quantity, and therefore gives only a very rough notion of the effect of the original.

The spoken portions of Greek tragedies are said by Aristotle to have been composed to begin with in the catalectic trochaic tetrameter, the metre imitated by Tennyson when he wrote:

Dreary gleams athwart the moorland, flying over Locksley Hall.

But before any tragedy now extant had been written, the trochaic tetrameter had been replaced as the normal metre of spoken verse by the iambic trimeter, which may be exemplified by the opening line of *Agamemnon*:

*thĕoūs | mĕn aī | tō tōnd' | ăpāll | ăgēn | pŏnōn.*

Tetrameters were reserved for animated episodes like the debate of the Elders after Agamemnon's murder, or the final stages of the altercation between the Chorus and Aegisthus at the end of the play. The chanted recitative which served as an intermediate between spoken and sung verse is in anapaestic dimeters; e.g., the prelude to the Parodos (1.40) begins:

# INTRODUCTION

*dĕkătōn mĕn ĕtōs | tŏd' ĕpeī Prĭămōū.*

At intervals, especially before a full stop, the last syllable is omitted (e.g. 1.59 *pēmpēi părăbăsĭn Erĭnȳn*). Lyric verse appears in a wide variety of metres, used for the most part in responsion (see above, p. v). Different kinds of metre may be combined to form the pattern of a stanza; and no such pattern is reproduced exactly in any other lyric passage.

The English style most akin to Aeschylus' is that of Elizabethan tragedy; but unfortunately no one translated Aeschylus into English before the last quarter of the eighteenth century. In our own time Louis MacNeice made a fine translation of the *Agamemnon*, notably faithful to the original; Richmond Lattimore and Robert Fagles have rendered the entire *Oresteia* with success. The present version makes no attempt to be poetic, or even literary; it tries to render the sense faithfully and to reproduce the impact made by the idiom of the original more faithfully than a translation with any literary ambitions could afford to do.

This version is not based on any published text of Aeschylus, though the text I have translated has more in common with the Oxford text of Sir Denys Page than any other. The text of all three plays (particularly the *Choephoroe*, which is preserved in a single very corrupt manuscript) rests on a most uncertain basis. Conjectural emendation is often necessary; gaps in the text occur; and many passages are the subject of dispute. The present work is not meant for professional scholars, and in the notes I have confined myself to what seemed essential for the readers for whom it is intended.*

By using such knowledge as we have of how earlier poets had treated the same story, we may hope to throw some light on Aeschylus' aims and methods. Agamemnon, king of Mycenae and leader of the great expedition of the Greeks to recover his brother Menelaus' wife Helen from Troy, where she had been carried off by Paris, is a central character in Homer's *Iliad*. There he appears as a brave fighter and, on the whole, a competent commander; but his pride and arrogance cause him to quarrel disastrously with his principal subordinate, Achilles. In open council he declares that

---

* The reasons for some of my disagreements with the Oxford text are given in my review of that work (*Classical Review*, n.s., 26, 1976, 6–8) and in my collections of notes at *Rheinisches Museum*, 103, 1960, 76–80, at *Harvard Studies in Classical Philology*, 73, 1968, 96–104 and at *Dionysiaca* (*Nine Studies in Greek Poetry by Former Pupils, Presented to Sir Denys Page on his Seventieth Birthday*), 1978, 45–59.

he prefers to his legitimate wife, Helen's sister Clytemnestra, Chryseis, a female prisoner who has been allotted to him as a prize.

In Homer's *Odyssey* the contrast between the fate of Agamemnon, his wife Clytemnestra and their son Orestes and that of Odysseus, his wife Penelope and their son Telemachus is a recurring theme of some importance. On leaving Troy Agamemnon commits his wife to the care of a trusted minstrel. But Agamemnon's cousin and deadly enemy Aegisthus sets out to captivate her; he decoys the minstrel to a desert island and there maroons him, and persuades Clytemnestra to accompany him to his own house. He posts a watchman to look out for the return of Agamemnon; and when Agamemnon does return, a storm drives him ashore near where Aegisthus lives. Aegisthus entertains his cousin to a feast, and there slaughters him 'like an ox at a manger'; Cassandra, daughter of Priam, king of Troy, whom Agamemnon has brought home as a concubine allotted to him out of the spoils of Troy, is killed by Clytemnestra. Zeus has already sent his messenger Hermes to warn Aegisthus of what will happen if he kills Agamemnon; and after seven years Agamemnon's son Orestes returns from exile in Athens and kills Aegisthus. Clytemnestra dies at the same time, we are not told how, and Orestes holds a funeral feast for both of them.

The story of how Agamemnon sacrificed his daughter Iphigenia to still the winds sent by Artemis to detain the Greek fleet off Aulis, on the coast of Boeotia, where it had assembled before sailing across the Aegean Sea to Troy was first told in the post-Homeric epic called the *Cypria*, probably a work of the seventh century B.C. According to this, Artemis was angry with Agamemnon because he had boasted that his skill in archery surpassed even hers, and the prophet Calchas warned him that the winds would not drop and allow his fleet to sail before he had sacrificed his daughter. The story is also told in the *Catalogue of Women*, a poem attributed to Hesiod, but perhaps written as late as the sixth century; in this Artemis at the last minute substituted a deer for Iphigenia, who was then turned into the goddess Hecate.

Another post-Homeric epic called the *Nostoi* (= The Returns of the Heroes) mentioned Orestes' great friend Pylades; since Pylades was the son of Strophius, king of Phocis, this seems to indicate that in that poem Orestes spent his exile not at Athens, as in the *Odyssey*, but in Phocis, near to Delphi and its famous oracle of Apollo. Aeschylus may have been influenced in important ways by the *Oresteia* of the sixth-century Sicilian poet Stesichorus, who wrote long poems in dactylic metres which although they counted as lyric verse resembled the epic in being recited to the accompaniment of the lyre. Unfortunately only a few fragments of this poem survive; it seems to have had a great influence upon the representations of the subject in Athenian painted pottery.

The death of Agamemnon supplied a particularly poignant subject for a tragedy. The greatest king of the heroic age, the successful commander in the greatest war of legend, seemed at the moment of his triumph to have attained the very peak of human felicity. Yet at that very moment, after having eluded all the dangers of the war and of the hazardous journey back that followed, he was struck down by a domestic conspiracy. Instead of having Clytemnestra move to the house of Aegisthus, Aeschylus allows her to remain at home. Stesichorus and Aeschylus' older contemporary, the Theban lyric poet Pindar, had transferred Agamemnon's capital from Mycenae to a city in Laconia, perhaps to please the Spartans, now the most powerful people of the Peloponnese; Aeschylus located it at Argos, the chief rival of Sparta in her own neighbourhood and an ally of Athens at the time in question. He reduced Aegisthus to the rank of a subordinate, and made Clytemnestra kill not only Cassandra, but Agamemnon himself, heightening the pathos by having the murder take place during the ritual bath, given to a man by his own wife or daughter, which traditionally marked the moment when after a long absence he resumed the enjoyment of his home and his possessions. Such a death was well designed to illustrate a central truth of Greek religion that was stressed over and over again by the tragedians, the infinite fragility of all human happiness, even that which seemed the most securely founded.

But the justice of Zeus had to be shown to be at work; and since the murder of Agamemnon was finally avenged, the theme of justice at work in successive generations lay ready to the poet's hand. First, how could Zeus have allowed the murder of Agamemnon to happen? Even before Aeschylus, revenge for Iphigenia had probably been thought to have been one of Clytemnestra's motives, though it was inextricably intertwined, as in Aeschylus, with guilty passion for Aegisthus. But could the sacrifice of Iphigenia alone account for Agamemnon's guilt? If he had refused to kill her, the great expedition against Troy could not have started, and clearly it was the will of Zeus that Paris and the Trojans should be punished for their offence against the laws of hospitality. Why, then, should Agamemnon have been confronted with the awful dilemma of having to choose between killing his daughter and giving up the expedition? We have seen that in the *Cypria* Artemis sent the winds to punish Agamemnon for an idle boast; Aeschylus says nothing of her motive, obviously because it does not seem to him important. What mattered to him was the question of why Zeus allowed him to be faced with his dilemma.

# INTRODUCTION

Legend supplied more than one point at which a poet might begin the history of the guilt that weighed upon the house of Agamemnon. He might start with a remote ancestor, the great Phrygian ruler Tantalus. Or he might start with Tantalus' son Pelops, who came from Asia to kill the tyrant Oenomaus, marry his daughter and occupy his throne; to him also a sinister legend was attached. Aeschylus chose to begin the chain of crimes and punishments with the brothers Atreus and Thyestes, either sons or grandsons of Pelops; Atreus was the father of Agamemnon. There are different versions of the quarrel between the brothers, some of which mention a dispute over the throne. Aeschylus says nothing of this, but mentions the seduction by Thyestes of his brother's wife. Atreus pretended to forgive him and entertained him to a feast; after he had eaten, he told him that he had been eating the flesh of his own children. That story is of capital importance in the *Oresteia;* for apart from supplying Thyestes' son Aegisthus with a motive for revenge upon his family, it constitutes the dark secret in the past history of the royal family which in the *Agamemnon* is many times hinted at but never revealed till it is exposed with devastating impact by the captive prophetess Cassandra.

In the *Oresteia* of Stesichorus, Orestes killed Clytemnestra and Aegisthus, and was pursued by the Erinyes for his murder of his mother (see the introduction to the *Choephoroe*): to keep them off, Apollo gave him a bow. Apollo and the Delphic oracle play an important part in Aeschylus, for Orestes consults Apollo as to how he shall avenge his father, and Apollo promises and gives advice and help. Orestes spends his exile in Phocis, near Delphi, as already in the *Nostoi*, and on the only occasion on which his friend Pylades, son of the king of Phocis, speaks (see *Cho.* 900ff.) it is to insist that Apollo's command must be obeyed. By making Clytemnestra personally kill Agamemnon, Aeschylus makes Orestes seem more sympathetic than he would have been if Aegisthus had been his father's killer, as he is in Homer. Athens, the scene of Orestes' exile in the *Odyssey*, in Aeschylus becomes the place where he takes refuge from the pursuing Erinyes. Before Aeschylus, poets had given their accounts of the foundation of the court of Areopagus. He seems to have been the first to claim that it was founded by Athena in order to judge the issue between Orestes and the Erinyes; and this story enables him to relate his theme of the working of divine justice to the fate and future prospects of his own city (see the introduction and appendix to the *Eumenides*).

The play begins with the actual moment of the fall of Troy. Agamemnon has arranged to have piles of brushwood heaped upon the summits of a series of mountains in places lying between Troy and Argos; once Troy

13

has fallen, the first such pile, upon Mount Ida behind Troy, is to be ignited, and then the others in succession until the news reaches Argos. Upon the roof of his own palace waits a watchman, not, as in the *Odyssey*, a creature of Aegisthus, but a loyal servant of Agamemnon, for ten years he has watched nightly for the beacon in the sky. It is he who speaks the prologue of the play; and while he is speaking it he sees the beacon. So we learn rapidly that this is the palace of the sons of Atreus; that the Trojan war is in its tenth year; that the watchman's task is set him by a woman with the will of a man; and that all is not well inside the house. When the watchman sees the beacon, he rejoices, looking forward to a reunion with his master that will not take place.

The Chorus consists of leading citizens of Argos, who form a council to assist the queen in government during the king's absence. They are men of advanced age, for they were too old to accompany the army when it left ten years earlier, and the stress laid on their infirmity prepares the audience for their inaction later. In the prologue to the Parodos, the first great choral ode, they tell of the launching of the expedition to inflict just punishment upon the Trojans for their offence against the laws of Zeus, and express their complete confidence in its final triumph. Then in the Parodos itself they sing of how the fleet was mustered ten years before at Aulis, and how a portent revealed to the prophet of the army that it was destined to triumph, but at grievous cost. Interpreting the portent in his riddling language, the prophet explained that Artemis was angry and might cause the fleet to be delayed, with far-reaching consequences.

At the moment when the Chorus sings of those events, ten years later, those consequences are still far from being exhausted; and so the elders think of the only power great enough to grant relief in such a situation, and celebrate the might of Zeus. Zeus has accorded to men a 'grace that comes by violence'; men, if they are wise, will show themselves aware that in the end Zeus is bound to punish crime. From here the Chorus goes straight on to tell of Agamemnon's struggle with his fearful dilemma, of his reluctant decision to sacrifice his daughter, and of the sacrifice itself.

The elders have assembled to inquire the reason for the sacrifice which Clytemnestra has ordered to be made after hearing the Watchman's announcement; and now Clytemnestra emerges from the palace to answer their inquiry. When she declares that Troy has fallen, they are reluctant to believe her; it is evident that their politeness masks distrust, based partly on a conviction of the unreliability of the female sex. The theme of antagonism between male and female is one of the motives that run through the *Oresteia;* although the early Greeks firmly maintained the supremacy of the male, their civilisation seems to have been the first in which doubts about the subjection of women found expression, and their poetry contains many instances of this. Clytemnestra explains ·how the beacons have conveyed the news from Troy to Argos, speaking as though the messenger had been a single fire that had travelled through the sky from Mount Ida till it swooped down upon the palace of the sons of Atreus. When she calls this 'a fire lineally descended from the fire of Ida', we see that in her mind it is a fire of vengeance, which has consumed Troy and will now fall upon its conqueror. Next she paints an imaginative picture of the scene inside the captured city; when she prays that the conquerors may respect the shrines of the city's gods, so that they may not be conquered in their turn, the audience senses that her pretended fears are her real hopes. Though she has offered no proof beyond the Watchman's word, the Chorus become infected by her moods and agree that Troy has fallen. In the prelude to the First Stasimon, the second great choral ode of the play, they give thanks for the victory to Zeus.

The Chorus declares that the punishment of the Trojans is an obvious instance of the working of Zeus' justice, and a signal refutation of those impious persons who believe that the gods take no thought of the crimes of men. It was provoked by the act of Paris in abducting Helen; and they go on to describe her fateful journey, and the desolation of the deserted Menelaus. The sorrow in the palace of the princes finds its counterpart in the sorrow in many houses throughout Greece, where in place of the men who have departed to the war urns carrying their ashes have come back. They speak of murmurs in the city against the sons of Atreus, who have sacrificed men's lives to recover Helen; the gods are resentful against those who have caused many deaths, and great triumphs may lead to great reverses. Finally the elders declare that they would not wish to have applied to them a term used in Homer and later to denote the chief|glory of Odysseus and others, the term 'sacker of cities'. What began as an ode of thanksgiving for victory has ended in anxious apprehension. So distressed are the elders that they revoke the assent which they have earlier given to Clytemnestra's claim that Troy has fallen and revert to their earlier scepticism, reinforcing it with a fresh expression of their low regard for women.

With no indication of a lapse of time, we are warned of the approach of the Herald whom Agamemnon after landing has sent ahead to announce his imminent arrival. In performance the thought that the king's landing would not have followed immediately upon the sighting of the beacon will not disturb the audience; the conventions of Greek tragedy allowed the poet full license in such matters. Like the Watchman, the Herald is a

loyal retainer of the king; he expresses the feelings natural in such circumstances, profound relief at the conclusion of the war and great satisfaction
at the punishment inflicted on the conquered enemy. The leader of the
Chorus salutes him, laying significant emphasis on his own relief at the
army's return. He means to convey a veiled warning that all is not well at
home; but the Herald finds his gladness at the event entirely natural and
embarks on a vivid description of the horrors of the campaign true to life in
laying more stress on the discomforts than on the dangers of the soldier's
lot.

At this point Clytemnestra enters the conversation. She has no need,
she says, to give thanks for victory, for she has already done so at a time
when the elders were unwilling to believe her news; as for the story of all
that has happened, she will hear it from the king's own lips when he
returns. She gives the Herald an effusive message of welcome for the king
that is charged with sinister ambiguity. Now the Chorus question the
Herald about the whereabouts of the king's brother, Menelaus. So far his
pathetic eagerness to preserve his status as the bearer of good news has led
him to avoid this subject; but now he is forced to admit that Menelaus is
missing, and to describe the terrible storm which has fallen upon the
returning fleet, separating the brothers. This together with the dangerous
complacency with which the Herald has spoken of the fate of Troy will lead
an audience familiar with tragedy to realise that Clytemnestra's pretended
fear but real hope that the Greeks may offend the gods by their conduct
in the moment of victory has been fulfilled. According to the traditional
story the Greeks by their behaviour during the sack of Troy, particularly
the slaughter of the aged Priam and the rape of the prophetess Cassandra in
the temple of Athena, so offended Athena, their most powerful helper among
the gods, that she joined forces with their enemy Poseidon to cause a great
storm to strike them on the way home. The absence of Menelaus is important in the play, for it makes it easier for Clytemnestra to carry out her plan;
his adventures in Egypt and elsewhere were depicted in the satyr-play that
accompanied the trilogy, the lost *Proteus*.

The news that Menelaus is missing reminds the Chorus of the unfaith-
ful wife who has been the cause of all his troubles; although she is not a
character in the play, Helen is presented in the *Agamemnon* in a way scarcely
excelled even by her depiction in the *Iliad*. Playing on her name, the Chorus
at the beginning of the Second Stasimon find her to have been fated from the
first to bring destruction. He who welcomes such a woman to his house is
like a man who takes in a lion-cub, at first a delightful pet for young and old
alike, but finally revealing its true nature by a bloody massacre of cattle.

16

# INTRODUCTION

With Helen there came at first a feeling of miraculous tranquillity as the love-god took possession of men's minds; later her marriage was brought to a grim conclusion by the deity that punishes crime, the Erinys. Helen is conceived as a being specially sent into the world by Zeus as an instrument of his destructive power; later in the play it will become clear that Helen's sister Clytemnestra is destined to fulfil the same punitive purpose.

From the thought of Helen as an instrument of divine punishment the Chorus pass to reflections on the working of divine justice. They reject the ancient superstition that the gods are jealous of human happiness, and therefore eager to destroy it; they insist that when disaster comes upon men, it comes as the punishment of crime. Justice shines out beneath the smoky rafters of humble dwellings, but leaves the palaces of the great but guilty; and it is she who guides all things to their appointed end. On that sombre note the Chorus ends the ode, immediately before the entry of Agamemnon.

The king enters in his chariot, accompanied by his retinue; with him is his prisoner Cassandra, who at first remains silent and immobile. In their speech of welcome the Elders admit that in the past they have been among his critics; but now that the war has been satisfactorily concluded, they are sincere in their rejoicing; others, they seem to imply, are less so.

Agamemnon in his answer shows his satisfaction at the ruthless extirpation of his Trojan enemies in a way that must remind the audience of the saying of the Chorus that 'the gods are not unmindful of the killers of many'. Taking the Elders' words of warning as an allusion to the quarrels between the Greek chiefs during the wars, he quite mistakes its drift; he promises, indeed, to hold an inquiry into the conduct of those who have remained at home, but cannot guess how little time he has. Now Clytemnestra appears, and greets him with an effusiveness that seems at times to teeter on the borders of hysteria. She urges him to make a triumphal entry into the palace, walking over tapestries meant for consecration to the gods, tapestries of a fabric so delicate that if once trodden on they will be unfit for any further use.

At first Agamemnon rejects her suggestion with an almost brutal firmness. Eulogy should come from outside a man's own family; and by laying the tapestries in his path his wife may bring the power of envy into action against him. Such honours are suitable only to a god; a man can be pronounced fortunate only after he is safely dead. Then by a series of penetrating questions Clytemnestra overcomes his resistance and forces him to do her will. At first he reacts correctly to the temptation; but instead of saying that he fears divine anger he says he is afraid of what

17

people will think, and then is led into minimising the importance of the issue and so giving way. His action in doing so should not be listed among the factors in his guilt; the value of the scene is symbolic; yet during performance the audience feels that if he succumbs to her persuasion he is in her power. After removing his boots in a futile gesture of appeasement he enters the palace, stepping upon the tapestries. His final protest at the extravagance of the proceeding provokes Clytemnestra to a superbly contemptuous reminder that they own a whole sea of purple dyes; for his life she would have sacrificed any quantity of the precious stuff. She ends with a prayer to Zeus to accomplish her design whose real meaning cannot be lost upon the audience. Now Agamemnon vanishes into the palace, and Clytemnestra follows; but Cassandra remains silent on the stage, perhaps hardly noticed by the audience.

The Chorus now sings the Third Stasimon, expressing an unaccountable sense of the imminence of trouble. They have witnessed Agamemnon's safe return, yet cannot rid themselves of an uncanny premonition of disaster. They recall the ancient superstition that a prosperous man may buy off envy provoked in the powers that control human affairs by his success by sacrificing a portion of his belongings. Wealth, they say, may be sacrificed and may always be renewed, but a man's life's blood, once spilt, can never be recalled. The thought of blood that may call for the shedding of more blood recalls knowledge which they possess but may not utter; were it not that respect forbade it, they would be pouring out a secret which as things are they must hold back. The respect is that which they owe to their royal house, and the secret is the dark secret lurking in its past.

The accumulated tension has now reached a point at which the audience will at any minute expect to hear the king's death-cry from inside the palace. Instead, Clytemnestra comes out once more; she has come to call in Cassandra, and does so with an icy cruelty that reveals what she has been hiding behind the carefully maintained facade. The Elders, speaking gently, second her demand that Cassandra shall go in; but Cassandra remains silent, and in the end Clytemnestra loses her patience and returns into the palace.

Noticing the statue of Apollo that stands before the palace door, Cassandra calls upon the god, mystifying the Elders; then they see that she is about to prophesy. First she alludes to a vision of the murdered children of Thyestes; then in the riddling mode of utterance peculiar to prophets she describes a vision of the murder which is about to happen. The Elders recognise the meaning of of her vision of the past, but are perplexed by what she says about the future: her words deeply disturb them, but they

18

conjure away their fears by telling themselves that no good comes to men from prophecy. Then Cassandra describes a vision of her own death; thinking back in time, she perceives the whole tenor of the sad destiny of Troy, from start to finish.

At the beginning of the scene Cassandra sings lyric verses and the Chorus replies in the verse of dialogue, reversing the usual relation between the utterance of an actor and that of the Chorus; gradually the Elders become infected by Cassandra's mood, so that they burst into song. But now after a pause Cassandra speaks in dialogue metre; by a supreme effort she attains a new clarity, and tells the Elders directly that the house of Agamemnon is never quitted by the Erinyes, the punishers of crime. By proving her knowledge of past events she might be expected not to know of, she hopes to force the Elders to believe her prophecies about the future; and she challenges them to deny the truth of what she has said about the children of Thyestes. Encouraged by their admission that it is true, she goes on to tell how Apollo endowed her with prophetic power as the price of her virginity, but she failed to fulfil her part of the bargain, and the god punished her by causing all to disbelieve her prophecies. The Elders assure her that they at least believe her; but though they can understand what she says about the past, they are and continue to be altogether baffled by what she says to them about the future.

A new access of prophetic vision now comes upon Cassandra; she sees a clear vision of the dead children, and senses the plotting of Clytemnestra and the complicity of Aegisthus, even though she does not name them. Once again the Elders fail to follow her, even when she tells them directly that they are about to witness Agamemnon's death. A vision of her own death follows, clearer than before; she tries to cast off the insignia of her prophetic office, and becomes aware of the presence of Apollo, seen by her alone, tearing them off before she herself can do so. Finally she prophesies the coming of Agamemnon's and her own avenger. Why, she asks, should she waste time in lamentation, she who has seen first the fate of Troy and now the fate of Troy's conquerors? The Elders ask why she makes no effort to escape, but she replies that it is useless. On the point of going through the door she hesitates, nauseated by what seems to be the smell of death and corruption. Then, summoning up her resolution, she calls upon the Elders to testify later to her courage, appeals to the all-seeing Sun to witness the guilt of her murderers, and speaks sadly of the evanescence of the life of men. Her final melancholy reflection upon human life is echoed by the Chorus as she leaves the stage.

The use he makes of Cassandra is the poet's master-stroke. The secret of the guilt from the past weighing upon the house of Atreus is finally revealed by the foreign prisoner, who has long remained silent, so that she has been supposed ignorant of Greek. A member of the Trojan royal family, who has witnessed the destruction of her own city and the massacre of her relations, is especially well qualified to deliver the comment upon human destiny which concludes the scene, bringing to a climax the principal theme which is proper to the *Agamemnon* among the plays making up the trilogy. These dramatic objectives are attained in a scene of unsurpassed poignancy, heightened by the poet's peculiar power to evoke a sense of the presence of supernatural beings and the workings of supernatural agencies.

Now at last Agamemnon's death-cry is heard from inside, and the Elders vainly debate whether they are to attempt to act. The scene is exposed to the ridicule of those who choose to view it from the standpoint of a naturalism foreign to the conventions of the Aeschylean stage; but the Elders themselves have prepared the audience for their helplessness by speaking of their great age and decrepitude, and realism in such matters is an irrelevant criterion here. Their futile discussion is interrupted by the appearance of Clytemnestra, standing over the bodies of her two victims.

With utter shamelessness she describes the murder of Agamemnon in his bath, gloating over her dead enemy in a fashion reprobated by Greek religion. The Elders wonder if she has partaken of some drug that has driven her mad, and proclaim that she is liable to death by stoning for her crime. They offered no resistance, Clytemnestra complains, when Agamemnon sacrificed her daughter; they employ a double standard, and in any case they are in no position to execute their judgment. Again the Elders declare that she is mad, but she replies that she is not afraid of them while she has the protection of her loyal friend Aegisthus, uttering a name not previously mentioned in the play. She finishes with further mockery of her dead enemies.

From this point on Clytemnestra replies in anapaestic recitative to the lyrics of the Chorus. The Elders lament for Agamemnon; once again they remember Helen and say that her evil work has now reached its climax. Clytemnestra will not allow Helen to be blamed; but when the Elders invoke the daemon of the house of Atreus, meaning the personified curse, she listens with more sympathy. When they lament once more and denounce her for her deed, she denies that the deed is hers; the avenging daemon, making himself manifest to her, has slain a mature man to atone for youthful victims. The Elders deny that Clytemnestra can cast off responsibility; and they are right; according to Greek religion a supernatural

20

being may inspire a human action, but the human actor can never shuffle off responsibility by saying so. Clytemnestra meets the lamentations and reproaches of the Chorus by repeating the charge against Agamemnon of murdering her daughter. Who, the Elders ask, shall render the king his due mourning and his due funeral laudation? This has nothing to do with them, Clytemnestra replies, and indeed these duties fell upon a dead man's family; she has killed him and she will bury him, without lamentation. For those funeral honours whose refusal was an act almost as heinous as the act of murder, Agamemnon will have to wait until the coming of his son Orestes.

The Elders admit that justice is difficult to attain; one death follows another to avenge it; but they remind Clytemnestra that so long as Zeus sits upon his throne the divine law demands that the doer shall suffer. That doctrine was first enunciated in the Parodos, and mention of it recurs again and again during the trilogy. The Elders declare that the family seems inextricably linked to its inheritance of ruin. Clytemnestra proclaims her willingness to strike a bargain with the daemon; she is willing to give up part of her possessions, if he will depart and plague another family. But the audience knows that no such bargain is possible. In the Third Stasimon the Chorus has said that wealth renounced to appease divine anger can always be replaced, but that blood once spilt can never be called back.

With the end of the great scene between Clytemnestra and the Chorus the real action of the play is over; but it is the custom of the Greek tragedians to bring the audience slowly down from the highest pitch of emotional intensity. Aegisthus enters with his bodyguard and with him the action loses several degrees of tragic grandeur. He sees the working of divine justice in his triumph, telling of the Thyestean feast in tones of matter-of-fact realism, and glorying in having plotted the destruction of his enemy in what by heroic standards must be thought a cowardly fashion. The Elders reproach him for his words and for his conduct, and pronounce against him, as they have done against Clytemnestra, the sentence of death by stoning. But like her, Aegisthus can point out to the Elders that they are in no position to execute their judgment, and he does this with brutal insolence. An undignified altercation follows; finally the Elders exasperate Aegisthus by threatening him with the vengeance of the young Orestes, and he calls upon his followers to draw their swords. In the end Clytemnestra intervenes to put an end to the unseemly wrangle.

Aristotle in his *Poetics* says that the characters in a tragedy are there for the sake of the plot and not their own, and his attitude reflects that of the tragedians. The ancients held that the characters in a drama should be

21

depicted as being the sort of people to perform the actions with which the story credited them; and ancient dramatists endowed their characters with individuality just so far as was necessary for this purpose and no further. The critics of the late nineteenth and early twentieth century imputed to Aeschylus, as they as they did to Shakespeare, their own excessive preoccupation with character-study; in consequence a reaction arose which in some quarters went so far as to deny him any interest in character. The truth lies between the extremes, as the characters of the *Agamemnon* help to show.

The two humble characters, the Watchman and the Herald, vivid as their utterances are, need only to show loyalty and simplicity. Aegisthus must be unfavourably presented, if Agamemnon is to seem relatively sympathetic; he is therefore made mean, cowardly and boastful, as the part he plays in the murder plot suggests that he is. The Argive Elders are given a consistent character, like all Aeschylean choruses. Old and decrepit as they are, they are lucid in speech and thought but incapable of action. Though critical of Agamemnon for having sacrificed men's lives to recover Helen, they are still his loyal subjects; and despite their helplessness at the crisis of the murder, they afterwards stand up courageously to Clytemnestra and Aegisthus, reminding them that divine justice will finally ensure that they are punished.

The Watchman in his prologue credits Clytemnestra with a 'man's mind in counsel'; so great are the cunning and ruthlessness with which Aeschylus' innovation in making her the actual killer requires him to invest her that she seems at times to acquire an almost Shakespearian degree of individuality. In the face of the barely concealed mistrust of the Elders she remains coolly and contemptuously polite. The effusiveness of the words of welcome which she speaks to the Herald and to the king himself serves to make it easier for an audience acquainted with the story to perceive the delicate ambiguity present in so much of her language. When she comes out to call in Cassandra, we see her for the first time with the vizor down; after the murder she casts aside all pretences, and openly proclaims her satisfaction in what she has accomplished. She insists upon the justice of her revenge for Iphigenia, and it is impossible for the Elders entirely to refute her claim. Yet the manner in which Agamemnon's dilemma at Aulis has been presented suggests that he deserves more sympathy than she is willing to accord him, and it is clear that a passion for Aegisthus is an important element among her motives, as Orestes in the second play certainly believes. The belief of some modern critics that she loses her resolution and self-confidence after the murder is utter nonsense; she firmly states her case against the Chorus, and when in the Choephoroe she realises her danger she calls at once for her 'man-slaying axe'.

The story requires that Agamemnon's character should be comparatively complicated. On the one hand he is the noble king, victorious in a just war, loved by his loyal subjects; on the other he is the son of the accursed Atreus, doomed from birth by the decree of Zeus' justice. At Aulis he has a choice between two crimes, and in choosing to kill his daughter adds to the guilt inherited from his father. More guilt accrues from the merciless revenge upon the Trojans of which he boasts with such complacency. In the First Stasimon it is suggested that the killers of many are in any case exposed to danger; that the sons of Atreus have right on their side in seeking to recover Helen, as the Chorus seems to imply in the prologue to the Parodos and at the beginning of the First Stasimon itself, seems at the end of the First Stasimon to be questioned. Aeschylus is not a philosopher but a poet, and we are in danger of oversimplifying and misrepresenting him if we try to work out with too great precision the apportionment of guilt and the operation of divine justice in his work. It is the essence of tragedy that two claims, propositions or principles, each of them just, should clash with one another. It is clear that Agamemnon is a predestined victim of Atê, the power sent by Zeus to blind men so that they commit disastrous errors. Yet neither the grimness of his responses to his wife's insinuating words of welcome nor the satisfaction with which he speaks of his revenge prevents us from feeling that he is far more favourably presented than are his murderers. Aeschylus has fully exploited the motive of the clash between man and woman; on the face of it the woman's claim seems, to be rejected; but the tragedy is concerned to present rather than to solve the permanent problems of human existence, and the assertion of male superiority by Apollo and Orestes matters less than the uncertain feelings which the treatment of the question in the trilogy leaves in the reader's mind.

A similar vagueness attaches to the poet's treatment of human guilt and of divine justice. Plato was unjust to Aeschylus in taking the statement of a character in his lost *Niobe* that 'the god manufactures guilt for men, when he has decided utterly to destroy a house' to mean that Zeus punishes the innocent. Now that a papyrus discovery has placed that statement in its context, we know that Aeschylus meant no such thing; and in the Second Stasimon of *Agamemnon* the Chorus declares that Zeus punishes only the guilty and their descendants. How, then, a philosopher would ask, does the chain of crimes and punishments begin? What was the origin of the guilt of Atreus? In Homer a human action is very often prompted by a god; but though the human actor may try to save face by pleading that the god overruled him, he cannot escape responsibility for an action which belongs to him. At the beginning of the *Odyssey*, Zeus claims that men blame the gods for wrong actions for which they alone are responsible. Are we to take his word for it? In general the archaic Greek poets did not do so. There is an uncertainty here which none of them quite resolves; if pressed for an answer, they might have said, as a character in Euripides infuriated Socrates by saying, 'It is best to leave these matters on one side'. They had a right to say this, because they were poets and not systematic theologians or philosophers.

# CHARACTERS

AEGISTHUS, cousin of AGAMEMNON

AGAMEMNON, king of ARGOS

CASSANDRA, Trojan captive

CHORUS, Argive elders

CLYTEMNESTRA, queen of Argos

HERALD

WATCHMAN

# AGAMEMNON

The play opens with the WATCHMAN lying on the
roof of AGAMEMNON's palace at Argos and gazing
out into the night.

WATCHMAN  *The gods I beg for deliverance from these toils,*
*From my watch a year long, through which, sleeping*
*upon the house of the Atreidae, like a dog,*
*I have learned to know the assembly of the stars of night*
*and those who bring winter and summer to mortals,*  5
*the bright potentates, shining in the sky,*

---

The WATCHMAN no doubt spoke from the roof of the wooden
building at the back of the stage serving as AGAMEMNON's palace.
In Homer the WATCHMAN waiting for AGAMEMNON's return is a
creature of Aegisthus. Aeschylus makes him a faithful servant of
AGAMEMNON (Agg *a memm' non*)

N.B.  The line numbers in the margins are those of the original
text, not those of the translation.

1  Aeschylus (*Es' keh lus*) likes to begin a play with a solemn and
resounding word; thus *Suppliants* starts with "Zeus" (*Zyuse*).

3  In the Middle East watchdogs still sometimes spend the night on
the roof.

5  The stars are called "potentates" because they "bring winter and
summer to mortals"; in Aeschylus' time the Greeks knew nothing
of astrology.

27

the stars, when they set and at their rising.
And now I am watching for the signal of the torch,
the gleam of fire bringing news from Troy
and the tidings of her capture; for such is the rule              10
of a woman's man-counseling, ever hopeful, heart.
And when I keep my couch that sends me wandering by night, my
 couch wet with dew,
this couch of mine that no dreams visit—
for Fear instead of Sleep stands by it,
so that I may not close my eyes fast in sleep—                   15
and when I have a mind to sing or hum,
incising this remedy of song against sleep,
then I weep, lamenting the misfortune of this house,
not now, as in time past, excellently kept in order.
But now may there come a happy deliverance from toil,            20
as the fire that brings good news shines through the darkness!

 He sees the beacon.

 Hail, lamp that shows by night the light of day,
and ordains the setting-up of many dances
in Argos for the sake of this event!
Hurrah, hurrah!                                                   25
To Agamemnon's wife I give clear signal,
that she may rise from her bed in all speed

---

11 The first oblique reference to CLYTEMNESTRA (*Klye tem nes' tra*).

13 The words used suggest the metaphor of a sickbed not visited by the proper doctor.

17 The two methods of ancient surgery were cautery and incision; here the remedy of song is described by a metaphor taken from the latter.

20 Notice the echo of the opening words of the speech.

22 The beacon is said to bring "the light of day" because "salvation" —the word has no moral overtones, but translates a term meaning "rescue" or "preservation"—here is commonly described in terms of the metaphor of day coming after night.

27 The word used to mean "rise" is a word commonly applied only to the rising of the sun, the moon, or the planets.

and raise a jubilant cry of thanksgiving at this torch,
if truly the city of Ilium
is taken, as the beacon's light announces.                                30
And I myself shall dance a prelude,
for my masters' throw has been lucky, and I will turn it to my
     advantage,
now that this beacon-watching has thrown triple six for me.
Well, may it come to pass that the lord of the house
comes back, and that I clasp his well-loved hand in mine.                 35
But for the rest I am silent; a great ox stands
upon my tongue; but the house itself, if it could find a voice,
could tell the tale most truly; for I of my choice
speak to those who know; but for those who do not know I forget.

> Exit the WATCHMAN. The CHORUS, consisting of
> old men of Argos, who as members of the Coun-
> cil help the queen to govern in the king's absence,
> enter and march around the orchestra until they
> take up their positions for the first ode (104).

*It is now the tenth year since Priam's*                                  40

---

31  The Greek game of dice was rather like backgammon; one needed
    both luck and skill; one tried by the exercise of skill to use to best
    advantage such opportunities as the throw of the dice might give.
    There is no need to suppose that the WATCHMAN actually dances
    on the stage.

34  The prayer is not destined to be fulfilled.

36  *a great ox* stands on my *tongue:* a proverbial way of saying, "I am
    inhibited from speaking out." Later in the play the house of the
    Atreidae (At rye' dee) will find a voice, which will be understood
    only by the captive Trojan prophetess CASSANDRA (*Kass and' ra*).

40  40–103 form a prelude to the first choral ode, the Parodos. The
    prelude is written in anapestic dimeters called "marching ana-
    pests," a meter which had an intermediate position between the
    trimeters (and occasional tetrameters) of dialogue and the lyric
    meters of choral odes and actors' arias; anapestic dimeters seem
    to have been chanted in a kind of recitative, midway between
    speech and song. The meter is commonly associated with marching,

great adversary at law,
King Menelaus and Agamemnon,
the pair of sons of Atreus mighty in honor,
put out with an Argive armament of a thousand ships     45
from this land,
to aid their cause in battle,
⎡uttering from their hearts a great cry for war
⎮ like vultures, who in grief
⎮ extreme for their children high above their beds     50
⎮ circle around,
⎮ rowed on the oarage of their wings,
⎮ having seen go for nothing the labor of guarding
⎣ the bed that held their chicks.
And on high Apollo, it may be, hears,     55
or Pan, or Zeus, the bird-voiced
shrill cry of these fellow dwellers in the sky
and sends on the transgressors her who brings punishment,

---

and so is suitable for the words the old men chant as they march around the orchestra. The ordinary unit is ∪∪– ∪∪– ∪∪– ∪∪–, varied with the occasional monometer (∪∪– ∪∪–) and with the paroemiac, a line minus the last syllable and usually occurring at the end of a period (∪∪– ∪∪– ∪∪– –). But a dactyl (–∪∪) or a spondee (– –) may be substituted for an anapest.

The issue between the Atreidae and the house of Priam is repeatedly described in legal language (cf. 534–37, 810–17). For the Greek tragedians, as for Marlowe, ("Is this the face that launch'd a thousand ships?") a thousand was the traditional number; Homer's Catalogue of Ships enumerates 1,186. AGAMEMNON and his brother MENELAUS (Men e lay′ us) are here the joint leaders of the expedition.

50   The Greek word for "children" used here is properly used of human children, not of the young of birds or animals.

55   Pan is appropriate as a god who lives in wild places. Zeus as the god to whom eagles and vultures (which the Greeks did not sharply distinguish from eagles) were sacred. Why Apollo is mentioned is hard to guess; perhaps it is because eagles and vultures circled over his shrine at Delphi as often in ancient times as they do now.

30

*though late, the Erinys.*
*And thus are the sons of Atreus sent*        60
*against Alexander by him whose power is greater,*
*Zeus, guardian of host and guest; for the sake of a woman*
   *of many men,*
*many wrestlings that wear down the limbs,*
*while the knee is brought low in the dust*
*and the spearshaft is snapped in the action before the*
   *sacrifice,*        65
*shall he ordain for the Danaans*
*and Trojans alike. The matter stands where now*
*it stands; and it shall be accomplished to its destined end.*
*Not by the persuasion of burnt offerings nor of libations,*
*of sacrifices that know no fire*        70
*shall he cajole aside unflinching wrath.*
*But we, who have not yet paid the debt due to our aged flesh,*
*we who were left behind from that expedition,*
*remain here; we guide with staves*
*our strength no greater than a child's.*        75

---

59   The hearer is kept waiting until the end of the sentence and the period for the sinister last word—Erinys (*Ee rine' iss*). The Erinyes, originally the personified curses of the dead, are the supernatural beings who are supposed to punish murderers of their own kin; they will play an important part in the *Oresteia*, and in its last play, *The Eumenides* (*Yū' men ih dēz*), they form the chorus. (See Introduction to *The Eumenides*.)

61   Zeus Xenios, "guardian of host and guest," refers to Zeus in one of his most important aspects.

65   The destruction of Troy is metaphorically compared to a sacrifice, in that a word that denotes the preliminaries to a sacrifice is used of the battles that preceded the destruction.

66   *Danaans*: pronounce *Dann' ay ans* = Greeks

71   "He" refers to Alexandros, who is the same as Paris (61).

72   The debt alluded to is death. The words may mean, "But we defaulters with our aged flesh. . . ."

75   Old men in Greece commonly walked with the aid of sticks; such sticks seem to have been a regular property of tragic choruses that represented old men (see note on 1650).

31

*For the fresh stuff of life that within*
*the breast holds sway*
*is like an old man's, and the war-god is not at his post;*
*and great age with the leaf already*
*withering on three feet*           80
*walks, and with strength no greater than a child's*
*like a dream seen by day wanders.*

The CHORUS turns to face the palace.

*But you, Tyndareus'*
*daughter, Queen Clytemnestra,*
*what is the matter, what the news, what have you learned,*     85
*what message*
*has prevailed on you, that you send messengers around and*
*sacrifice?*
*The altars of all the gods that guide the city,*
*gods on high and gods below the earth, gods of the doors*     90

---

78   *the war-god:* the warlike instinct.

80   There is a clear allusion here to the riddle of the Sphinx, which had certainly been mentioned in one of the now lost epics on the Theban saga that were known to Aeschylus. The Sphinx used to ask, "What creature is it that walks on four legs in the morning, on two during the middle of the day and on three during the evening?" Oedipus guessed that the creature was man.

82   Tyndareus, (*Tin' dar yuse*), king of Sparta, was the husband of Leda and father of Castor and CLYTEMNESTRA; Helen and Polydeuces (Pollux) were Leda's children by Zeus.

83   CLYTEMNESTRA has summoned the CHORUS, and they address her although she is not present on the stage. Some suppose that because she is addressed, she must necessarily be present. But in the Parodoi of two other tragedies, Sophocles' *Ajax* and Euripides' *Hippolytus* (*Hip al' ih tus*), absent persons are addressed by the CHORUS, and although the circumstances are not quite the same, the fact is relevant. Dramatically, it would not be suitable to have CLYTEMNESTRA present during the delivery of the Parodos, and her formal greeting from the CHORUS at 258 probably marks her first appearance.

90   *gods of the doors:* an emendation for "gods of heaven," introduced

*and of the market-place,*
*blaze with offerings;*
*and from this side and that as high as heaven*
*torches send up their light,*
*charmed by the hallowed unguent's*
*soft guileless coaxing,*                                                95
*the royal offering from the inmost store.*
*Of these matters tell us what you can and may,*
*and become the healer*
*of this anxiety.*
*Now it carries thoughts of ill,*                                       100
*and now from the sacrifices you reveal*
*springs hope that gives protection, so that worry insufferable*
*[cannot grieve my heart].*

### STROPHE 1

*I have power to tell of the auspicious command of the*
*expedition, the command of men*

---

because "gods of heaven" would be synonymous with "gods on high."

103    The final words are hopelessly corrupt, but the sense may be guessed with confidence.

104    The Chorus now sings the Parodos proper, "the longest and richest chorus extant in Greek tragedy" (Fraenkel). It falls into three sections, differentiated by sense as well as meter. The first (104–59) is in dactylic meters, similar to the dactylic hexameter of Homer and other epic poets, but interspersed with iambic passages that look forward to the iambics that are the prevailing meter of the last section. The second section (160–91) is in trochees, a meter felt to be closely akin to the iambic; a trochee is $-\cup$, an iambus $\cup-$, and since both meters can be varied by the syncopation or resolution of some of the syllables, trochees and iambics are sometimes very much alike. Most of the second section is occupied by the hymn to Zeus (160–83); that the second section also includes the beginning of a narrative shows how closely the hymn is woven into the fabric of the ode. The third and final section is in iambics mixed with trochees and following easily on the trochees that precede.

*in authority; for still from the gods am I inspired*      **105**
*with persuasive power, my strength in song, by the life that has*
    *grown up with me:*
*to tell how the two-throned command of the Achaeans, of the*
    *youth of Hellas*
*the concordant leadership,*      **110**
*was sped with avenging spear and arm*
*by the warlike bird of omen to the Teucrian land,*
*the king of birds appearing to the kings of the ships,*
*the black eagle and behind it the white one,*      **115**
*appearing near the palace on the hand in which the spear*
    *is brandished,*
*in seats conspicuous,*
*feeding upon the hare, her womb teeming with young,*
*checked from running her final course.*      **120**
*Sing sorrow, sorrow, but may the good prevail!*

### ANTISTROPHE 1

*And when the trusty prophet of the army saw it, he knew*

---

**105** *in authority*: from an emendation; the transmitted text means "grown men," which seems odd in this context. The sense of the next sentence is, "I am still young enough to be inspired with persuasive strength from the gods." The word rendered by "life" means "lifetime," or "vital force"; this is imagined as having grown together with the speaker.

**109** The lofty periphrasis "the two-throned command of the Achaeans" (pronounce A kēē ans) for AGAMEMNON and MENELAUS is in keeping with the exalted style of this whole passage, a style full, like the meter, of reminiscences of epic.

**112** *Teucrian (Tyuke′ ri an)*: "Trojan."

**115** Or perhaps "the one that is white behind," alluding to a particular kind of eagle.

**116** The right-hand side; "in the palace" simply refers to wherever the kings are staying; there is no need to worry about whether there was a palace in Aulis (Orl′ is).

**122** Calchas (Kall′ khas), the son of Thestor, in the *Iliad* is the prophet of the Greek army.

*the warlike tearers of the hare for the two Atreidae, two in temper,*
the chiefs who launched the expedition; and thus he spoke,
  interpreting the portent:      125
"In time does this expedition capture Priam's city,
and all the abundant herds —
of the people before the walls
shall Fate violently ravage.
Only let no envy from the gods cast into darkness,
struck beforehand, the great bit for Troy's mouth
that is the army encamped. For in pity holy Artemis is angry  135
with the swift hounds of her father    *Eagles*
that sacrifice the wretched hare with all her young before the birth;
she loathes the feast of the eagles.
Sing sorrow, sorrow, but may the good prevail!

       EPODE

Kindly as is the Fair One  *Artemis*    140
to the helpless young of savage lions
and delightful to the breast-loving whelps
of all beasts that roam the wild,
she begs that these portents be made valid;
favorable, but not faultless, are the signs.     145

---

124 *two in temper:* this phrase is puzzling; it presumably means "different in temper."

129 *herds of the people:* "the herds that are the people." Using the riddling language of prophecy, Calchas speaks of the Trojan people as a great herd of cattle that is to be slaughtered. Cattle were sacrificed in the days of peace before the walls (cf. 1168), and many of the Trojan warriors died fighting before the walls.

133 I have not softened the violent mixture of metaphors in the Greek.

140 Artemis (*Art' em is*) was the patroness of wild beasts and also of hunters; but the eagles and the hare stand for the sons of Atreus (*Ay' trē uhs*) and the Trojans, so that the real meaning here is that Artemis loves Troy, as she does in the *Iliad*, and prays to Zeus for vengeance on those who are destined to destroy it.

144 Her prayer can only be addressed to Zeus.

*I call upon the blessed Healer,*
*that Artemis may not bring to pass delay in port through adverse*     150
*winds, long lasting, holding fast the ships,*
*working to bring about another sacrifice, one without song or feast,*
*an architect of quarrels grown up with the family,*
*with no fear of the husband. For there abides, terrible, ever again*
     *arising,*
*a keeper of the house guileful, unforgetting, Wrath child-avenging."*     155
*Such were the fateful words that Calchas shrieked, together with*
     *great good,*
*as he read the omen of the birds by the way for the royal house;*
*and in harmony with these*
*sing sorrow, sorrow, but may the good prevail!*

STROPHE 2

*Whoever Zeus may be, if this name*     160

---

146    Paian, "The Healer," is a title of Apollo, who is implored to intercede with his sister Artemis.

152    Song and feast normally accompanied a sacrifice.

153    Observe the dark hints not only at IPHIGENEIA's (*Eye phi gen eye' a*) sacrifice ("another sacrifice"), but at the curse brought upon the house of Atreus by the Thyestean (*Thye ess' te an*) feast, hints whose import will be revealed only much later (see Introduction, (p. 13).

155    *keeper of the house:* here the Wrath; it is not a direct reference to CLYTEMNESTRA.

156    Prophets were often said to shriek their predictions in a mantic frenzy.

160    The refrain is a feature of the most primitive poetry, and its use at the end of each stanza of the opening section of the ode (121, 139, 159) is one of the many features of the choruses of this play that recall the influence on tragic lyrics of the poetry of religious worship. The refrain concludes with a conventional prayer that all may turn out well; and the CHORUS follows up the prayer by a special appeal to Zeus, recalling in many ways the actual hymns used in worship. For the worshiper it is important to address the god by his correct

36

*is pleasing to him,*                                                   ✗
*by this name I address him.*
*I can compare with him,*
*measuring all things against him,*
*none but Zeus, if from my mind the vain burden*        165
*may be cast in sincerity.*

### ANTISTROPHE 2

*Not even he who in time past was great,*
*abounding in boldness irresistible,*
*he shall not even be counted, since he was of the past;*       170
*and he who then came into being*
*is gone, having met his victor in three falls.*
*But he who gladly sings the triumph of Zeus*
*shall hit full on the target of understanding:*            175

---

name; otherwise he may not hear or may not listen. This is why some poets who address prayers to the gods call upon them by many of of their names or epithets; others adopt compendious formulas like the one found here: "by whatever name you like to be called, by that name do I call you." At the same time, the formula as it is used here recalls the saying of the fifth-century philosopher Heraclitus: "One thing, the only truly wise, does not and does consent to be called by the name of Zeus."

165    If one needs to shift from one's shoulders the vain burden of worry —vain because worrying is no use—the one source of relief is Zeus.

168    The first ruler of the universe was Ouranos; he was defeated and deposed by his son Kronos (*Krŏ' nŏs*); Kronos in his turn was defeated and deposed by his son Zeus (Hesiod, *Theogony* 453f.). The words used to describe the struggles for the lordship of the universe suggest the wrestling matches that were an important feature of the Greek athletic festivals at Olympia, Delphi, and elsewhere. The victorious wrestler had to throw his adversary in three bouts; his victory would in all likelihood be celebrated in a hymn of triumph, such as the hymns of Pindar.

### STROPHE 3

of Zeus who put men on the way to wisdom
by making it a valid law
that by suffering they shall learn.
There drips before the heart instead of sleep
pain that reminds them of their wounds;                    180
and against their will there comes discretion.
There is, I think, a grace that comes by violence from the gods
seated upon the dread bench of the helmsman.

### ANTISTROPHE 3

And then the senior chieftain
of the Achaean ships,                                      185
blaming no prophet,
letting his spirit go with the sudden blasts of fortune

---

176   We should strongly resist any attempt to import Christian notions
into the doctrine of learning by suffering here set out by Aeschylus.
"Justice always defeats Hybris in the end," says Hesiod in a famous
passage of the Works and Days (218f.); "it is only the foolish man
who learns by suffering." The wise man, it is implied, understands
that it is foolish to defy the will of Zeus; the foolish man, who fails
to understand when he is warned, will learn only when disaster
teaches him. It is not safe to suppose that suffering was thought to
purify or to ennoble.

179   The fear of divine punishment is compared to an old wound that
aches at night and keeps a man from sleep. The "wisdom" and
"discretion" here enjoined mean simply the good sense a man needs
to have in order to realize the folly of breaking Zeus's law of reciprocal justice.

183   The "grace that comes by violence" consists in the knowledge that
injustice against other men will inevitably be punished by the cham-
pion of justice, Zeus. "The helmsman's bench" is a metaphor for
"the seat of power"; "seated high on the helmsman's bench" is an
epithet of Zeus in Homer.

184–  The sentence that starts here is never finished; the clause beginning
87    "when" in line 181 goes on so long that the poet abandons his

38

*when a delay in port that kept their stomachs empty*
*pressed hard the host of the Achaeans,*
*as they held the shore opposite Chalcis*                    190
*in the region of Aulis where the seas roar to and fro,*

STROPHE 4

*and the winds coming from the Strymon*
*causing a cruel delay, bringing starvation, evil for ships at anchor,*
*making men wander,*
*unsparing of ships and cables,*
*doubling the length of passing time,*                       195
*with wasting wore away the flower of the Argives;*
*and when another remedy*
*against the cruel storm*
*more grievous for the chiefs,*
*was shrieked out by the prophet,*                           200
*putting forward Artemis as cause, so that the Atreidae*

---

original contraction and starts again at 205. Such an anacoluthon is not unusual in Aeschylus.

190–  The Achaean expedition to Troy assembled at Aulis on the Boeotian
91    coast. Across the Euripus (*You ripe′ us*), the strait that separates Euboea from the mainland, lies the town of Chalcis (*Khall′ sis*).

192   The Strymon is one of the great Thracian (*Thrāy′ shun*) rivers; cutting north winds blow from the snowy mountains of Thrace and vex the Aegean (*Ee gee′ an*). At this point the meter changes from trochees to iambics; the use of syncopation to slow the movement of the verse makes the rhythm marvelously expressive of the frustration of the delay. From 199 on, in the description of the means of appeasing Artemis proposed by Calchas, the meter becomes choriambic ($-\cup\cup-$ instead of $\times-\cup-$); two lines (199–200) consist of two choriambs, the second of which halts the rhythm (catalexis) by the omission of a syllable, but then follows a continuous run of nine choriambs down to the catalexis at the end of the stanza, giving a rhythm well suited to express the violent reaction of the princes to the prophet's words.

196   *Argives:* pronounce *Ar′ gӯves* (hard "g").

beat the ground with their staves
and could not hold back a tear,

ANTISTROPHE 4

then the senior prince gave tongue and said,                205
"A grievous doom is disobedience,
and a grievous doom it is
if I massacre my daughter, the pride of my house,
polluting with streams of slaughtered maiden's blood
a father's hands hard by the altar.                          210
Which of these courses is free from evil?
How am I to become a deserter of my ships,
losing my allies?
For that they should long
for a sacrifice to still the winds and for a maiden's blood
with passion exceeding passion                               215
is right in the eyes of heaven. May all be for the best!"

STROPHE 5

And when he had put on the yoke-strap of compulsion,
his spirit's wind veering to an impious blast,
impure, unholy, from that moment
his mind changed to a temper of utter ruthlessness.          220
For mortals are made reckless by the evil counsels
of merciless Infatuation, beginner of disaster.
And so he steeled himself to become the sacrificer
of his daughter, to aid a war                                225
fought to avenge a woman's loss
and to pay beforehand for his ships.

---

212   The meaning might be, "failing in my alliance," i.e., "failing in
      my duty as an ally."

218   On the dilemma of AGAMEMNON, see Introduction, page 12. The
      CHORUS in this passage certainly speaks of the sacrifice of IPHIGENEIA
      as a wicked action, but this does not necessarily imply that AGAMEM-
      NON had any choice but to perform it. What is here called "infatua-
      tion" (parakope, 223) is identical with what is usually called "de-
      struction" (ate); see 385f., etc.

### ANTISTROPHE 5

And her prayers and cries of "Father!"
and her maiden years they let go for nothing,
those arbiters eager for battle; 230
and her father told his servants after a prayer
to lift her face downwards like a goat above the altar,
as she fell about his robes to implore him with all her heart,
and by gagging her lovely mouth 235
to stifle a cry
that would have brought a curse upon his house;
using violence, and the bridle's stifling power.

### STROPHE 6

And with her robe of saffron dye streaming downwards
she shot each of the sacrificers 240
with a piteous dart from her eye,
standing out as in a picture, wishing
to address each by name, since often
in her father's hospitable halls
she had sung, and virginal with pure voice 245
had lovingly honored the paean

---

230   Either "arbiters" is a synonym for "chiefs" or the Atreidae are compared to umpires in an athletic contest.

231   A prayer normally preceded a sacrifice.

233   The usual gesture of a suppliant was to clasp the knees of the person supplicated. Whoever performed a sacrifice wore a long robe.

237   The sense is not that IPHIGENEIA would have cursed her father, but that her cry would have brought a curse upon him.

242   The point of comparison with a figure in a picture is that both seem as if they would speak, but no speech comes.

245   The paean was a song in honor of the gods (most often of Apollo), and is here said to accompany the third libation at banquets, poured in honor of Zeus in his aspect as preserver (Soter). No other author indicates that young girls in the heroic age were brought in to sing at the men's banquets.

*of felicity at the third libation*
*of her loving father.*

ANTISTROPHE 6

*And what came next I did not see, nor do I relate it;*
*but the arts of Calchas do not fail of fulfilment,*
*and Justice sways the balance,*
*bringing to some learning by suffering. The future*   250
*you may learn when it comes. Rejoice in it before it comes!*
*But all is one if we lament before;*
*for it will come clear with the rays of dawn.*
*Well, in what follows may achievement turn out prosperous,*  255
*as is the will of this nearest*
*sole bulwark of the Apian land!*

Enter CLYTEMNESTRA.

CHORUS I have come, Clytemnestra, in reverence for your
power;
for it is right to honor the wife of a king
when the throne has been made empty of the male.   260
And whether you have heard good news or have not,
but sacrifice in the hope of happy tidings,
I would in loyalty learn; nor shall I resent your silence.

---

250 See 177 with note.

251 The text and meaning are uncertain.

255 Some think that the "bulwark" is CLYTEMNESTRA, but it is certainly
the elders of the CHORUS themselves. There is no instance of a
CHORUS introducing an actor who enters the stage before the singing
of the ode is finished.

257 *the Apian (Apé i an) land:* an ancient designation of the Peloponnese, at this time under the rule of AGAMEMNON. Once again (cf.
122, 139, 159, 217) we find the prayer for good fortune with which
cult-hymns commonly concluded.

258 For the first time CLYTEMNESTRA enters the stage. See note on
83 above.

CLYTEMNESTRA Happy tidings, as the proverb has it,
may the dawn bring as she comes from night her mother.    265
But greater than hope is the joy you shall hear of;
for Priam's city is taken by the Argives.

CHORUS How do you say? Your words have escaped me, since
they were beyond belief.

CLYTEMNESTRA That Troy is in the hands of the Achaeans;
do I speak clearly?

CHORUS Delight steals over me, calling forth a tear.    270

CLYTEMNESTRA Yes, your eye proclaims your loyalty.

CHORUS What sign do you trust? Have you any proof of this?

CLYTEMNESTRA I have; of course I have, if a god has not deceived me.

CHORUS But do you respect as persuasive the visions seen in
dreams?

CLYTEMNESTRA I would not accept the fancy of a slumbering
mind.    275

CHORUS But has some wingless rumor encouraged you to believe this?

CLYTEMNESTRA You greatly scorn my intelligence, as though
it were a young girl's.

---

264 CLYTEMNESTRA catches the words "hope" and "happy tidings"
from the speech of the Coryphaeus (Kor' ih fee' us). "Happy
tidings" is an expression of good omen, and serves her in her
opening prayer, but she vigorously rebuts the suggestion that she
has no better reason for sacrificing than mere hope. No one knows
what the proverb was to which her opening words allude; perhaps
it was something like "like mother like child in beauty."

268 Here we have the formal kind of dialogue called "stichomythia"; see
Introduction, page 7.

273 What god is meant is stated only at 281.

276 wingless rumor: presumably a false rumor.

43

CHORUS But within what space of time has the city been
taken?

CLYTEMNESTRA I say, during the night that lately gave birth
to the light we see.

CHORUS And what kind of messenger could arrive with such
speed as this? 280

CLYTEMNESTRA Hephaestus, sending from Ida a bright flame.
And beacon began to send beacon this way by means of the courier
fire;
Ida sent it to the rock of Hermes
in Lemnos, and as the mighty torch came from the island
Zeus's crag of Athos was third to receive it. 285
And rising aloft to skim the surface of the sea
the might of the traveling torch . . . . . .
the pine, like another sun, passing on
the golden light of its flame to the watchers of Macistus.
And he delayed not, nor was he in heedlessness overcome 290
by sleep, so as to neglect the duty of a messenger;
but far off the beacon's light
signaled to the guards upon Messapion its coming over the waters
of Euripus.

---

281 Hephaestus (*He feest' us*), as the fire-god, is identified with the fire
of the chain of beacons lit on heights that has brought the news
across the Aegean and all the way to Argos.

283 Ida (*Eye' da*) is the great mountain behind Troy; Lemnos (*Lemm'
nos*) is an island off the coast of Asia Minor.

285 Mount Athos (*Aye' thos*) on the Thracian coast, like many mountains, was sacred to Zeus.

287 A line seems to have been dropped out after 287.

289 According to an ancient grammarian's note here, Macistus (*May
sis' tus*) was the name of a mountain in Euboea; but there is no
other evidence for this, and it may be nothing better than a guess.
If it is the name of a place, then in 290 that place is personified.

293 The Euripus is the strait between Euboea and the mainland, and
Messapion (*Mess aye' py on*) is a mountain on its western side, in
Boeotia.

And they shone an answering light and passed far on the message,
kindling fire in a heap of gray brushwood.                                    295
And in strength the torch and not yet growing dim,
leaping over the plain of the Asopus,
like a radiant moon, to Cithaeron's rock
awoke another succession of convoying fire.
And the light sent from afar was not rejected                                 300
by the watch; it burned more than was appointed;
and the light plunged beyond the lake of the Gorgon face,
and reaching the mountain of the wandering goats
urged that the covenant of the fire be not [neglected?].
And kindling the fire with unstinting strength the men sent ahead     305
the great beard of flame, so that it passed far beyond
the headland that looks upon the crossing point of Saron,
blazing as it went. Then it plunged downwards, and reached
to the peak of Arachne, the watch close by the city.
And then it plunged down upon this house of the Atreidae,             310

---

297    The Asopus (*Aye sō' pus*) is the main river of Boeotia; Cithaeron
       (*Sith ee' ron*) is the great mountain range that separates Boeotia
       from Attica to the south.

302    The identity of "the lake of the Gorgon face" and of "the mountain
       wandered over by goats" is a complete mystery. Perhaps these are
       riddling descriptions of real places; if so, the "lake" may refer to
       the western half of the Saronic (*Sarr onn' ic*) gulf (mentioned at
       306-7) and the mountain to the island of Aegina, whose name
       suggests the word for "goat."

304    The word rendered by "be not neglected" depends on a dubious
       conjecture.

307    The Saronic Gulf.

309    *Arachne*: pronounce *Ar akh' nē*: Mount Arachnaion, now called
       Arna, stands north of the highway from Argos to Epidaurus.

310    Throughout, the fire of the beacons is described as though it were
       the same fire, journeying from Mount Ida across the Aegean and over
       eastern Greece to Argos. It is hard not to suppose that the fire, "not
       without an ancestor in the fire of Ida," which speeds rapidly across
       the Aegean and "plunges down upon the house of the Atreidae"
       stands for the avenging power of Zeus, which, having punished

AGAMEMNON

*this light not without an ancestor in the fire of Ida.*
*Such are the laws that govern my torch-bearers;*
*each is supplied in relays from another;*
*and victory belongs both to the first and to the last to run the*
*course.*
*Such is the proof and token that I tell you of,*     **315**
*since my husband has sent the news from Troy to me.*

CHORUS   To the gods, lady, I shall address my prayer later;
*but for this tale of yours, I would hear it to the end*
*again and exhaust my wonder at it.*

CLYTEMNESTRA   *Troy is this day in the hands of the Achaeans.*   320

---

Priam and his city for their crime against Zeus's law, will now punish the conqueror of Priam, AGAMEMNON.

312   Torch-races were held each year at Athens in honor of Prometheus (*Pro mē' thē us*), Athene (*A thē' nē*), and Hephaestus, and later in honor of the Thracian goddess Bendis. The race was a relay race in which the torch was passed from one member of each team to the next. It is these torch-races that the beacon system is compared to in this passage.

The following beacon-stages are mentioned:

1. Ida–Lemnos: over 90 miles.
2. Lemnos–Mount Athos: about 50 miles.
3. Mount Athos–Macistus (if in Euboea): about 100 miles.
4. Macistus–Mount Messapion: if Macistus is in Euboea, about 15 miles.
5. Mount Messapion–Mount Cithaeron: about 26 miles.
6. Mount Cithaeron—"lake of the Gorgon face" and "mountain of wandering goats"—[?].

Once the beacons reach Greece, the stages become much shorter, and it is clear that realism is less important than the effect of the sonorous proper names.

317   It would be normal for the CHORUS to render immediate thanks to the gods for the reported victory; but before doing so it demands that CLYTEMNESTRA repeat her announcement. The imaginative picture she now paints of the fall of Troy (330 f.) in no way amounts to the "sure proof" that the Coryphaeus calls it (352); but for the time being the CHORUS is convinced.

46

Cries, I think, that will not blend ring out in the city.
If you pour vinegar and oil into the same vessel,
you may say they stand apart in no friendly fashion;
so also one may hear apart from one another the voices
of conquered and conquerors, voices of their different fortunes.     325
For the conquered, falling about the bodies
of men, brothers and fathers,
of children and aged men, from a throat no longer free
lament the end of their dear ones.
As for the conquerors, the toil that sends them wandering in the
     night after the battle     330
assigns them, starving, to places where they breakfast off what the
     city holds,
not by means of any duly allotted billet,
but as each has drawn the lot of chance.
In the Trojan houses captured by their spears
they dwell already, from the frosts and dews beneath the open sky     335
released; and as men favored by the gods
they shall sleep all night long without a watch!
If they reverence the city-keeping gods
of the conquered land and the divinities' abodes,
then the conquerors shall not be conquered in their turn.     340
But may no longing first come on the army
to ravage what they should not ravage, vanquished by love of gain!
For they still need to win their way safe home,

---

336   CLYTEMNESTRA's pretended fears are her secret hopes; she knows
that the triumphant army may easily commit excesses that spur
divine vengeance and so forward her plan to murder AGAMEMNON.
According to the poetical tradition of the post-Homeric epics, followed also by the tragedians, the Greeks committed atrocities during the sack of Troy that provoked the gods to punish them. In
particular, Neoptolemus butchered the aged Priam at the altar of
Zeus, where he had taken refuge as a suppliant, and the lesser Ajax
violated CASSANDRA in the temple of Athene, where she had fled to
implore the protection of the goddess. In consequence the Greek
fleet as it rounded the southern promontory of Euboea was scattered by a terrible storm; Ajax and many others lost their lives, and
the survivors were dispersed.

to round in due course the second bend of the racecourse.
And even if the army should return without offense against the gods, 345
the agony of the dead might awaken;
may it wreak no sudden havoc!

Such is the tale you hear from me, a woman;
but may the good prevail, in no uncertain fashion;
for many are the blessings whose enjoyment I now pray for. 350

CHORUS Lady, you speak wisely, like a prudent man.
And now that I have heard from you sure proofs,
I make ready to address in praise the gods;
for not unworthy of our labors is the return they have accomplished.

O Zeus the King and kindly Night, 355
possessor of great glories,
you who hurled upon the towers of Troy
a net without holes, so that none full grown

---

344 In a Greek race course the runner turned at the end of the track
and ran back along a track parallel with the first.

348 CLYTEMNESTRA's mention of her sex shows that she is looking back
to the opening of her conversation with the Coryphaeus, in which
he was reluctant to accept her story.

349 Again the prayer that all may turn out for the best (see n. on 255).

350 Many people believe that CLYTEMNESTRA leaves the stage here, or
after 354.

352 The CHORUS will now perform the duty of rendering thanks, which
was postponed at 317.

355 Like the Parodos, the First Stasimon is preceded by a prelude in
anapestic dimeters (see note on 40). Its train of thought is directly developed at the beginning of the ode (367f.).

355 According to the usual account, Troy fell at night. The "great
glories" are presumably the stars and planets, but the word rendered
"possessor" is unusual and may be corrupt.

358 The metaphor of the net is taken from Homer (*Iliad* 5. 487f.), and
the statement that neither old nor young can leap beyond it certainly alludes to a fable about a fisherman's net, in which the
big fish were captured but the little ones escaped (*Babrius* 4).

48

*nor any of the young could overleap*
*slavery's mighty*                                                        360
*dragnet, of all-capturing destruction.*
*It is the mighty Zeus, lord of host and guest, that I revere,*
*he that has accomplished this; against Alexander*
*long since he has been bending his bow*
*so that neither short of the mark nor beyond it*                         365
*should the bolt of the stars fall vainly.*

STROPHE 1

*They may speak of a stroke from Zeus;*
*that at least can be traced out.*
*He has accomplished it as he ordained. Men have said*
*that the gods did not deign to attend to mortals*                        370
*by whom the grace of things inviolable*
*was trampled; but such men are impious.*
*And the penalty for daring what may not be dared has been revealed*

---

366   *the bolt of the stars:* the thunderbolt; *asterope* or *astrape* (lightning) was derived from *aster* or *astron* (star).

367   The prevailing meter of the First Stasimon is the lyric iambic, which we have already encountered in the third section of the Parodos (see p. 39). The first stanza, however, concludes with an abbreviated (catalectic) choriambic dimeter of the kind described on page 27 (380–98); and at the end of the third (446–51 —466–70) there is a run of lines consisting of a choriamb (–ᴜᴜ–) followed by an iambic metron (x–ᴜ–) running down to a final catalexis. Further, each strophe is followed by a type of refrain in which the same words are not repeated (as in the first section of the Parodos; see p. 36) but which consists of a brief pendant to the stanza in a different meter; two pherecrateans (–x –ᴜᴜ –x) are followed by a glyconic (–x –ᴜᴜ –ᴜx) and then another pherecratean. The effect is one of an almost primitive simplicity, and in each case the content matches the rhythm; this is undoubtedly an archaic feature derived from cult poetry.

374   The text in this line is uncertain, and this affects the sense of the whole sentence; the version here adopted represents the easiest way of extracting sense without violent change, but the corruption

to the descendants of those whose pride is greater than is right,   375
when their house abounds with wealth in excess,
beyond what is best. May it be granted me
to have good sense, so that the gods
are content to leave me free from harm!   380
For there is no defense
for a man who in the surfeit of his wealth
has kicked the great altar
of Justice out of sight.

ANTISTROPHE 1

He is overborne by relentless Persuasion,   385
child irresistible of forecounseling Destruction.
And every remedy is vain; not hidden,
but conspicuous, a lurid-shining light, is the plague.
And like bad bronze   390

---

may go much deeper. Still, the sense seems to be that the descendants of criminals may have to pay the penalty for the crimes of their ancestors, a doctrine prominent in this play (see p. 69).

378   By a slight emendation that is usually adopted the text is made to mean, "But may a fate [or "wealth"] without pain be granted, so as to content a man well endowed with sense." But the unemended text, as I have rendered it, suits the context better. The run of the thought is, "May I be well endowed with sense, so that the gods are content to leave me unscathed; for if a man offends against the altar of Justice, nothing can protect him."

381   The sense might quite well be, "For wealth cannot protect a man against satiety, once he has kicked. . . ." Koros, literally "satiety," is sometimes almost synonymous with "hybris" (see p. 70).

386   The meaning is not that the victim is "persuaded" by another person but that he succumbs to the persuasive power of whatever temptation causes his undoing. In Paris' case this was the power of love, and Persuasion (Peitho) is often represented as a minor diety attending upon Aphrodite (Aff rō dye' tē).

390   bad bronze: bronze that has been adulterated with lead; when such bronze suffers wear and contusion, it turns black.

when rubbed and battered
he is stained with a black indelible;
for he is like a boy that pursues a flying bird.                    395
Unbearable the affliction he has brought upon his city.
His prayers none among the gods will hear,
and him that has dealings with such men
Justice brings down.

Such a one was Paris, who went                                      400
to the house of the Atreidae
and shamed the hospitable board
by the theft of a wife.

### STROPHE 2

And she, leaving for her fellow citizens the din
of shields, the forming of companies
and fitting out of ships,                                           405
and bringing to Ilium as her dower destruction,
sped swiftly through
the gates, daring a deed beyond daring; many were the groans
of the prophets of the house as they spoke these words:
"Alas, alas for the house, for the house and for the princes!       410
alas for the bed she shared with her husband!
we may see the dishonored silence of one
sitting apart, not reviling, not beseeching.
And as he longs for her that is beyond the sea
a ghost shall seem to rule the house.                               415

And the charm of her beautiful statues
is hateful to her husband;

---

395  "To chase something that has wings" is a proverbial way of describing the quest of the impossible.

409  Prophets were part of a chief's household in the heroic age (cf. *The Libation Bearers*, 87).

411  Literally "alas for the bed and her husband-loving steps!"

412  These lines are corrupt and not to be restored with certainty, although the general sense is probably correctly given.

*and in the absence of her eyes*
*gone is all the power of love.*

ANTISTROPHE 2

| | |
|---|---|
| *And visions seen in dreams, persuasive,* | 420 |
| *are there, bringing a pleasure that is deceitful.* | |
| *For deceitfully, when he thinks he sees his beloved* | |
| *slipping through his arms* | |
| *the vision is gone, never afterwards* | 425 |
| *on its wings following the paths of sleep."* | |
| *The sorrows in the house, at the hearth,* | |
| *are these and worse than these;* | |
| *and everywhere for them that went forth from the land of Hellas* | |
| *a mourning woman, one that suffered much,* | 430 |
| *is found in each one's house;* | |
| *yes, there is much to cut to the very heart.* | |
| | |
| *For those they sent away* | |
| *they know, but instead of men* | |
| *to each one's home* | 435 |
| *there come back urns and ashes.* | |

STROPHE 3

*And Ares, the gold-changer of bodies*

---

418   The Greeks believed that love was implanted in the lover by a ray
from the eyes of the beloved. Hence the absence of the beloved's
eyes is singled out for mention. Other scholars find here a reference
to the emptiness of Menelaus' eyes in Helen's absence.

422–   The words rendered by "when he thinks he sees his beloved" are
23    partly corrupt.

430   In each house there is a mother or a wife lamenting.

433   In Homer the ashes of the dead were not sent to their homes,
except according to an interpolated passage in *Iliad* 7. 334f.
Aeschylus probably had in mind the custom of his own countrymen,
which seems to have been introduced only five years before the
production of the *Oresteia.*

437   The gold-changer gives gold, perhaps gold dust, in exchange for

52

and holder of the scales in the battle of the spear
from Ilium sends to their dear ones
heavy gold dust that has felt the fire,                                      440
dust bitterly bewailed; with ashes
that were once men he loads the urns, easily stowed.
And they lament them, praising this man                                      445
as skilled in battle,
and that as having died a noble death amid the slaughter—
"for the sake of another's wife."
These are the words they mutter low;
and over them comes grief with resentment                                    450
against the champions of justice, the Atreidae.
But the men where they fell about the wall
in all their beauty occupy
their tombs in Ilium's earth;
and the enemy land covers its occupiers.       .                             455

### ANTISTROPHE 3

Grievous is the talk of the citizens when they are angry;
The curse the people has pronounced ordains that a penalty must
      be paid.
My anxious thought waits to hear
a thing shrouded in darkness.                                                460
For the killers of many do not go
unwatched by the gods; and the black

---

heavy articles; so Ares (Air' ēs), the war-god, sets up his scales in
the battle and gives dust, i.e., ashes, in return for bodies. His gold
dust is "heavy," a word that besides its literal sense often carries
the meaning "grievous."

454 Commentators quote Coleridge's "The Ancient Mariner":
> The many men so beautiful,
> And they all dead did lie.

456 The pronouncing of the curse is conceived as creating an obliga-
tion the person cursed must discharge to his own cost; the subject of the sentence is indefinite, but the Atreidae are in the mind
of the CHORUS.

Erinyes in time consign to darkness
him who is fortunate without justice,
wearing away his life while his fortune is reversed,               465
and among the vanished
he has no protection.
The burden of excessive praise
is heavy; for by the eyes of Zeus
the thunderbolt is hurled.                                         470

My choice is prosperity that brings no envy.
May I not be a sacker of cities,
nor yet, myself the captive of others
eat away my life!

                                    EPODE

At the bidding of the fire that brought good news               475
through the city runs the swift
message; but if it is true
who knows, or if it is some lie sent by the gods?

---

463   The name of Hades, the ruler of the underworld, was derived by
      the early Greeks from an adjective meaning "unseen," "invisible."
      "Darkness" in this line and "the vanished" in 466 both suggest
      the world of the dead below the earth.

469   It seems likelier than not that the eye of Zeus was thought to dart
      its lightning at transgressors. The thunderbolt, then, through its
      close association with lightning could be said to be hurled by the
      eye of Zeus. But the evidence adduced is unsatisfactory, and the
      passage may be corrupt.

475   What began as an ode of rejoicing for the great victory of AGAMEM-
      NON over Troy ends, like the Parodos, with an expression of ago-
      nized apprehension. Saddened by the realization of this fact, the
      CHORUS revokes its earlier acceptance of CLYTEMNESTRA's assur-
      ance that Troy has fallen. Seeing that the conventions of Greek
      tragedy, and particularly early tragedy, are wholly remote from
      modern naturalism, we should not be unduly perplexed by this
      volte face, which enables the poet to secure a startling effect when
      the HERALD enters at the beginning of the following scene.

Who is so childish or so far shaken out of his senses
as to let his heart take fire                                                                  480
at the new message of the beacon
and then to suffer when the story is changed?
It is like a woman's rule
to join in approving thanksgiving before the thing is manifest.
Too persuasive, a woman's ordinance spreads far,                         485
traveling fast; but dying fast
a rumor voiced by a woman comes to nothing.


CLYTEMNESTRA   Soon shall we know about the beacon-watchings
and the fire-transmissions of the light-bearing torches,                   490
whether they tell the truth or, as is the way of dreams,

---

483   The CHORUS once more expresses a contempt for women that has
      already been apparent in its opening dialogue with CLYTEMNESTRA
      and will be observed again later. The opposition between man and
      woman is one of the play's recurrent themes. So is the masculine
      quality of CLYTEMNESTRA (11, etc.).

489   If CLYTEMNESTRA went off after 350 or 354, she returns now. The
      manuscripts are certainly right in giving this speech to CLYTEMNESTRA
      Many editors have transferred it to the CHORUS leader, because they
      think it impossible that CLYTEMNESTRA should speak here and then
      remain silent on the stage from 501 to 587, all the more since at
      549–50 the Coryphaeus tries to convey to the HERALD a veiled
      warning against her. But the speech well suits CLYTEMNESTRA and
      has to be emended in order to be taken away from her; also, 501–2
      constitutes a common type of brief utterance of the Coryphaeus
      that could hardly be appended to a speech by him. Perhaps CLYTEM-
      NESTRA goes off after 537 and returns just before she speaks at 587,
      but there is no indication of this in the actual text, and most probably
      she is present throughout. The warning against her is not openly
      given, and although later tragedians might have arranged for her to
      be off stage during its delivery, I am not sure that Aeschylus would.
      [Oliver Taplin, *The Stagecraft of Aeschylus*, 1977, 294 f. pleads for
      the other view.]

491   The Greeks believed that dreams were sometimes sent by the gods
      to deceive mortals; Zeus sends such a dream to AGAMEMNON at
      the beginning of the second book of the *Iliad*.

this light that brought joy in its coming has beguiled us.
I see here a herald from the shore, his brow
shaded with twigs of olive; and mud's brother
and neighbor, thirsty dust, attests this much,                    495
that he is not voiceless, nor will you find him kindling
the flame of mountain brushwood to make signals with a fire that is
    illusion.
But either he will speak out, so that we rejoice the more . . .
but the opposite news is less to my liking.
May we have good besides the appearance of good!                  500

CHORUS   May whoever prays otherwise for our city
reap in his own person the fruit of his mind's evil!

    Enter the HERALD.

HERALD   Hail, earth of my fathers, earth of the Argive land!
In the light of this <u>tenth year</u> have I come home to you;

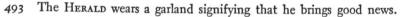

493   The HERALD wears a garland signifying that he brings good news.

494   An expression like "mud's brother and neighbor, thirsty dust" is
    called by the Icelandic name "*kenning*"; in Greek literature up
    to about the middle of the fifth century this archaic style is not
    uncommon.

497   *fire*: literally "a smoke of fire."

499   *the opposite news* . . . : literally "the report opposite to this I no
    longer like"; compare Hector's words in Homer: "Polydamas, what
    you say is no longer to my liking" (*Iliad* 12.231, and 18.285).

501   The HERALD first addresses the land of Argos; then (508f.) the
    Sun, Zeus, and Apollo; then (513f.) the gods whose altars stood
    together in the "divine assembly" of the marketplace, singling out
    Hermes (*Herm' ēs*), the patron of heralds; and finally—by an
    easily forgivable anachronism—the heroes. Next, he speaks to the
    palace itself, to the benches in front of it where kings customarily
    sat to give judgment (519), and to certain obscure divinities whose
    statues stood nearby. Before the Coryphaeus addresses him at 538,
    he shows no awareness of the presence of the CHORUS.

504   By a familiar metaphor the tenth year's coming is compared to
    sunrise after darkness.

many hopes were shattered, but this one have I had fulfilled.    505
Yes, never did I think that in this land of Argos
I should die and have right of burial in soil most dear.
Now I say hail to my country, and hail to the sun's light,
and to you, supreme Zeus of the land, and you, Pythian king,
with your bow no longer darting your shafts against us.    510
The enmity you showed us by Scamander's banks was enough;
but now be once more our preserver and healer,
lord Apollo! and I address all the gods
in their assembly, and the guardian of my privilege,
Hermes, beloved herald, whom heralds revere,    515
and the heroes who were our escort; in kindness once again
may they receive the army that the spear has spared!
Hail, palace of our kings, beloved house,
and seats revered, and gods that face the sun!
Long ago, I think, with gladness in those eyes    520
did you wish us farewell; and now with. . . . . .
honor welcome the king after long lapse of time.
For he is come, bringing light in darkness to you
and to all present here together, the lord Agamemnon.
Come, give him good greeting, for it is proper,
him who has uprooted Troy with the mattock of Zeus who does
 justice    525
with which the soil has been worked over.

---

507  It was a great sorrow for a Greek to think that he would be buried
 abroad, with no kindred near to perform rituals at his tomb (cf.
 452f. above).

509  *Pythian:* pronounce *Pie' thi an:* Apollo, so called from Pytho, a name
 of his oracle at Delphi. The HERALD remembers the plague sent
 upon the Greeks by Apollo with his arrows and described in the first
 book of the *Iliad.*

511  *Scamander:* pronounce *Ska man' der.*

523  A line from some lost epic runs, "If he were to be done by as he
 did, then would true justice have been done." The expression "to
 be done by as one did" is proverbial and is used of the Persians,
 who invaded Greece with Xerxes, soon after the mention of their
 destruction of the temples in the passage just alluded to (*The Persians,* 813f.).

And the altars and the seats of the gods are vanished,
and the seed is perishing from all that land.
Such is the yoke that he has cast about the neck of Troy,
the senior chief born of Atreus, a man dear to the gods,   530
he that is come, worthiest of honor among men
now living! for neither Paris nor Paris' confederate city
boasts that what they did was more than what they suffered.
For cast in a suit for rapine and for theft
he lost his booty, and in utter destruction   535
brought down the house of his fathers with his land.
Double was the atonement paid by the sons of Priam.

CHORUS Herald of the Achaeans from the army, I wish you joy!

HERALD I rejoice; and if the gods wish my death, I shall no
longer say no.

---

527 This line is almost identical with 811 of Aeschylus' *Persians*, which
has encouraged certain scholars to think it has been interpolated
here. They want to be rid of it because they do not believe AGA-
MEMNON's HERALD would have boasted of the impious action of
destroying the temples. The usual story, however, was that the
HERALD did so boast; it is clear from CLYTEMNESTRA's speech at
320f. that she is hoping that the victorious Greeks may provoke
divine anger, and that this hope is likely to be fulfilled. The line
is very hard to remove from its context and is doubtless genuine.

534 Paris carried off not only Helen, but much property with her,
according to the *Iliad*. Once again legal language is used to describe the crime of Paris and its punishment (see note on 40f.).

537 See note on 489.

539 The line is corrupt, and the sense cannot be guessed at with any
certainty. The Coryphaeus has saluted the HERALD with the normal greeting, which is an imperative meaning "Rejoice"; the
HERALD replies, "I do rejoice"; after that, the text is uncertain.
The usual view is that the HERALD is saying, as characters in
tragedy often do, "Now that my dearest wish has been granted,
I am content to die." This is a development from the common
usage by which one said, "May I die, if only this or that prayer
is first granted" (see 1610–11 for an example).

CHORUS  Is it longing for this your native land that has afflicted
you?                                                           540

HERALD  Yes, so that my eyes fill with tears of joy.

CHORUS  Then this was an agreeable malady that was upon you.

HERALD  How so? if you instruct me I shall be master of this
saying.

CHORUS  Because they for whom you were smitten with desire
returned your longing.

HERALD  Do you mean that this land longed for the army that
longed for it?                                                 545

CHORUS  Yes, so that I sighed often from a darkened spirit.

HERALD  From where came this dejection? It was on the army
that this oppression lay.

CHORUS  Long since silence has been my remedy against harm.      ✕

HERALD  How so? in the absence of the princes, were there some
you feared?

CHORUS  So that, in your words, even death would be a great joy.  550

HERALD  Yes, for success has been achieved; and of these things
in all the length of time

---

540  The Coryphaeus' reason for insisting that those at home missed
the army as much as the army missed them is that he wishes to
convey to the HERALD a veiled warning that all has not been well
during the army's absence. The HERALD, however, is slow to understand him. When he finally takes the point, at 549, he assumes
at once that any danger has been ended by the army's triumphant
return, and he wrongly interprets the words of the Coryphaeus at
550 to be a kind of prayer for death that, if the usual interpretation of 539 is right, he himself has expressed. The scene has much
of the archaic stiffness that in Aeschylus usually marks the kind
of dialogue known as stichomythia (see Introduction, p. 7), in
which each character speaks one or two lines at a time; it is well
to remember that naturalism was not attempted.

a part, one may say, has fallen out well
and part, again, may be faulted; but who except the gods
is without pain for his whole lifetime's length?
For if I were to tell of our labors and hard bivouacs,     555
the narrow gangways, with their wretched bedding . . . and what
    groans
did we not utter, when we did not receive our daily portion?
And other things, again, happened on land, and·these were yet more
    hateful;
for our beds were up against the walls of the enemy;
and from the sky and from the meadowland     560
dews drizzled down upon us, to the constant ruin
of our clothing, filling our hair with creatures.
And if one were to tell of the winter, killer of birds,
intolerable as the snow of Ida made it,
or of the heat, when the sea in its noonday     565
repose without a wind lay where it had fallen with no wave. . . .
Why should I lament for this? Our toil is past,
past so that the dead, for their part, care not even to rise again.
Why must I tell the tale of those who perished,     570
and why must the living groan again over malignant fortune?
I hold that what has happened warrants us even to feel great joy.
And for us who are left from the Argive army
gain prevails, and sorrow does not countervail it:
so that we may rightly boast to this sun's light,     575
as our fame flies over sea and land:
"After taking Troy once did the Argive host

---

553   That only the gods are free from pain is a commonplace often stated by the Greek poets.

555   The HERALD's description stresses not the dangers of war but its discomforts. Aeschylus experienced much active service, as one might almost have guessed from this emphasis. The Syntax is unusually abrupt at many places in this speech, and the sense at several points is uncertain. How far this is due to textual corruption and how far to an incoherence meant to characterize the HERALD is not easily determined.

577   The language resembles that found in actual dedications of the spoils of war.

nail up these spoils to the gods of Greece,
an ancient glory for their shrines."
When men hear such words, they must praise the city        580
and her generals; and the grace of Zeus,
that accomplished these deeds, shall be honored. You have heard
    all I have to say.

CHORUS  Your words prevail on me, and I do not reject them;
for eagerness to learn is always a renewal of youth for the old.
But it is proper that this should concern the house and Clytemnestra   585
most, and that I should share the wealth it brings.

CLYTEMNESTRA  I raised the cry of triumph long since,
when there came the first message of the fire,
telling of the taking and the razing of Ilium.
And there were some who rebuked me, and said, "Persuaded by   590
the beacons, do you think Troy has been sacked?
Indeed it is like a woman to let her feelings carry her away."
By such words as these I was made to seem to wander in my wits;
but nonetheless I sacrificed, and as is women's custom
one here, one there in the city uttered                    595
the jubilant cry, giving praise in the gods' abodes,
lulling the fragrant flame that feeds on incense.
And now, for the full story, what need have you to tell it me?
From the king himself I shall hear all the tale.           600
But that I may make best haste to receive my honored husband
on his return—for what day's light
dawns sweeter for a woman than this,
when a god has brought her man safe home from a campaign
and she unbars the door? . . . —take this message to my husband!
May he come as soon as possible, the city's darling, ✗     605

---

587  If CLYTEMNESTRA left the stage at 537 (see note on 489), she re-enters
     now. Her opening words meant that she did what the WATCHMAN
     (28) wished her to do.
590  She has in mind the incredulity of the CHORUS (268f., and 475f.).
594  Cf. 86f.
603  The speaker changes the construction of the sentence in midstream,
     as often in Aeschylus.
605  The word translated "darling" is undignified and almost offensive.

and may he find his wife faithful in his house,
just as he left her, the watchdog of the palace,
loyal to him, an enemy to his ill-wishers,
one alike in all things; in the length of time
she has destroyed no seal set there by him.
I know no more of delight—nor of censorious rumor—     610
coming from another man, than I know how bronze is dipped.
Such is my boast, a boast replete with truth,
not shameful for a noble lady to utter.

    Exit CLYTEMNESTRA.

    CHORUS   Thus has she spoken; if you understand     615
through clear interpreters, her speech looks fair.
But you speak, Herald! It is of Menelaus that I ask,

---

609   The notion of the "seal of chastity" may be deliberately suggested
here.

611   *bronze is dipped:* literally "the dipping of bronze"; this might refer to tempering (provided we suppose that "bronze" is being used
loosely to refer to iron, as it may be) or to a coloring process. We
have no early evidence for a coloring process of this sort, and it may
be that it is chosen as an example of something that is impossible. In
any case, this latter explanation is to be preferred, as yielding a most
effective tragic irony. CLYTEMNESTRA will show presently that she
knows just as much about "how to color bronze" as she knows
about delight and censorious rumor.

612   The manuscripts give these lines to the HERALD; they are obviously
wrong (N.B.: if "my" were in the Greek, this would be even more
obvious, but its addition here is due to the requirements of the
English idiom). For the HERALD to make such a comment at the
end of CLYTEMNESTRA's speech, before the comment of a familiar
type made by the Coryphaeus, would be contrary to the rules of
Aeschylean technique.

615   The text is doubtful and the sense uncertain; a warning seems to
be conveyed in riddling terms. The separation of Menelaus from
his brother is a matter of special importance for the plot, for
the absence of Menelaus made it easy for CLYTEMNESTRA and
AEGISTHUS (*Ee gisth' us*; soft "*th*") to carry out their plan. The
wanderings of Menelaus were described in the satyr-play *Proteus*,
now lost, which was produced together with the *Oresteia*.

*whether safely returned once more*
*he will come with you, a power dear to this land.*

HERALD It cannot be that I speak what is false as fair,   620
so that my friends harvest it for the long time ahead.

CHORUS If only you can tell good news and still speak truth!
When good news and true news are severed, it is not easy to conceal.

HERALD The man is vanished from the Achaean host,   625
he and his ship; what I say is no lie.

CHORUS Did he put out in your sight from Ilium,
or did a storm, a sorrow to all alike, snatch him from the army?

HERALD You have hit the mark, like a master archer;
and a long tale of woe you have briefly voiced.

CHORUS Was it as living or as dead   630
that rumor on the other voyagers' lips told of him?

HERALD No one knows so as to give clear report,
except the Sun that nurtures life upon the earth.

CHORUS Then how do you say the storm came upon the fleet,
and how did it end, by the anger of the gods?   635

HERALD It is not fitting to mar the day of good news

---

621 The news the HERALD brings is compared to a crop that will have
to feed a community for some length of time.

626 One story was that AGAMEMNON and Menelaus quarreled, and
that Menelaus set off from Troy alone. Aeschylus glances at this
version, but follows the other, according to which the ships of the
brothers were separated by a storm.

633 The Sun was believed to travel each day from the far east to the
far west, returning during the night to its starting point in a golden
cup that sailed across the sea; during its daily journey, it could
see all that happened upon the earth.

636 Throughout the scene the HERALD shows himself pathetically
anxious to insist that he brings good news and most reluctant to
allow the longed-for hour of triumph to be marred by the recol-

with the tongue of ill report; apart is the honor paid to the gods.
But when a messenger brings to a city news of calamity to be prayed
  against,
with gloomy countenance, news of its army's fall—
telling how one wound afflicting the whole people has befallen the
  city,                                                                     640
and how many men have been hounded forth from many homes,
by the double scourge that Ares loves,
a two-tipped spear of ruin, a bloody pair of yokefellows:
when a messenger is loaded with such woes as these,
then it is proper to utter this paean of the Erinyes.                       645
But when with good news of events bringing salvation
he comes to a city rejoicing in prosperity . . .
how shall I mix good with the bad, telling
of the storm that afflicted the Achaeans, not without the wrath of
  heaven?
For a covenant was sworn by those former enemies,                           650
fire and sea, and they gave earnest of their friendship
by destroying the unhappy host of the Argives;
and in darkness evil arose from the stormy waves.

---

lection of those features of the situation that are unpleasing. The
Greeks did not allow religious celebrations of a joyful character
to be interrupted by any note that might seem ill-omened; that is
what is meant by "apart is the honor paid to the gods."

642 A scourge is sometimes called "double" in Greek simply because
it has two points; but the scourge is probably called that here in
view of the distinction between public and private calamity that
has just been drawn.

645 The paean was originally a song in honor of Apollo, and therefore
joyful; the Erinyes (see note on 59), like other gods of the underworld, had no place in any joyful form of worship, so that the
notion of a paean of the Erinyes carries an effect of powerful
paradox.

651 Fire and sea are compared to businessmen who give one another
guarantees by engaging in a joint enterprise.

The ships were dashed against each other by the winds of Thrace;
and they, butting against each other of necessity 655
beneath the storm of the hurricane and the spray of beating rain,
vanished out of sight, like sheep scattered by an evil shepherd.
And when the sun's bright light arose,
we saw the Aegean sea flower with the corpses
of Achaean men and with the wrecks of ships. 660
But we and our ship, its hull unscathed,
were stolen away or else begged off
by some god who set his hand to the tiller.
And preserving fortune graciously took her seat upon our vessel,
so that we had not to stay at anchor and fear the welter of the waves, 665
nor did we run aground upon a rocky shore.
And then, having escaped a watery Hades,
in the bright light of day, not believing in our fortune,
we let our thoughts seek remedy for our new reverse,
for the host had suffered and been sorely pounded. 670
And now, if any of them yet breathes,
they speak of us as dead, of course;
and we suppose their fate to be the same.
May it turn out as well as possible! As for Menelaus,
first and chiefly, expect that he will come. 675
Well, if some ray of the sun finds him out
still flourishing in life, by the contrivance of a Zeus
who does not yet wish to exterminate his house,
there is some hope that he may come back home.
Know that in hearing so much you have heard the truth! 680

    Exit HERALD.

### STROPHE 1

CHORUS  *Who can have named her*

---

654   For the icy north winds that blow over the Aegean from this direction, see 192f.

674   Some think that part of the text is missing after 674; this is unlikely.

681   The disastrous news that Menelaus is missing brings the thoughts of the CHORUS back to the wife of Menelaus, Helen, who has been the agent of disaster (cf. 225, 403f., 447). In trochaic meter

*with such utter truth?*
*Was it perhaps some unseen one*
*who in foreknowledge of what was fated*
*guided his tongue rightly?*                                    685
*Her, the bride of the spear, the object of contention,*
*Helen? For in a manner fitting to her name*
*destroyer of ships, destroyer of men, destroyer*
*of cities from the delicate tissues*                          690
*of her bower she sailed,*

---

like that in the hymn to Zeus (160f.), it etymologizes her name,
deriving it from a word that means "destroy"; then in ionics
(ᴜᴜ‒‒), mostly in the 'anaclastic' form known as anacreontics
ᴜᴜ‒ᴜ/‒ᴜ‒x), it returns to her voyage to Troy. In the corresponding antistrophe, it dwells on the disastrous end of her marriage to Paris; strophe and antistrophe are rounded off with a final
piece consisting (probably) of three pherecrateans (‒x ‒ᴜᴜ ‒x).
The fable of the lion cub that follows is an appropriately
simple meter, glyconics (xx ‒ᴜᴜ ‒ᴜx) and pherecrateans, some
with a slight variation (‒ᴜᴜ ‒ᴜᴜ ‒x), then again two catalectic
trochaic dimeters, then a glyconic and a pherecratean to finish. The
third strophe (736f.) opens with iambics and finishes with ionics and
anacreontics; the fourth (763f.) is in the iambics that play such
an important part in the choruses of AGAMEMNON. The Greeks
of the archaic period believed in the mystical significance of
etymologies, and not only poets but even philosophers might
attach importance to them. Etymology was then in a primitive
state, and many of the etymologies that were taken seriously were
false, as this one is; names were thought to give a clue to the fate
of their bearers. The name "Helen" is treated as though the first
part were connected with the root "*hele-*," meaning "kill," "destroy."

683   What "unseen one" was imagined as the possible giver of the
name? Not, I think, a god or spirit, but more likely a person now
dead; by a false etymology of the name of Hades from an adjective
meaning "not seeing" or "not seen," the dead were sometimes
called "the unseeing" or "the unseen ones."

*sped by the breeze of Zephyrus the giant.*
*And many huntsmen that bore shields*
*were gone in the wake of the oars*      695
*when they had put in to Simois'*
*leafy shores*
*through the work of bloody strife.*

### ANTISTROPHE 1

*And for Ilium was a* kedos *true to its name*
*accomplished by a wrath that fulfilled its purpose;*    700
*for the dishonoring of the guest-table*
*and of hospitable Zeus in later time*
*it exacted vengeance from those who loudly*
*celebrated the song in the bride's honor,*     705
*the song which then fell to the bridegroom's kin to sing.*
*And learning a different tune*
*Priam's aged city,*      710
*a tune of many sorrows,*
*loudly, I think, laments, calling upon*
*Paris of the disastrous marriage.*

---

692   *Zephyrus:* pronounce *Zeff' ir us:* Zephyrus was the west wind, not normally called a giant. But it was thought that if the gods had a special reason for wishing it, a journey might be accomplished with uncanny speed; we find the same notion in Aeschylus' *The Suppliants,* 1046–47.

693   *huntsmen . . . shields:* the armed warriors of the Greek army; huntsmen do not normally carry shields, but these huntsmen on the track of Helen did so.

696   *Simois:* pronounce *Simm' oe is.*

699   *kedos:* this word can mean either "a connection by marriage" or "mourning." None of the translators whose work is known to me has found an English expression that adequately preserves the play on the two senses of the word here.

704   See note 61; cf. 399f.

705   In this case the bride's kin were not there to perform the office that should have been theirs.

67

*She has endured a life of ruin*
*and of lamentation through her citizens'*
*piteous slaughter.*                                                715

## STROPHE 2

*A man reared a lion's offspring*
*in his house, unsuckled, just as it was,*
*in the beginnings of its life*                                    720
*gentle, dear to children*
*and a delight to the aged.*
*And often he took it in his arms*
*like a new-born child*
*bright-eyed, and fawning on the hand*
*as its belly's needs compelled it.*                               725

## ANTISTROPHE 2

*But in time it showed the temper*
*it had from its parents; for returning*
*kindness to those that reared it*
*with horrid slaughter of their cattle*                            730
*it made a feast unbidden,*
*'and the house was befouled with blood,*
*woe irresistible to the servants,*
*a vast havoc of much slaughter.*
*And by the act of a god a priest of Ruin*                         735
*had been reared within the house.*

---

717  We should beware of supposing that there must be an exact parallel
between the lion's career and that of Helen; there is not, for Helen
was only the instrument, not the agent, of the destruction of the
Trojans. CLYTEMNESTRA's career is far more similar to the lion's.

735  The word "priest" is chosen because priests performed the act of
sacrifice; the slaughtered cattle are imagined as being a sacrifice to
Ate, the personification of destruction.

### STROPHE 3

And at first I would say there came to Ilium's city
a temper of windless calm, 740
and a delicate adornment of wealth,
a soft dart of the eyes,
the flower of love that stings the heart.
And after bedding them together she brought about
a bitter end of the marriage, 745
evil in her sojourn, evil in her company
sped to the sons of Priam
by the guidance of the hospitable Zeus,
she that brings tears to brides, the Erinys.

### ANTISTROPHE 3

And long has there been current among men an ancient saying, 750

---

737 The shift to the slower iambic rhythm is perfectly adapted to the
sense. The CHORUS is saying that two things came to Ilium
(*Eye' li um*): first, a feeling of calm, and next, love; it is not
describing Helen.

742 The matron who presides over the nuptials is in this case none
other than the avenger of Zeus Xenios (see note on 61), the
Erinys; the audience is kept waiting until the end of the sentence
and stanza for the awful name (cf. 55–59).

750 Closely linked by strophic responsion with the preceding stanza
is the beginning of one of the most significant passages of theological reflection in Aeschylus; it continues until the end of the
stasimon. The CHORUS strongly insists that the gods do not punish
humans out of mere jealousy of their good fortune; crime alone
provokes their vengeance, which may be delayed to fall on the
descendants of the criminal. But the great and powerful are more
liable to temptation than the poor and humble. The "ancient
saying" referred to in the opening passage states the widespread
primitive belief in the divine envy that is provoked by the overabun-
dant prosperity of certain mortals. But more than a century before
Aeschylus it had been rejected by Solon, a writer particularly well
known at Athens (fr. 1, 9f.; fr. 5, 9–10). We must not, therefore,

that a man's great prosperity, brought to completion,
has offspring, and does not perish childless;
and that from good fortune for a family                    755
there is born insatiable woe.
And I am apart from others, alone in thought;
for the impious act
begets more after it,
like to the stock from whence they come.                   760
For the fate of houses that walk straight in the paths of justice
is a fair offspring of their former fate.

### STROPHE 4

But ancient insolence is used
to beget an insolence that has its youth
among the woes of mortals, soon or late, when the appointed time    765
of birth is come, and a spirit
irresistible, unconquerable, is brought forth,
the recklessness that is Ruin, black for the house,        770
like to its parents.

### ANTISTROPHE 4

Justice shines
beneath smoky rafters

---

take the CHORUS' protestation (757) that it is alone in its opinion
as a personal utterance of the poet, something which, common as
it is in choral lyric poetry, would be surprising in tragedy of this
early date.

758　The metaphor of procreation is often applied in Greek poetry to the
relationship of such abstractions as surfeit, insolence (hybris), and
ate (destruction); thus Solon had said (fr. 5, 9, mentioned above),
"Surfeit begets Hybris." Just so, the fate of just men is a "fair
offspring" of the fate of their ancestors.

766　The text is uncertain, but the general sense seems not to be in
doubt.

773　Dike, the personification of Justice, is commonly called (first by
Hesiod) a daughter of Zeus and is said to sit at his right hand and

*and honors the righteous life;* 775
*but the gold-bespangled halls where there are hands unclean*
*she quits with eyes averted*
*and goes to what is holy, having no respect for*
*the power of wealth made counterfeit with praise.* 780
*And she guides all things to their appointed end.*

Enter AGAMEMNON in his chariot, accompanied by
CASSANDRA.

CHORUS  *Come, king, sacker of Troy,*
*offspring of Atreus,*
*how am I to address you? How am I to revere you,* 785
*neither overshooting nor falling short of*
*the right measure of my gratitude?*
*Many among mortals give preference to seeming,*
*transgressing against justice.*
*To echo the groans of the unfortunate* 790
*each one is ready; but the sting of pain*
*does not reach their hearts.*
*And seeming as though they share his joy,*

---

tell him which among men are just and which unjust. In one lost
play of Aeschylus she appeared as a character; see the interesting
fragment that is preserved (No. 282 in the Loeb edition; No. 281
probably belongs to the same play). In this stanza Aeschylus may
have in mind a famous passage of Hesiod's *Works and Days*, which
describes how Aidos and Nemesis (Respect and Right Apportionment) will one day desert the earth and fly up to heaven in indignation at the wickedness of men (197f.).

781    Originally the word "Dike" may have meant something like
"custom," "the appointed way in which things happen"; this made
it easy for "Justice" to be imagined as the appointed order of the
universe. The stasimon closes on an ominous note for AGAMEMNON,
whose entry immediately follows its conclusion.

782    As the king enters, the CHORUS welcomes him in marching anapests
(783–809: see note on 40f.). The stress they lay on the difference
between sincere and false praise is significant; they are aware that
CLYTEMNESTRA's words will not be sincere.

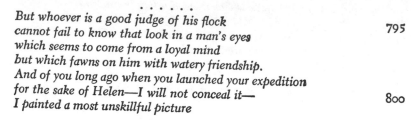

*constraining their mirthless faces*

. . . . . .

*But whoever is a good judge of his flock*
*cannot fail to know that look in a man's eyes*
*which seems to come from a loyal mind*
*but which fawns on him with watery friendship.*
*And of you long ago when you launched your expedition*
*for the sake of Helen—I will not conceal it—*
*I painted a most unskillful picture*

795

800

. . . . . .

*and as not wielding well the tiller of your mind,*
*trying by sacrifices to bring back*
*courage to dying men* [?].
*But now not from the mind's edge nor without friendship*
*I say, "Sweet is toil to them who have accomplished."*
*And in time shall you learn by inquiry*
*which of the citizens has guarded the city justly*
*and which has failed to keep the proper limit.*

805

AGAMEMNON   First Argos and the gods of the land,
It is right that I address,

810

---

799   Compare 466–74.

803   Text uncertain; I have translated an emendation which may well be wrong.

805   Again the text is not certain, but some proverbial phrase bearing the meaning given in the translation must be used.

810   Like the HERALD (503f.), AGAMEMNON first salutes the land of Argos and its gods. In saying that the gods have helped him to return and have helped him in punishing the Trojans, he uses a word meaning "share in the responsibility," which some scholars have taken as a proof of his arrogance. But a Greek might claim without blasphemy to share the credit for an achievement with the gods who had helped him. A Greek hero was expected to do his best, and then a god might help him; in such a case, the god would not claim all the credit. Jehovah might inspire Samson to slaughter countless Philistines with an ass's jawbone; but then all the credit would belong to Jehovah.

72

they that have a share in
my safe return and in the satisfaction exacted
from Priam's city. For by no spoken word the gods
heard the parties' pleas, and in no uncertain fashion          815
their votes for the death of men and ruin of Ilium
they put into the urn of blood; and to the opposite vessel
hope of a hand approached, but the vessel was not filled.
And even now the smoke marks out the conquered city.
Destruction's storms have life; and dying with the city
the embers waft forth rich breaths of wealth.                 820
For this must the gods with very mindful gratitude
be paid, since their arrogant rapine
has been avenged, and for a woman's sake
their city was ground to dust by the Argive monster,
the offspring of a horse, the shield-bearing army,            825
which launched its leap as the Pleiads set.
And the ravening lion leaped over the wall,
and licked his fill of the blood of kings.
To the gods I have drawn out this prelude.
But as for what you think, I have listened and remember,      830
and I too say the same and you have me as a fellow advocate.
For in few among men it is inbred

---

813   In a fifth-century Athenian law-court there was an urn of condem-
      nation and an urn of acquittal; the juror received one pebble, which
      he put into one or the other of them. He may have taken care to
      preserve the secrecy of the ballot by approaching the other urn also
      and pretending to put his pebble into it; but we do not have to
      suppose this in order to understand the text.

824   The Wooden Horse.

826   Troy fell at night, according to a tradition that is first attested to
      in the post-Homeric epic, *Little Iliad*. Properly speaking, "as the
      Pleiads (*Pleye′ ads*) set" should denote a season of the year, early
      November; the usual story was that Troy fell in early summer.
      Probably the poet simply meant to indicate night rather than day.

829   Now AGAMEMNON turns to the CHORUS; he expresses agreement
      with what it has said, but the CHORUS' warning does not alert him
      to the immediate danger.

to pay respect without envy to a friend in his prosperity.
For the poison of hatred lodged near the heart
doubles the burden for him who has the malady;                    835
he is burdened with his own sorrows,
and he groans as he looks upon another's happiness.
I can speak from knowledge—well I know
the mirror of society, the image of a shadow,
those who seem most kindly towards me.                            840
But only Odysseus, who sailed against his will,
once yoked proved a ready trace-horse for me;
whether he is alive or dead, I say
this of him. But for the rest, in the sight of the city and the gods
we shall hold general conclave in full assembly                  845
and shall take counsel. As for that which is well,
we must plan that it continue well.
But as for that which has need of healing remedies,
either by burning or by the kindly knife
we shall try to turn back the pain of the disease.               850
But now I shall come to my halls and to the house where lies my
    hearth,
and my first greeting shall be for the gods
who sped me far and have brought me back;
and since victory has attended me, may she abide!

      Enter CLYTEMNESTRA.

CLYTEMNESTRA  Men of the city, honored lords of Argos here,  855
I shall feel no shame to speak to you
of the love I bear my husband; for in time timidity
dies away for human kind. It is not from others

---

838  Text uncertain.

841  Apart from the famous quarrel with Achilles that is described in
the *Iliad* and the quarrel with Ajax, which led to the latter's sui-
cide, AGAMEMNON was stated in the *Odyssey* (3, 130f.) as well as
in a post-Homeric epic, *Nostoi* by Agias, to have left Troy alone
because of a quarrel (see note on 1640, below).

849  The two principal methods of ancient surgery were cautery and
excision.

that I have learned; I shall speak of my own life of sorrow
so long as this man was beneath Ilium.           860
First, for a woman far from her husband
to sit in her house alone is a fearful grief,
hearing many a malignant rumor;
as one messenger follows another
bringing yet worse tidings, uttering sorrow for the house.   865
And if this man has endured as many wounds
as rumor channeled to our house
made him, he is riddled with more holes than a net.
And if he had been dead, as many stories reported,
then with three bodies, like a second Geryon,         870
he could have claimed to receive a threefold cloak of earth
—much earth above, I do not speak of that below!—
perishing once under each aspect.
Because of such malignant rumors as these
many nooses were knotted for my neck and hung on high,   875
untied by others by force after they had seized me against my will.
This, I say, is why our son does not stand here,
the warrant of your pledges and of mine,
as he should have stood, Orestes; do not be surprised at this.
For he is the guest of a kindly ally,          880
Strophius the Phocian, who warned me of trouble
on two accounts, of your peril

---

870    Geryon (*Gee′ ry on*; hard "*g*"), or Geryones, was a monster with
three bodies and three heads who lived near Tartessos in Spain
(in the neighborhood of Cadiz) and was killed by Heracles. Lines
870–73 are puzzling; some have thought them corrupt, or interpolated; 872 in particular has been suspected, perhaps rightly.

875    If one is trying to prevent someone from hanging himself, one
must first hold him fast to prevent his moving and then get someone to untie the noose.

877    One story was that Orestes was rescued, either by Electra or by a
faithful nurse, at the time of the murder. Strophius (*Stroff′ i us*),
king of Phocis, was the father of Pylades, Orestes' (*Or′ est′ ēs*)
great friend, who appears in *The Libation Bearers.*

881    *Phocian:* pronounce *Fō′ shun.*

before Ilium, and of how the people's lawless clamor
might overthrow the council, since it is inbred
in mortals to kick the man who has fallen.                              885
Such a pretext carries no deceit.
For me the gushing fountains of my tears
have run dry, and no drop is left in them;
and my late-watching eyes are sore
with weeping for the beacon-fires for you                              890
left ever unattended. And in my dreams
the light sounds of a gnat's trumpeting
would wake me, since I saw more sufferings concerning you
than the time through which I slept had room for.
Now, having endured all this, with a heart free from mourning         895
I can call my husband here the watchdog of the fold,
the forestay that preserves the ship, the firmly grounded pillar
of the lofty roofs, only-begotten child to a father,
land appearing to sailors beyond hope,
fair weather seen after the storm,                                     900
for the thirsty traveler the water of a fountain;
it is a joy to escape any manner of constraint.
Such are the appellations of which I hold him worthy.
But let envy be absent; for many are the sufferings
which I bore in time past; and now, dear one,                         905
descend from this your chariot, not setting upon the ground
your foot, O king, the foot that conquered Troy!
Handmaids, why do you delay, you who have assigned to you the task
of strewing the ground he walks on with tapestries?

---

886   The pretext alluded to is the pretext just mentioned for the sending
      away of Orestes.

895   The long series of hyperbolical comparisons takes the form of what
      is called a "priamel," a word derived from *praeambulum* (preamble)
      and denoting "a series of detached statements which through con-
      trast or comparison lead up to the idea with which the speaker
      is primarily concerned." The effect is one of almost nauseating
      flattery.

902   A somewhat feeble line, perhaps an interpolation. If it is genuine,
      then the comparison to the joy that comes to one pent up in
      escaping is the last item in the series of compliments.

At once let his path be spread with purple,          910
that Justice may lead him to the home he never hoped to see!
And for the rest, may forethought not overcome by sleep
accomplish all justly with the gods' aid as it is fated!

AGAMEMNON   Offspring of Leda, guardian of my house,
your speech matches my absence;          915
for you have drawn it out at length. But to give me
fitting praise, that is an honor that should come from others.
And for the rest do not in woman's fashion
pamper me; do not as if I were a barbarian
gape at me with prostrations and loud cries;     920
do not by strewing my path with raiment make it exposed
to envy. It is the gods you should honor with such things;
and to walk, being a mortal, on embroidered splendors
is impossible for me without fear.
I tell you to honor me with honors human, not divine.     925
Apart from footwipers and embroideries
the voice of fame resounds; and good sense

---

910   The irony is obvious to the audience. Note that it is tapestries,
not carpets, that CLYTEMNESTRA proposes to have spread upon the
floor for AGAMEMNON to walk upon during his triumphal entry. It
is made clear that such tapestries were reserved for the service of
the gods, that they were enormously valuable, and that they were
so delicate that after being trodden upon they could not be used
again.

914   AGAMEMNON's tone in speaking to his wife is noticeably dry; but
it is impossible to say whether rumors of her infidelity had reached
him. His first reaction to her proposal that he should walk upon
the tapestries is the correct one; but presently, by a series of shrewd
and penetrating questions, CLYTEMNESTRA will overcome his resistance.

921   In ancient Greece, as in some parts of India and Persia today, the
distinction among tapestries, carpets, and robes was not altogether
sharp.

926   The sense could conceivably be "Different sound the word 'footwipers' and the word 'embroideries.'"

is the god's greatest gift. We must pronounce him fortunate
who has ended his life in the prosperity he cherishes;
and if in all things I may fare so, I do not lack confidence.          930

CLYTEMNESTRA   Come, tell me this, not against your judgment.

AGAMEMNON   My judgment, be assured, I shall not suppress.

CLYTEMNESTRA   Would you have vowed to the gods, in a moment of fear, that you would act after this fashion?

AGAMEMNON   Yes, if any with sure knowledge had prescribed
this ritual.

CLYTEMNESTRA   What do you think Priam would have done,
had he accomplished this?          935

AGAMEMNON   Indeed he would have walked upon embroideries,
I think.

CLYTEMNESTRA   Then feel no scruple for the reproach of men.

AGAMEMNON   Yet talk in the mouths of the people has great
power.

CLYTEMNESTRA   But he of whom none is jealous is not envied.

---

928   It is a commonplace of Greek popular thought that a man can only
be pronounced fortunate after his death.

931   *tell me this*: CLYTEMNESTRA means "say that you will do this
thing."

933   This question is sophistical; an action taken in order to fulfill
a vow would not be the same as one taken to glorify oneself.
AGAMEMNON's answer implies that he recognizes this distinction.

935   Again the question is sophistical; Priam, an Oriental and also
an offender against the law of Zeus, is not a good example. Again
AGAMEMNON's answer shows that he is not deceived.

938   This time AGAMEMNON's answer is less satisfactory. He should have
said, "It is not men, but gods whose anger I fear"; instead he
weakly remarks that public opinion is a great force.

939   CLYTEMNESTRA makes use of what seems to be a commonplace
among the Greeks, that it is precisely the great man who arouses

AGAMEMNON  *It is not a woman's part to desire contention.*  940

CLYTEMNESTRA  *But for the fortunate even to yield up victory
is becoming.*

AGAMEMNON  *Do you in truth value victory in this contest?*

CLYTEMNESTRA  *Be persuaded; you are the winner, if willingly
you leave all to me.*

AGAMEMNON  *Well, if this is your pleasure, let someone swiftly
loose*
*my boots, which serve my feet as slaves;*  945
*and as I tread upon these purples of the gods,*
*let no eye's envy strike me from afar.*
*For I feel much reluctance to waste the house's substance with my
feet,*
*ruining wealth and tissues bought with silver.*

---

jealousy; Such a man, she says, must necessarily be envied. A
brother of the Sicilian tyrants Hieron and Gelon was actually
named Polyzalos, "he who arouses much jealousy." Still, to agree
directly with CLYTEMNESTRA would be dangerous, and AGAMEMNON
will not do so. But instead of pointing out the danger, he feebly
protests that it is unbecoming for a woman to be so insistent.
He is triumphant, she answers, and it becomes him to give way; if
he willingly surrenders, he is the victor. After making the futile
gesture of removing his boots, AGAMEMNON yields and enters the
palace, while CLYTEMNESTRA mocks at his parsimony.

One must beware of overrating the significance of this scene,
as though the trampling of the tapestries made a significant addition to the guilt of AGAMEMNON; its importance is symbolic
rather than actual. But in performance it is most effective; as
AGAMEMNON enters the palace the audience knows that he will
never re-emerge. The scene's effect is truly tragic, for AGAMEMNON
knows that what his wife proposes is wrong, and yet she persuades
him to act against his better judgment. Would it be possible for
her to persuade him, if he were not under a curse, so that in the
phraseology common to Aeschylus and Homer, Zeus sends Ate
to take away his wits?

For this, so much; but in kindly fashion                               950
bring in this stranger; on him who is gentle in the use of power
the god from afar looks favorably;
for none of his own will bows to the yoke of slavery.
And she came with me as the chosen flower
out of much wealth, the army's gift.                                   955
But since I am constrained to defer to you in this,
I will go into the halls of the palace, treading upon purple.

    CLYTEMNESTRA    There is a sea—and who shall dry it up?—
that breeds a gush of much purple, precious as silver,
ever renewed, for the dyeing of garments.                             960
And a store of such stuffs by the gods' grace, king,
is here for us to have; the palace does not know poverty.
And I would have vowed the trampling of much raiment,
had it been prescribed at the seat of an oracle,
in contriving the homecoming of this man's life.                      965
For while the root survives, the leaves return to the house,
stretching their shade over against the dogstar;
and with your return to the hearth of the palace,
you signal warmth in winter by your coming.
And when Zeus makes from the unripe grape                             970
wine, then at once is there coolness in the house,
while a man of power walks about the palace.
    Exit AGAMEMNON.
Zeus, Zeus with power to accomplish, accomplish my prayer;

---

950    It was a common practice in the heroic age for an army that had
sacked a city to bestow upon its chiefs female captives as a token
of regard. These women enjoyed the status of a secondary wife, and
sometimes had children by their captors who themselves attained
heroic status, although inferior in position to the children of the
chief wife. Thus Hesione, daughter of the Trojan king Laomedon,
was given to Telamon, and her son Teucer, although a hero, was
subordinate to his half-brother Ajax, Telamon's son by his wife
Eriboea. Thus at Troy Chryseis (*Khrise ee′ is*) was given to AGA-
MEMNON, Briseis (*Bry see′ is*) to Achilles, and after the city's
capture Andromache, Hector's widow, to Achilles' son Neoptolemus.

958–72    During this speech AGAMEMNON is slowly entering the palace.

965    My rather awkward translation results from an attempt to bring
out an ambiguity that is not accidental.

80

and may what you are about to accomplish be your care!

Exit CLYTEMNESTRA.

### STROPHE 1

CHORUS  Why, ever constant, does this                               975
terror, set before my divining heart
hover,
and prophecy speaks in a song unbidden, unpaid for,
nor does trustful confidence
sit on my mind's throne                                              980
so that I can spurn it away
like a dream hard to interpret?
Time has passed its youth
since the cables were thrown
onto the sandy shore,                                                985
when to Ilium
the army came in its ships.

### ANTISTROPHE 1

And I learn with my own eyes

---

975   The meter of the first strophe and antistrophe (975–87, 988–1000)
      is mainly trochaic; at 979 ⁓ 92 there are dactyls, and 983–87 ⁓ 997–
      99, cretics and iambics. The second strophe (1001) and antistrophe
      (1019) begin with cretics; then come anapests, and then dactyls;
      from 1011 ⁓ 25 to the end the metre is again trochaic, with dactyls
      at 1014–15 ⁓ 1031–32.

977   The early Greeks believed the seat of the intelligence to be the
      heart; the importance of the brain was realized by the fifth-century
      medical writer, Alcmaeon of Croton.

978   The minstrels who sing in the halls of kings in the Homeric poems
      perform only at the bidding of their patrons, who later reward
      them for their performances. The CHORUS compares its presen-
      timent of evil with a song of a different nature; the comparison is
      made easier because the presentiment is called a prophecy, and
      prophets often put their predictions into verse.

984   The text is uncertain, but probably mentions the ship's cables
      being thrown onto the shore as a preliminary to making her fast.
      This is found in several epic descriptions of a ship's landing.

of his return, myself my witness;
but nonetheless the dirge without a lyre                          990
is chanted,
the dirge of the Erinys is chanted by my mind, self-taught
within me, altogether lacking
the cherished confidence of hope.
And my inward parts do not speak vainly,                          995
while near a mind instinct with justice
my heart swirls in eddies
that bring fulfillment.
Yet I pray that from my
expectation these things may fall
so that they fail to be fulfilled.                               1000

### STROPHE 2

Indeed great good health
is never content with its limits. For sickness,
a neighbor that shares a wall, presses it hard;
and a man's fortune, steering a straight course               1005
strikes a hidden reef.
But if beforehand any part of the possessions

---

992 A Homeric minstrel might boast of being self-taught, claiming that the gift of song had been given to him by a god; here the self-taught singer is the anxious mind that "chants the dirge of the Erinys."

995 Words used to denote mental organs, like "mind" or "spirit," were originally words used to denote physical organs where the mind or spirit was thought to be located; here the dividing line between physical and mental is very indistinct.

1001 The text is most uncertain. "The limit of health is never satisfied," if right, presumably means, "Men are never satisfied with whatever limit of health [i.e., prosperity, good fortune] they may attain." But then what follows does not come naturally.

1005 A line must be missing either before or after this line, probably before it.

1008 It was sometimes believed that a man whose great prosperity exposed him to divine envy might appease the gods by the

*that he owns is hurled by apprehension*
*from the derrick of moderation—*                    1010
*then the house entire does not sink,*
*overfull of abundance,*
*nor does the hull plunge beneath the waves.*
*Great and abundant is the gift that comes from Zeus,*
*which from the furrows of each year's harvest*      1015
*destroys the plague of famine.*

### ANTISTROPHE 2

*But the black blood that has once*
*poured to the ground in front of a man*             1020
*in death who could call back*
*with incantations?*
*Even him that knew well*

Bad Blood
no atonement

---

voluntary sacrifice of part of his possessions. Thus Herodotus (III. 40f.) describes how the Samian tyrant Polycrates tried to propitiate the gods by throwing into the sea a favorite ring, only to have it reappear inside a fish served to him at table. On hearing this story the Egyptian king Amasis abandoned his alliance, feeling sure Polycrates would come to a bad end. This concept is here expressed in a metaphor, the jettisoning of cargo in a storm. The point of 1014f. is that abundant harvests in the future may be trusted to make up losses incurred by sacrifices of this kind.

1010   A derrick is an apparatus for slinging off cargo which is to be jettisoned.

1017   This affords a convenient transition to the thought that, although the loss of possessions can always be made up, the loss of life is irremediable; the latter is a thought that recurs at several places in the *Oresteia*.

1021   Incantations were part of the apparatus of the Homeric doctor.

1022   The reference is to Asclepius, son of Apollo by the mortal woman Coronis, who was so great a physician that he could restore the dead to life. According to the early legend, he restored Hippolytus to please Artemis, and for doing so he was killed by Zeus with the thunderbolt. This legend became less prominent in later times,

*how to raise men up from the dead*
*Zeus checked in no gentle fashion.*
*And did not one portion appointed*                    1025
*by the gods restrain another*
*from going beyond its due,*
*then my heart would outstrip*
*my tongue and would be pouring this forth.*
*But as things are it murmurs in darkness*             1030
*full of sad thoughts and having no hope*
*of accomplishing any timely purpose,*
*while fire is kindled in my mind.*

Enter CLYTEMNESTRA.

CLYTEMNESTRA   Bring yourself in, you too, I mean Cassandra!   1035
Since without anger Zeus has made you with our house
a sharer in lustral water, with many slaves
taking your stand near the altar of Zeus, god of possessions,
descend from the chariot here, and do not be proud.

---

when the cult of Asclepius had attained great importance and his shrines at Epidaurus, Cos, and Pergamum had become places of pilgrimage.

1025   The sense may be disputed, but I believe it to be, "If it were not that the god-given rights of one man (AGAMEMNON, a king) restrain those of another (me, a subject) from exceeding their due (i.e., from speaking of things discreditable to the royal house), I should now be explaining why I feel so much afraid." The Argive elders are afraid because they know that Atreus' crime against Thyestes (*Thie ess' tēs*; soft "*th*") brought a curse on the royal house, and so the sinister intentions of CLYTEMNESTRA may be realized. The reason for their fears will become clear to the audience only with CASSANDRA's revelation.

1035   At this point an audience will expect to hear AGAMEMNON's death-cry. Instead, CLYTEMNESTRA comes out of the palace to call in CASSANDRA, who has remained on the chariot without speaking a word. Her words are not calculated to console the daughter of Priam or to content her with her new servile status.

Why, they say that even the son of Alcmene once      1040
endured to be sold. . . . . .
At least, if the constraint of this lot befalls one,
one should feel much gratitude at having lords whose wealth is
    ancient;
for those who have reaped a fair harvest which they never hoped for
are cruel to slaves in all things, and according to strict rule     1045
     . . . . . .
I have told you the nature of our custom.

CHORUS  *It is to you she speaks, a clear speech, and now she
    pauses.*
*Caught as you are in the toils of fate,*
*obey her if you will; but perhaps you will not.*

CLYTEMNESTRA  Why, if she is not, like a swallow,     1050
possessed of an unintelligible barbarian tongue,
I speak within the compass of her wits [?], and try to prevail on her
    with my words.

---

1037   Before a Greek sacrifice those present wetted their hands, and
     after it they were sprinkled with lustral water.

1038   Zeus Ktesios (Zeus the god of possessions) was worshipped in the
     storerooms of houses; his symbol was an urn containing ambrosia,
     a mixture of water, honey, and various fruits.

1040   *Alcmene:* pronounce *Alk meen' ē* (mother of Heracles): Heracles
     was punished for his treacherous murder of Iphitus by being taken
     to Lydia by Hermes and there sold to the queen Omphale, whom
     he served for a period (see Sophocles, *The Women of Trachis*
     248f.).

1041   The end of the line is corrupt; there is probably a reference to
     the humble fare eaten by slaves.

1050   The Greeks called foreigners, particularly Orientals, by the con-
     temptuous name *"barbaroi"* ("barbarians"), originally descriptive
     of what they thought to be their incoherent speech, which was
     sometimes compared to the twittering of swallows.

1052   The text and sense are uncertain; the first part of the line is
     probably corrupt.

CHORUS (to CASSANDRA)   Go with her; what she orders is best
   as things now are.
Obey, leaving your seat here on the wagon.

CLYTEMNESTRA   I have no time to linger here by the door;     1055
for the cattle of Hestia of the central navel-stone
stand there already, sacrifices to reward the fire,
for us who never hoped to have this joy.
And you, if you have a mind to obey any of my orders, make no delay;
but if you lack understanding and do not take in my words,     1060
then instead of speech make indication with barbarian hand.

CHORUS   The stranger seems to need a clear interpreter;
and her manner is that of a newly captured beast.

CLYTEMNESTRA   Indeed she is crazy and obeys the prompting
   of a mischievous mind,
she who has come leaving a city newly conquered     1065
and does not know how to bear the bridle

---

1056   At a sacrifice it was customary to reward the fire for its work
     in consuming the victim or victims with a preliminary sacrifice
     to Hestia, goddess of the hearth, that took place at the very
     start of the proceedings. But the words translated "sacrifice to
     reward the fire" depend on an emendation that is far from certain.

1057   This line is cut out by some editors as an interpolation; they may
     well be right.

1061   There is no incongruity in CLYTEMNESTRA's telling CASSANDRA
     in Greek what she is to do even if CASSANDRA does not understand
     Greek; in such circumstances people do attempt to communicate
     by speaking in their own language, trying to make their meaning
     clear by the tones and gestures that accompany their words. For
     the word "barbarian," see the note on 1061 above, although the
     word used here is not "barbaros" but a synonym.

1063   This seems to show that while remaining on the chariot,
     CASSANDRA is not motionless, but on the contrary highly agitated.

1066   The bit is attached to the bridle. We possess several specimens
     of the Greek bit, which is a very cruel instrument. At the
     slightest hint of disobedience the rider could cause the spiked
     rolls of the bit to tear the delicate membrane of the tongue and
     draw blood.

*till she has spent her strength in bloody foam.*
*I say I will not waste more words to be insulted.*

Exit CLYTEMNESTRA.

CHORUS  *But I will not be angry, for I pity her.*
*Come, unhappy one, desert this carriage,*                     1070
*and bowing to constraint submit to the unaccustomed yoke.*

CASSANDRA utters a cry of distress.

CASSANDRA  *Apollo, Apollo!*

CHORUS  *Why do you utter cries of woe, invoking Loxias?*

---

1072  Not every actor in an Aeschylean tragedy sings lyrics in addition
to speaking dialogue. CLYTEMNESTRA, for instance, who has
the largest part in what survives of Greek tragedy, never sings
lyrics, although she chants marching anapests. In *Agamemnon*
the only character who sings besides speaking is CASSANDRA. It
is not uncommon for a chorus to sing short lyrical passages and
an actor to reply in trimeters or in marching anapests. What we
have here is more unusual, for it is the actor, CASSANDRA, who
sings while the CHORUS replies in trimeters. Usually, the CHORUS'
state of mind is more exalted than that of the actor; here the
opposite is true, and this explains why CASSANDRA sings while
the CHORUS speaks. But as the exchange between them proceeds,
the CHORUS gradually becomes infected by CASSANDRA's mood,
and at 1121 they suddenly burst into sung lyrics. The meter of
the lyrics throughout the scene is the dochmiac, whose prevailing
rhythm can easily be grasped by means of Sir Richard Jebb's
mnemonic: "Thĕ wise kān gărōōs/Rĕsēnt leathĕr shōēs"; it is
particularly appropriate to excited utterance of the kind found here.
In the end CASSANDRA by a great effort calms herself, and in
speech instead of song, and in a much clearer and more explicit
way, she reiterates her warning (1178f.). From then until CAS-
SANDRA leaves the stage at 1330 the meter, apart from one or two
interjections, is in trimeters, symmetrically distributed between
CASSANDRA and the Coryphaeus.

1074  The Olympian gods, and Apollo in particular, can have no part
in scenes of mourning (cf. note on 645). *Loxias* (*Lox' i as*) is

*He is not such that a singer of dirges should come his way.*　　1075

　　CASSANDRA utters another cry.

CASSANDRA　*Apollo, Apollo!*

CHORUS　*Once more she calls with voice ill-omened on the god,*
*one in no way suited to stand by when tears are shed.*

CASSANDRA　*Apollo, Apollo!*　　1080
*You of the roadside, my destroyer.*
*For you have a second time easily destroyed me.*

CHORUS　*She will prophesy about her own sorrows;*
*the god's gift remains in her mind, even in servitude.*

CASSANDRA　*Apollo, Apollo!*　　1085
*You of the roadside, my destroyer!*
*Ah, where have you brought me? To what house?*

CHORUS　*To that of the Atreidae; if you do not understand this,*
*I tell it you; and you shall not say that it is false.*

CASSANDRA　*No, to a house that hates the gods, one that knows* 1090
*many sad tales of kindred murder . . . ,*
*a slaughter-place for men, a place where the ground is sprinkled.*

CHORUS　*The stranger seems to have keen scent, like a hound,*
*and she is on the track of those whose blood she will discover.*

CASSANDRA　(pointing to the door of the palace) *Yes, for here*
*are the witnesses that I believe.*　　1095

---

　　a title of Apollo, especially associated with his aspect as a god of prophecy.

1081　CASSANDRA has noticed the statues of Apollo Agyieus, Apollo of the Roadside, standing by the door of the palace. Such statues were conical pillars standing outside the doors of houses and could be seen there on the tragic and the comic stage.

　　There is a pun on the name Apollo and a verb meaning "to destroy."

1082　The first occasion will be told of later (1202f.).

1091　The text is corrupt; the sense conjectural.

1095　For the feast of Thyestes, see Introduction, page 13.

*These are children weeping for their slaughter,*
*and for the roasted flesh their father ate.*

CHORUS   Indeed we had heard of your prophetic fame;
*but we seek no interpreters of the gods.*

CASSANDRA   O horror, what plot is this?                    1100
*What is this great new agony?*
*A great evil is being plotted in this house,*
*unbearable for its friends, hard to remedy;*
*and protection stands far off.*

CHORUS   These prophecies I know not;                       1105
*but the others I recognized; for it is the talk of all the city.*

CASSANDRA   Ah, wretched one, will you accomplish this?
*The husband who shares your bed*
*you have washed in the bath, and . . . how shall I tell the end?*
*For soon this shall be; and she stretches forth hand*       1110
*after hand, reaching out.*

CHORUS   I do not yet understand; for now her riddles
*leave me perplexed at her obscure oracles.*

CASSANDRA   Ah, ah! Alas, alas, what is this that comes into
       *view?*
*Indeed it is some net of Hades.*                           1115
*But it is the net that shares his bed, that shares the guilt*
*of murder. And let that company whom the family can never sate*
*raise a shout over the sacrifice that stoning must avenge!*

CHORUS   What Erinys do you bid raise her cry

---

1106   The crime of Atreus is what the CHORUS has in mind.

1110   CASSANDRA incoherently describes a vision of CLYTEMNESTRA
       about to perform the murder.

1116   What object CASSANDRA has in mind will become clear only at
       1382f.

1117   She means the Erinyes (see 1186f.). Atrocious crimes against
       the whole community were punished in early times by ston-
       ing; the CHORUS will threaten CLYTEMNESTRA with this fate at
       1615f.

over the house? Your words give me no joy. 1120
And to my heart runs a drop of saffron dye,
the drop that for men who fall by the spear
accompanies the rays of life's sun as it sets;
and swiftly comes destruction.

CASSANDRA   Ah, ah! Look, look! Keep away the bull 1125
from the cow! In the robe
she has caught him with the contrivance of her black horn,
and she strikes; and he falls in the vessel of water.
It is the stroke struck by the cauldron of cunning murder that I
    speak of.

CHORUS   I would not boast of being a master judge of oracles, 1130
but this seems to me like some evil thing.
But from oracles what good message
is sent to men? For through evil
the wordy arts of soothsayers
bring fear to their listeners. 1135

---

1121   The text and sense are uncertain. If the emendation presupposed
by this translation is right, the allusion is to a belief that in
moments of great terror the blood runs to the heart, leaving the
other parts of the body, thus causing pallor. "Yellow" rather than
"white" is the color used to describe pallor by the Greeks, and
Homer speaks of "yellow fear." The blood is called "the drop of
saffron dye," not because it itself is yellow, but because it makes
the face go yellow.

1125   In the riddling language characteristic of prophetic utterances
and found in the words of CASSANDRA, as it has been in the
speech of Calchas reported in the Parodos (126f.), people are
often referred to by the names of animals.

1126   Difficult. If I am right, the cow who stands for CLYTEMNESTRA
is said to gore the bull who stands for AGAMEMNON with her
black horn.

1130   Although the early Greeks believed strongly in their oracles and
prophets and predictions in their poetry always come true, distrust
of oracles is often expressed—by Hector, for example, in a famous
passage of the Iliad (12. 237f.).

CASSANDRA    *Oh, oh! The unhappy fate of me in my misery!*
*For I speak of my own agony; another cup has been poured out.*
*Where have you brought me, one unfortunate?*
*For nothing but to share your death? Why else?*

CHORUS    *Your wits are crazed and a god carries you away,*    1140
*and over yourself you chant*
*a song unmusical, like that tawny one,*
*who, never tired of crying, cries, alas, with sad heart*
*lamenting for Itys, for Itys throughout a life*
*with sorrow beset on both sides, a nightingale.*    1145

CASSANDRA    *Oh, oh! The end of the songful nightingale!*
*For about her the gods cast a winged body*
*and give her a happy ordeal, free from cries of pain.*
*But for me there waits a rending with the two-edged spear.*

CHORUS    *From where have you the rushing pangs of possession*
*by a god,*    1150
*pangs that are in vain*
*and you shape your song of fear with ill-omened shriek*
*and in piercing notes alike?*
*From where have you the boundaries of your prophetic way*
*that tell of evil?*    1155

---

1142    The nightingale was originally Procne, daughter of Pandion, king of Athens and wife of Tereus, king of Thrace. Her sister Philomela was ravished by Tereus, who cut her tongue out to keep his crime secret, but Philomela by depicting the story on a tapestry informed her sister. Together they took revenge on Tereus by killing Itys (*Eye' tis*), his infant son by Procne; then the gods changed Procne into the nightingale, Philomela into the swallow. Philomela becomes the nightingale, as far as we know, only in Roman poetry.

1145    The word rendered "flourishing on both sides" is an adjective used in the language of religious ritual to denote a child who has both parents living and who was thus qualified to perform certain religious duties.

1146    Procne was simply transmuted into a nightingale, but CASSANDRA will die a painful death.

1150    The CHORUS learns the answer to this question only at 1202.

CASSANDRA   O the marriage of Paris, deadly to those he loved!
O my native stream of Scamander!
Then I was reared and grew
about your banks, ah me!
But about the shores of Cocytus and of Acheron          1160
I am likely soon to prophesy.

CHORUS   Why have you voiced this saying, all too clear?
A child might hear and understand.
And I am struck once more by a deadly pang,
by your grievous fate, listening to your shrill plaintive notes     1165
shattering for me to hear.

CASSANDRA   O the sorrows, the sorrows of my city
that perished utterly!
O my father's sacrifices before the walls,
prodigal in slaughter of cattle that cropped the grass!          1170
But they did not suffice for a remedy
to save the city from suffering as was fated.
And I whose mind is all aflame shall soon fall to the ground. [?]

CHORUS   These utterances follow on those before;
and some malignant spirit falls
grievously upon you and makes you                   1175
sing of sorrows full of tears and charged with death.
And the end I do not know.

CASSANDRA   Now shall my oracle be no longer one that looks forth
from a veil, like a newly wedded bride,
but as a bright, clear wind it shall rush              1180
toward the sunrise, so that like a wave

---

1160   Cocytus (Kō kye' tus), which means "the river of weeping," and
        Acheron, which was popularly derived from a word meaning
        "sorrow" (cf. 1557), were two of the rivers of Hades.

1172   The text is uncertain, probably corrupt.

1178   At this point CASSANDRA begins to speak in trimeters instead of
        singing in lyrics; she becomes more controlled and more articulate.

1180   The oracle is compared to a wind that blows toward the rising
        sun and drives the waves to a point where they may be clearly
        seen.

there shall surge toward the light a woe far greater
than this; no more in riddles shall I instruct you.
You bear me witness, running beside me as I scent out
the track of the ills accomplished long ago!                          1185
For this house is never left by a choir
that sings in unison, yet with no pleasant sound; for not pleasant
    are its words.
Yes, and it has drunk—so that it grows all the bolder—
of human blood, and stays in the house, a band of revelers
not easily sent away, composed of the Erinyes bred with the family.   1190
And the song they sing as they beset the rooms
is one of destruction that began it all; and each in turn they spit
on a brother's marriage-bed that brought harm to its violator.
Have I missed the mark, or do I like an archer make a hit?
Or am I a false prophet who knocks at doors, a babbler?               1195
Speak out in witness, taking oath that I know
the crimes of the house, old in story!

---

1186    After a *symposion* (drinking party), the guests would often take
part in a *kōmos* (a word sometimes translated "revel" and sometimes "serenade," according to the context; Milton's Comus derives his name from it). Carrying torches, they would set forth to
serenade one house after another in their more or less drunken
state; such scenes are sometimes depicted on Greek vases. The
members of this *kōmos* have drunk deep, not of wine but of
blood, and instead of going from house to house, they remain at
the house of the Atreidae.

1192    Thyestes first seduced Aerope, the wife of his brother Atreus, and
had her hand over to him the golden lamb that was the token of
Atreus' sovereignty, a story perhaps glanced at at 1585. Atreus
took vengeance by killing all his brother's children except one (he
killed a dozen, if the text at 1605 is sound) and serving them to
him at a banquet.

1196    A Greek prophet was supposed to know not only the future but
also the present and the past. This claim is made for Calchas in
*Iliad* 1. 70. A prophet will try to secure belief in the accuracy of
his prediction of the future by showing that he knows of past
events which are known to his audience, but which he cannot possibly have learned of except by supernatural means. This is why

CHORUS   And how could the plighting of an oath, though truly
    plighted,
avail for remedy? But I marvel at you,
that though bred beyond the seas you speak truly                    1200
of a foreign city, as though you had been present.

CASSANDRA   It was the prophet Apollo who set me in this office.

CHORUS   Struck with desire, god though he is?

CASSANDRA   Earlier, modesty made me not speak of this.

CHORUS   Yes, we are all fastidious when we have great good
    fortune.                                                       1205

CASSANDRA   Well, he was a wrestler who mightily breathed his
    grace upon me.

CHORUS   Did you come to the act of getting children, as is the
    way?

CASSANDRA   I consented, and then played Loxias false.

CHORUS   Being already seized by the prophetic arts?

CASSANDRA   Already I was foretelling to the citizens all their
    sufferings.                                                   1210

CHORUS   How then were you unscathed by the wrath of Loxias?

---

CASSANDRA insists that the CHORUS swears that what she has said
about the past history of the house of Atreus is the truth; for it
is of vital importance to her that they shall believe her when she
warns them of what is about to happen in the near future.

1202   Behind the myth of CASSANDRA there probably lies an ancient no-
    tion of the prophetess, inspired by the prophetic god Apollo, as
    the bride of the god. At Delphi the prophetess of Apollo, the
    Pythia, had to be a virgin.

1206   It is impossible to be certain whether this is merely a metaphorical
    way of saying that Apollo desired CASSANDRA or whether actual
    physical wrestling took place before they struck their bargain.

1208   See note on 1074.

CASSANDRA   *I could make none in anything believe me, once I*
    *had committed this offense.*

CHORUS   Yet to us your divinations seem worthy of belief.

   CASSANDRA   *Ah, ah! O misery!*
*Once more the dread pain of true prophecy whirls me round,*      1215
*troubling me with sinister preludes.*

*Do you see here sitting near the house*
*these young ones, like to the shapes we see in dreams?*
*Children slain, as it were, by the hands of their kindred,*
*their hands full of the meat of their own flesh;*      1220
*the vitals with the entrails I see them holding,*
*a pitiful load, of which their father ate.*
*For these, so I declare, there is one who plots revenge*
*a cowardly lion, tumbling in the bed,*
*watching at home, alas, for the master on his return,*      1225
*my master—for I must bear the yoke of slavery.*
*And the commander of the fleet, the destroyer of Ilium*
*does not know what kind of hateful bitch's tongue,*
*uttering and drawing out at length, with welcoming smile, its plea,*
*shall hit, with an evil hitting, upon the target of crafty destruction.*   1230
*Such is her daring; the female is the murderer of the male.*
*She is—what is the proper name for me to give*
*the hateful monster?—an amphisbaena, or a Scylla*
*living in the rocks, a bane to sailors,*

---

1219   Some scholars want to emend this line, on the ground that CAS-
     SANDRA could not know from the look of the ghosts of Thyestes'
     children who had been their murderer. One ought not to have to
     point out that she *feels* it; she knows it by a prophetic intuition.

1229   The reference is to CLYTEMNESTRA's speech of welcome at 855f.

1233   An amphisbaena is a mythical monster, a snake with a head at
     both ends. Scylla was the many-headed monster who lived oppo-
     site the whirlpool Charybdis, and in the twelfth book of the
     *Odyssey* ate six of Odysseus' (*Od iss' yuse*) crew (see *The Liba-*
     *tion Bearers*, 612f., with my note).

a raging hell-mother, breathing truceless war                                  1235
against her own! And how she cried out in joy,
she who dares all things, as though at the turning point of battle!
And she seems to revel in his safe homecoming.
And if I fail to convince you of this, all is one; how can it be other-
    wise?
The future will come; and soon you shall stand here                             1240
to pronounce me, in pity, a prophet who spoke all too true.

CHORUS   Thyestes' feast upon his children's flesh
I understand and shudder at, and fear possesses me
as I hear it truly told and not in images.
But when I hear the rest I lose the track and run off the path.                 1245

CASSANDRA   I say that you shall look on Agamemnon's end.

CHORUS   Unhappy one, lull your voice to utter no ill-omened
    word!

CASSANDRA   But no healer stands by while this word is uttered.

CHORUS   No, if indeed it must be so; but may it not happen!

CASSANDRA   You utter prayers, but others are about the business
    of killing.                                                                 1250

CHORUS   Who is the man by whom this woeful deed is being
    brought about!

CASSANDRA   Far, indeed, you have been thrown from the track
    of my oracles.

---

1236   See 973f.

1245   In spite of the words of the Coryphaeus at 1213, Apollo's curse
    is working (see 1212).

1247   The Coryphaeus has demanded that CASSANDRA refrain from ill-
    omened utterances. Such abstinence was commonly demanded
    before the performance of religious rites, especially rites concern-
    ing the worship of Apollo, one of whose titles was "The Healer."

1252   The word "man" has shown CASSANDRA that the CHORUS has
    completely failed to understand her warning.

CHORUS   Yes, for I do not understand the scheme of him who
will accomplish it.

CASSANDRA   And yet I know the Greek tongue all too well.

CHORUS   So do the oracles of Pytho; yet they are hard to under-
stand no less.                                                                            1255

CASSANDRA   Ah, ah! It is like fire, and it comes over me!
Oh, Lycean Apollo, woe is me!
This two-footed lioness that beds
with the wolf in the noble lion's absence
will kill me, poor wretch; and as though brewing                          1260
a potion she will put in the cup a wage for me also.
She boasts, as she sharpens the sword for the man,
that he shall pay with murder for his bringing of me.
Why do I preserve these things to mock myself,
this staff and these fillets of prophecy about my neck?              1265
You I shall destroy before my death!
Go you to ruin! As you fall, so I pay you back!
Make rich with destruction some other instead of me!
But see, Apollo himself stripping me
of my prophetic raiment, he who has watched me                          1270
mightily mocked even with these ornaments upon me
by friends turned enemies, mocked without doubt in vain.
And like a wandering mendicant
I bore with being called beggar, wretch, starveling;
and now the prophet has undone me, his prophetess,                      1275
and has hailed me off to such a deadly fate as this.

---

1255   For Pytho, see note on 509.

1257   Apollo was often invoked as "Lycean" (*Lie see' an*) under his
aspect as an averter of calamity.

1266   CASSANDRA is addressing the insignia of her prophetic office
(1265), which she now begins to take off and destroy.

1272   *friends turned enemies:* CASSANDRA's own family, who under the
influence of Apollo's curse mocked at her prophecies; their mocking was "without doubt in vain" because the prophecies have now
been fulfilled.

Instead of my father's altar, a chopping-block awaits me,
soon to be red with my hot blood when I am struck before the
    sacrifice.
Yet shall my death not go without vengeance from the gods!
For there shall come another to avenge us in turn,        1280
a son that slays his mother, an atoner for his father;
an exile and a wanderer, estranged from this land
he shall return to put the coping-stone on this destruction for his kin.
For a great oath has been sworn by the gods,        1290
that the stroke that laid his father low shall fetch him home.    1285
Why do I make this pitiful lament,
now that I have seen Ilium's city
faring as it fared, and those that took the city
have come off like this in the judgment of the gods?
I shall go and act; I shall endure to die;        1289
and I call on these gates as gates of Hades.        1291
I pray I may receive a mortal stroke,
that without a struggle my blood may gush forth
in easy death, and I may close these eyes of mine.

    CHORUS  Woman much to be pitied and very wise,    1295
your speech has been long. But if truly
you know your fate, why like a cow whom the god
impels, do you go fearlessly to the altar?

    CASSANDRA  There is no escape, strangers, for any further length
    of time.

    CHORUS  But the last of one's time is valued most.    1300

    CASSANDRA  This day is come; little shall I gain by flight.

    CHORUS  Well, know that your endurance comes from a valiant
    heart.

---

1277  Priam was cut down by Neoptolemus, son of Achilles, at the altar
    of Zeus, at which he had taken refuge as a suppliant.

1297  If a sacrificial victim seemed to go willingly to the altar, it was
    considered a good omen.

1299  The words rendered as "for any further length of time" depend
    on an uncertain emendation.

CASSANDRA   *None among the fortunate hears such words.*

CHORUS   *But a glorious death is happiness for a mortal.*

CASSANDRA   *Alas for you, father, and for your noble children!*   1305

> CASSANDRA *starts to advance toward the door of the palace, but starts back.*

CHORUS   *What is the matter? What fear turns you back?*

CASSANDRA   *Ah, ah!*

CHORUS   *Why do you cry, "Ah"?—unless it is some repulsion in your mind.*

CASSANDRA   *The house breathes slaughter, dripping blood.*

CHORUS   *How so? This is the smell of the sacrifice at the hearth.* 1310

CASSANDRA   *The same scent as from a tomb assails me.*

CHORUS   *It is no Syrian incense, giving splendor to the house, of which you speak.*

CASSANDRA   *See, I go and in the house to lament my fate*
*and Agamemnon's. Enough of life!*
*Ah, my hosts!*                                                1315
*I cry not out in terror, like a bird before a bush,*
*but in death bear me witness to this,*
*when a woman shall die in return for me, a woman,*
*and a man for a man unfortunate in his wife.*

---

1305   CASSANDRA thinks of her father Priam and his sons and daughters.

1309   To the prophetess the house seems to smell of blood; thus in the *Odyssey* (20, 351f.) the prophet Theoclymenus has a vision of the hall of Odysseus with its walls covered with blood, portending the destruction of the suitors of Penelope.

1316   The bird that hath been limed in a bush
       With trembling wings misdoubteth every bush
                       (Shakespeare, 3 *Henry* VI, V. vi. 13f.).

1318   This prediction will be fulfilled during the action of the second play of the trilogy, *The Libation Bearers.*

And I call on you thus, my hosts, as one about to die.                    1320

   CHORUS   Poor lady, I pity you for the end you have foretold.

    CASSANDRA   I wish to make one speech more, or sing a dirge
over myself: I pray to the sun's
last light that to my avengers
my enemies may pay for my murder also,                    1325
for the death of a slave, an easy overthrow.
Alas for the affairs of men! When they are fortunate,
one may liken them to a shadow; and if they are unfortunate
a wet sponge with one dash blots out the picture.
And I pity this far more than that.                    1330

    CASSANDRA goes into the house.


    CHORUS   Of prosperity all mortals can never
have too much; and from the halls
to which men's fingers point none bars it
and turns it away with these words:
"Enter no more."
To this man the blessed ones granted                    1335
That he should take Priam's city,
and honored by the gods he returns home.
But now if he is to atone for the blood of some who are of the past
and by dying for the dead is to ordain
a penalty that consists in other deaths,                    1340
who, who among mortals may boast himself born
with a fortune beyond reach of harm?

---

1323    The text is corrupt and the sense uncertain.

1330    If the text is right, CASSANDRA is saying that she pities the unfortunate more than she does the fortunate. We should expect her
to say that she pities both equally, and there is much to be said
for an emendation that has her say, "And I do not pity this much
more than that."

1331    The CHORUS sings a brief interlude in marching anapests, designed simply to separate the preceding scene from the scene during which the murder happens.

AGAMEMNON (offstage)  *Oh, I am struck deep with a mortal blow!*

CHORUS  *Silence! Who tells of a blow, mortally wounded?*

AGAMEMNON  *Oh! Yet again, a second time I am struck!*    1345

CHORUS  *I think the deed is done, from the king's cries of pain.*
*But let us take counsel together, in the hope that there is some*
*safe plan.*

CHORUS 1  *I for my part tell you my opinion;*
*we should sound a summons to the citizens to bring help here to the*
*palace.*

CHORUS 2  *But I think we had best break in at once,*    1350
*and prove the deed while the sword is newly streaming.*

---

1343  The scene that follows has incurred much ridicule, and from a
naturalistic point of view would deserve it; but Aeschylean tragedy
did not aim at naturalism. It is important to remember that the
CHORUS has prepared the audience for its ineffectiveness at this
crucial moment by the stress it has laid on its own age and decrepitude (72f.).

AGAMEMNON's voice is heard from inside the palace; his utterances at 1343 and 1345 are in trimeters, but the words of the
Coryphaeus at 1344 and 1346–47 are in trochaic tetrameters. The
rhythm of this meter corresponds to that of Tennyson's, "Dreary
gleams athwart the moorland, flying over Locksley Hall." Aristotle
says that it was originally the regular meter of tragic dialogue, but
before the time of our earliest complete tragedy—*The Persians* of
Aeschylus, produced in 472 B.C.—it had been displaced by the
iambic trimeter, although *The Persians* contains two scenes in it.
Later it came to be reserved for scenes of special haste and anima-
tion, such as these lines and the last scene of *Agamemnon* (1649–
73).

1348  Each of the twelve members of the CHORUS in turn speaks two
trimeters.

CHORUS 3   *I too join in such a proposal,*
*and vote for action; it is no time for delay.*

CHORUS 4   *It is clear; their prelude is that of people*
*whose acts betoken tyranny for the city.*                      1355

CHORUS 5   *Yes, for we loiter; but they tread underfoot*
*the fair fame of the goddess Delay, and show themselves awake with*
*   actions.*

CHORUS 6   *I do not know what plan I can hit on and put for-*
*   ward;*
*it is to the doer that deliberation too belongs.*

CHORUS 7   *I too am of like mind, for I am at a loss*        1360
*for how to raise up the dead again with words.*

CHORUS 8   *Are we even to protract our lives while yielding thus*
*to these defilers of the house as leaders?*

CHORUS 9   *Why, it cannot be borne, but death is better;*
*for that is a gentler fate than to have tyranny.*             1365

CHORUS 10   *Must we truly, inferring from his cries of pain,*
*guess that the man has perished?*

CHORUS 11   *We should know for sure before we discuss this*
*   matter;*
*for guessing is different from sure knowledge.*

CHORUS 12   *All my votes go for approving this opinion,*     1370
*that we should know for certain how it is with the son of Atreus.*

> CLYTEMNESTRA comes into view, standing over
> the dead bodies of AGAMEMNON and CASSANDRA.

CLYTEMNESTRA   *Before I said much to suit the time,*
*but I shall feel no shame to say the opposite.*

---

1359   The speaker gives up the attempt to think out a correct course of
action, preferring to leave deliberation about the consequences of
the deed to those who have performed it.

1371   Text uncertain.

For if one has in hand acts of enmity against enemies
who seem to be friends, how else can one fence up the nets          1375
of harm to a height beyond overleaping?
For me this contest, sprung from an ancient quarrel,
has been matter for thought long since; but in time it has come;
and I stand where I struck, with the deed done.
And I so acted—and I will not deny it—          1380
that he could neither escape nor ward off death.
A covering inextricable, like a net for fish,
I threw around him, an evil wealth of raiment;
I struck him twice; and while uttering two cries
he let go, where he was, his legs; and after he had fallen          1385
I added a third stroke, a votive offering
for the Zeus below the earth, the savior of corpses.
So did he fall and quickly breathed away his life,
and spouting out a sharp jet of blood
he struck me with a dark shower of gory dew,          1390

---

1375   The image is that of a hunting-net, which was fixed between two
trees so that the game could be driven into it.

1382   The word translated by "covering" means literally "that which is
thrown over something"; although it may be used to mean a
fishing-net, it is found in tragedy in a more general sense. A late
writer (Apollodorus, epitome 6. 23; Loeb edition, ii. 269) describes the thing that was thrown over AGAMEMNON as "a garment with no holes for the neck or arms." This is confirmed by a
red-figure calyxkrater of the Dokimasia Painter, probably painted
about the time of the Oresteia's first production and lately pur-
chased by the Boston Museum of Fine Arts (63. 1246). One side
shows the death of AGAMEMNON, the other the death of AEGIS-
THUS. AGAMEMNON is covered by a "garment" of the kind described.

1386   At banquets it was customary to pour three libations, the third
in honor of Zeus, the Savior or Preserver (cf. 245f.). Hades, the
god of the underworld, is called "the Zeus below the earth" in the
Iliad (9. 457) and by Aeschylus in The Suppliants. CLYTEM-
NESTRA takes advantage of this usage to utter a kind of parody
that conveys the bitterest irony (cf. 645, with note).

while I rejoiced no less than the crop rejoices
in the Zeus-given moisture at the birth of the bud.
So stands the case, my honored lords of Argos here;
rejoice, if you will rejoice, but I exult in it.
And if one could pour over a corpse libation of a fitting liquid,          1395
it would be just to pour this, no, more than just!
Such a mixing bowl of evils, sprung from the curse, did he
fill up in the house and return himself to drain!

    CHORUS  We wonder at your tongue, at its audacity,
that you utter such a speech over your husband.          1400

    CLYTEMNESTRA  You make trial of me as though of a foolish
    woman;
but I with fearless heart speak to those who know—
and whether you wish to praise or blame me,
all is one—this is Agamemnon, my husband,
and a corpse, the work of this right hand,          1405
a just workman. So stands the case.

---

1392  Zeus as the sky-god sends the rain. The choice of an object of comparison has an effect comparable to that of the blasphemy of 1386–87.

1393  Cf. 855.

1395  In the *Odyssey* (22, 411f.) Odysseus stops the old nurse Eurycleia from uttering a cry of exultation over the bodies of the massacred suitors, saying, "It is not holy to exult over slaughtered men." The saying became proverbial, and is echoed by the seventh-century poet Archilochus (fr. 65 Diehl).

1396  *this*: refers to the blood of which CLYTEMNESTRA has been speaking.

1406  The CHORUS sings a short lyric stanza, almost all in the dochmiac meter that prevails in the lyrics of the first part of the CASSANDRA scene; 1426–30 have the same metrical pattern. Each stanza is answered by CLYTEMNESTRA in a speech in trimeters (1412–25, 1431–47). The CHORUS finds CLYTEMNESTRA's words so astonishing that it supposes them due to the effects of poison; in the responding stanza (1426f.) the CHORUS claims that she shows symptoms of madness.

CHORUS   Woman, what evil
food nurtured by the earth or what drink
sprung from the flowing sea have you tasted,
that you have put on yourself this murder, and incurred the people's
    curses?                       1410
You have cast away, you have cut away; and away from the city shall
    you go,
an object of grievous hate to the citizens.


CLYTEMNESTRA   Now you pass judgment on me of exile from
    the city
and declare that the citizens' hate and the people's curse shall be
    mine,
though then you raised no opposition to this man,
who holding it of no special account, as though it were the death of
    a beast,                       1415
where sheep in their fleecy flocks abound,
sacrificed his own child, a travail
most dear to me, to charm the winds of Thrace?
Was it not he whom you should have driven from this land,
as penalty for his polluting act? But when you take cognizance    1420
of my actions, you are a harsh judge. But I bid you
utter such threats, being prepared
that if in fight on equal terms you vanquish me
you shall rule; but if a god ordains the opposite,
you shall have a lesson, and shall learn, though late, discretion.    1425


CHORUS   Great is your daring,
arrogant your words; just as your mind
is maddened by the bloody deed,
the blood-fleck in your eyes is clear to see.

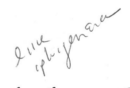

---

1425   The CHORUS takes the opposite line from the common Greek
      notion that it is undignified to be a late learner (cf. CHORUS at
      709f., at 584), as Solon did when he wrote the famous verse, "And
      I grow old, ever learning much" (fr. 22, 7 Diehl).
1427   Bloodshot eyes were thought to be a symptom of madness. The
      idea that CLYTEMNESTRA's eyes are actually stained with blood is

In requital yet you must, deprived of friends,
pay with blow for blow.                                    1430

CLYTEMNESTRA   This too you are hearing, the solemn power of
   my oath!
I swear by the justice accomplished for my child,
and by Ruin and the Erinys, to whom I sacrificed this man,
for me no expectation walks the hall of fear,
so long as the fire upon my hearth is kindled by            1435
Aegisthus, as in time past loyal to me;
for in him I have no slight shield of confidence.
Low he lies, he who did outrage against me his wife,
the darling of each Chryseis beneath Ilium!
And this woman here, the captive and soothsayer            1440
and bedfellow for him, the trusty prophetess
who shared his couch, the public harlot
of the sailors' benches! They have not failed to get the honor due
   them.
For he lies as I have described, and she after singing
like a swan her last lament in death                       1445

---

wholly foreign to the conventions of Greek tragedy, which dis-
dained this kind of realism.

1430   The expression is semiproverbial (cf. note on 523); the notion
recurs several times during the Oresteia.

1436   This is the first overt naming of AEGISTHUS in the play.

1439   In the first book of the Iliad, AGAMEMNON quarrels with Achilles
because of having had to give up Chryseis, daughter of Chryses,
priest of Apollo, a captive who has been handed over to him in
accordance with the custom described in the note on 950. In
open council AGAMEMNON declares that he prefers Chryseis to
CLYTEMNESTRA, whose equal she is in all respects (Iliad 1. 113f.).

1443   The expression translated "public harlot" is not certainly intelligi-
ble and may be corrupt.

1444   This is the earliest allusion to the belief that swans sing before
they are to die, a belief mentioned also in a moving passage of
Plato's Phaedo (84 E). The swan is often said to be sacred to
Apollo.

lies beside him, his lover; when he brought in
a side-dish for his bed, he pandered to my delight!

### STROPHE 1

CHORUS *Alas! If only swiftly, without grievous pain,*
*and with no watching of the sick-bed,*
*some Fate would come bringing to us*                              1450
*the sleep that never ends, now that he is slain,*
*the kindest of guardians!*
*He suffered much for a woman's sake; and at a woman's*
*hand has he lost his life.*

### REFRAIN 1

*Ah, ah, mad Helen,*                                              1455
*you who alone destroyed the many, the very many*
*lives beneath Troy,*

---

1446   The last sentence is difficult, but not, I believe, corrupt. Some
       scholars find it unthinkable that CLYTEMNESTRA should say that
       the pleasure of having killed her husband's concubine should
       heighten her own sexual satisfaction. This seems to be an insuffi-
       cient reason for refusing to accept the meaning that the words
       appear to bear.

1448   The CHORUS sings three lyric strophes (1448f., 1481f., 1530f.)
       and its corresponding antistrophes (1468f., 1505f., 1560f.), six
       stanzas in all. Each strophe is followed by a pendant in the form
       of a lyric stanza called an "ephymnium" (1455f., 1488f., 1537f.);
       the ephymnium following the second is repeated after the cor-
       responding antistrophe (1513f.). Each ephymnium begins with
       the cry of lamentation "Io!" The meter of the first two strophic
       pairs is iambic mixed with aeolic; that of the third is iambic; all
       three ephymnia are for the most part anapestic, with iambic or
       aeolic at the end of the stanza. Each lyric utterance of the CHORUS
       is answered by CLYTEMNESTRA in marching anapests. The lyrics
       are well suited to express passionate lamentation and despair, the
       anapests to express grim, confident satisfaction.

1455   Yet again does the CHORUS refer to Helen (cf. 62, 403f., 681f.).

107

*now you have put on yourself the last, the perfect garland,*
*through the blood not washed away. Truly there was then in the*
  *house*          1460
*a strife strong to conquer, a sorrow for the husband.*

CLYTEMNESTRA   *Do not pray for the fate of death,*
*grieved by this event!*
*Do not turn your wrath against Helen,*
*calling her a destroyer of men, one who alone*      1465
*took the lives of many Danaan men*
*and accomplished a woe none might resist!*

### ANTISTROPHE 1

CHORUS   *Spirit that falls upon the house and the two*
*sons of Tantalus,*
*and through women holds an evil sway,*        1470
*a sway grievous to my heart,*
*over the body like an evil crow*
*you stand and glory in singing with discordant note*
*a song of evil!*

CLYTEMNESTRA   *Now you have set right the opinion you pro-*
  *nounce,*
*calling on the thrice glutted*             1475
*spirit of this race!*
*For by his will a lust to lick blood*

---

1459   "The last, the perfect garland" seems to be a metaphorical reference to the guilt incurred by her who has caused, after so many
others, this final deed of blood. The "blood not washed away" is
first and foremost the blood of the children of Thyestes.

1468   *Tantalus*: pronounce *Tan' tal us.*

1469   Tantalus was father of Pelops, who in the usual genealogy was
father of Atreus. But Pleisthenes (*Plice' then ēs*) is sometimes inserted in the pedigree, at one place or another (cf. 1569, 1602).
"Daimon" can mean a god, a minor divinity, or a spirit; here it
is the personified curse upon the family.

1473   Two syllables are missing; the sense can be guessed at reasonably
enough.

is nurtured in its belly; before the old agony
ceases, there flows fresh pus.                                    1480

### STROPHE 2

CHORUS  Mighty for this house
is the spirit you tell of, heavy his wrath.
Alas, alas, evil is your tale,
never satiate of baneful fortune.
Woe, woe, through the act of Zeus,
cause of all, doer of all;                                        1485
for what is accomplished for mortals without Zeus?
Which of these things is not god-ordained?

### REFRAIN 2

O my king, my king,
how shall I weep for you?                                         1490
What word shall I utter from a loving heart?
And you lie in this spider's web,
gasping out your life in an impious death—
alas, on this shameful bed,
brought low by a guileful death,                                  1495
by a two-edged weapon sped by [your wife's] hand.

CLYTEMNESTRA  You aver that this deed is mine.
But do not consider
that I am Agamemnon's consort!

---

1479  The comparison is to a suppurating wound.

1484  All that happens is in accordance with the will of Zeus; even so at
the beginning of the *Iliad* (1. 5) Homer says that "the design of
Zeus was fulfilled," and at the end of Sophocles' *Women of
Trachis* the Chorus says, "None of these things is not Zeus."
But this does not imply a belief in any kind of determinism; the
early poets saw no inconsistency between the belief that Zeus
determines all things and the freedom of men to make their own
decisions.

1496  The supplement [your wife's] seems necessary to complete the
sense.

*But manifesting himself to this dead man's wife*  1600
*the ancient savage avenger*
*of Atreus, the cruel banqueter,*
*slew him in requital,*
*sacrificing a grown man after children.*

## ANTISTROPHE 2

CHORUS  *That you have no guilt*  1505
*for this murder, who shall bear witness?*
*How, how can it be so? But the avenger*
*from his father's time may have been your helper.*
*And amid streams*
*of kindred blood black Ares*  1510
*forces his way to where he shall pay atonement*
*to the gore congealed of the children that were devoured.*

## REFRAIN 2

*O my king, my king,*
*how shall I weep for you?*
*What word shall I utter from a loving heart?*  1515
*And you lie in this spider's web,*
*gasping out your life in an impious death—*
*alas, on this shameful bed,*
*brought low by a guileful death,*
*by a two-edged weapon sped by [your wife's] hand.*  1520

CLYTEMNESTRA  *Neither, I think, was this man's death*
*shameful . . . . . .*
*For did not he accomplish guileful*
*destruction in the house?*
*But my child raised up from him,*  1525
*Iphigeneia, much bewailed,—*
*unworthy was what he did to her, worthy was what he suffered!*

---

1501  *ancient savage avenger*: identical with the Daimon.

1510  The name of the war-god stands for violence.

1522  Probably not more than a line or two is missing.

*Let him utter no loud boast in Hades,*
*now that he has paid with death for what he began.*

### STROPHE 3

CHORUS  *I do not know, deprived of meditation's*                    1530
*resourceful thought,*
*which way to turn, while the house falls.*
*I fear the beating of the rain that brings the house low,*
*the rain of blood; and the drizzle ceases.*
*Justice is sharpened for another deed of harm*                    1535
*on other whetstones by the hand of Fate.*
*O earth, earth, would you had received me,*
*before I saw him occupy the lowly bed*
*of the bath with silver walls!*                    1540
*Who shall bury him? Who shall lament him?*
*Shall you dare to do this, to slay*
*your husband and then lament him,*
*and for his soul decree thanks that are no thanks*                    1545
*in return for his mighty deeds?*
*Who shall pronounce with tears*
*praise at the tomb over the godlike man,*
*laboring in sincerity of heart?*                    1550

CLYTEMNESTRA  *It does not fall to you to take thought for this*
*duty; by my hand*
*he fell, by my hand he died, and my hand shall bury him,*
*to the accompaniment of no weeping from the house.*
*But gladly Iphigeneia,*                    1555
*his daughter, as is fitting,*
*shall meet her father at the swift*

---

1541  For the dead man's spirit to be deprived of its right to proper
lamentation by the next of kin and of respectful burial was a
grievous injury, according to Greek religious belief. Thus in the
Sophocles' *Ajax* and *Antigone*, much of the action turns on the
question of whether or not the dead heroes Ajax and Polynices are
to receive proper burial.

1556  *swift ferry of sorrows:* Acheron (see note on 1160).

111

*ferry of sorrows*
*and cast her arm round him and kiss him.*

### ANTISTROPHE 3

CHORUS Taunt is now met with taunt, 1560
and it is hard to judge;
the plunderer is plundered and the slayer slain.
But it abides, while Zeus abides upon his throne,
that he who does shall suffer; for it is the law.
Who shall cast out the brood of curses from the house? 1565
The race is fastened to destruction.

CLYTEMNESTRA With truth you have come upon
this oracle. But I for my part
am willing to swear a covenant with the demon
of the Pleisthenids so that I bear all this, 1570
hard though it is to endure; and he may go for the future
from this house and wear away some other family
through deaths at the hands of kindred.
Even if my share of possessions
is small, I shall be content with all things, 1575
if I have rid our halls
of the frenzies in which we shed each other's blood.

Enter AEGISTHUS, accompanied by his bodyguard.

AEGISTHUS O kindly light of the day that has brought justice,

---

1564  See 532–33, with note.

1568  *Pleisthenids:* pronounce *Plise'* then *ids.*

1571  It is an ancient belief, common to many different civilizations,
that in conjuring a god or spirit not to afflict oneself or one's
friends one must offer him another victim (cf. the English rhyme,
"Rain, rain, go to Spain"). Of course no such compact with the
Daimon as CLYTEMNESTRA speaks of is possible. It is absurd to
think that her behavior in this scene shows any sign of remorse
or contrition; she remains defiant to the last line of the play. But
in the debate between her and the CHORUS, the CHORUS succeeds
in establishing a valid point.

now I can say that as guardians of the rights of men
the gods from above look upon the woes of earth,
now that I have seen this man lie here
in the woven robes of the Erinyes, to my delight,
paying for the deed his father's hand contrived.
For Atreus, ruler of this land and this man's father,
drove my father, Thyestes—to put the matter clearly—
his brother, since his power was challenged,                    1585
away from the city and his home.
And when he returned as a suppliant at his hearth,
poor Thyestes found a safety,
in that he did not in death stain with his blood his native earth
himself; but by way of hospitable entertainment the godless father
        of this man here,                                        1590
even Atreus, more a willing than a kindly host,
seeming to keep the day of meat-eating with good cheer,
served to my father a feast of his children's flesh.
The footparts and the ends of the hands
he chopped up small above . . . . . . . . . . . . sitting each by himself. 1595
And taking at once in ignorance a part that could not be recognized,
he ate, a meal bringing ruin to his family, as you see.
And then he understood the monstrous act
and cried out, and fell back, spewing out the butchery,
and called down on the Pelopids a fate unbearable,              1600
kicking over the table to mark the justice of his curse,
that so might perish all the race of Pleisthenes.
So it has come about that you can see this man fallen here;
and I am the just schemer of this murder.
For he left me, the thirteenth child, and with my wretched father  1605

---

1580   The thing cast over AGAMEMNON is not really a robe (see note on
       1382), so that this is a metaphorical description.
1585   See note on 1192.
1594   The text is either corrupt or partly missing, perhaps both.
1600   Pronounce *Pell' op ids.*
1601   See note on 1469.
1605   Some scholars emend "thirteenth" to "third," because they find
       thirteen a surprisingly large number. It seems to me unsafe to as-
       sume that Aeschylus would have felt this; in *Suppliants,* Danaus
       has fifty daughters and his brother Aegyptus fifty sons.

113

he drove me out, an infant in swaddling clothes.
But when I had been reared up, Justice brought me back,
and from far off I laid my finger on this man,
stitching together the whole scheme of the fatal plan.
So even death is agreeable to me,                                         1610
now that I have seen this man in the toils of Justice.

CHORUS  Aegisthus, insolence over others' misfortune is a thing
    I care not to practice.
And do you say that you deliberately slew this man,
and that you alone planned this piteous murder?
I say that on the day of reckoning your head shall not escape,        1615
know it for certain, the curses that bring stoning at the people's
    hands.

AEGISTHUS  Do you speak thus, seated at the oar below
when those upon the bench are masters of the ship?
Old as you are, you shall learn that a lesson comes hard
to one of your years, when discretion is enjoined.                    1620
Bonds and whips and the pangs of hunger
are excellent prophet-doctors
for the wits. Have you eyes, and do you not see this?
Do not kick against the pricks, so that you do not strike them and
    feel pain.

---

1610  See note on 539.

1616  See note on 1117.

1617  The metaphor like that of the "ship of state" is common (cf. 183)
and persists in our word "government" (which derives from the
Latin word for "steering").

1622  prophet-doctors: an expression that seems to have originated as a
title of Apollo, who was both these things.

1623  For the proverb, cf. Mark 8:18 (Matthew 13:13); the proverb is
common in classical literature.

1624  The proverb occurs at Apostles 26:14; this proverb too was well
known during the classical period. AEGISTHUS' constant use of the
tritest cant sayings seems to be one of the features meant to
characterize him as a mean and contemptible person.

CHORUS  Woman, do you do this to those newly returned from
    battle—                                                  1625
keeping the house and shaming the husband's bed
did you plot this death for the general?

AEGISTHUS  These words too are the breeders of a race of tears.
But you have a tongue the opposite of that of Orpheus.
For he led all things with his voice by means of the delight he
    gave;                                                   1630
but you stir up anger by your foolish barkings,
and shall be led; once mastered you shall show yourself more tame.

CHORUS  So you are to be tyrant of the Argives,
you who when you had plotted death against him,
did not dare to do this deed with your own hand!         1635

AEGISTHUS  Yes, for the deception was clearly the woman's part,
and I, an ancient enemy of the house, was suspect.
And with his possessions I shall try
to rule the citizens; and him that will not obey
I shall yoke with a heavy yoke; no trace-horse          1640
fed on barley, he! But the hateful housemate
of darkness, hunger, shall see him grow soft.

CHORUS  Why with your cowardly heart did you not
kill this man yourself, but with you a woman

---

1625  *woman*: addressed to AEGISTHUS, not to CLYTEMNESTRA; a parti-
        ciple in the next line has been changed from masculine to feminine
        by someone who missed the point. Effeminate men are sometimes
        addressed in this way in tragedy, and in this case it is clear that
        the whole dialogue is between the Coryphaeus and AEGISTHUS and
        that CLYTEMNESTRA takes no part in it.

1629  Rocks and trees were alleged to have followed Orpheus (*Orf' yuse*)
        in order to hear his song. The feeble comparison is one more mark
        of the contemptible character of AEGISTHUS.

1640  The trace-horse, which ran to the right of the pair pulling a
        chariot or wagon in order to lend assistance when a special effort
        was required (cf. 842 above), was better fed than other horses.

1641  For this type of phrase, cf. 494-95 with note.

—polluting the land and its gods— 1645
killed him? Does Orestes somewhere see the light,
that he may return here with favoring fortune
and become the all-prevailing slayer of both these two?

AEGISTHUS *Well, since you wish to act and speak thus, you
shall soon learn!*

CHORUS *Come now, dear comrades, the work to be done is
near at hand!* 1650

AEGISTHUS *Come now, let each make ready his sword with hand
on hilt!*

CHORUS *I too have hand on hilt and do not refuse death.*

AEGISTHUS *We accept the omen when you speak of death; and
we choose to take what will come to pass.*

CLYTEMNESTRA *By no means, dearest of men, let us do further
harm;*
but even this is much to reap, a sad harvest. 1655
There is enough of ruin; let us shed no blood.
Go . . . . . ., elders to the house, yielding

---

1649 AEGISTHUS threatens the CHORUS, and in reply the Coryphaeus
calls his comrades to offer resistance. At this point the meter
changes from trimeters to tetrameters, which are used, as often
in later tragedy, to indicate excitement and animated movement
(cf. on 1345). The attributions of lines to speakers at the beginning of the scene have become confused in the manuscripts, because it was assumed that "dear comrades" in 1650 must be
addressed by AEGISTHUS to his bodyguard. The word rendered by
"comrades" is indeed a military word, but it is one that can quite
well be addressed by the Coryphaeus to his fellow members of the
CHORUS. What is decisive is that the old men carry staves (cf. 75)
and not swords; the swords must be carried by AEGISTHUS' bodyguard, who do not speak but are addressed by AEGISTHUS at 1651.

1657 Corrupt; the concluding lines from this point on have suffered a
good deal of damage.

*to Fate before you suffer; you must acquiesce in this as we have
done it.*
*If we could have had enough of these troubles, we should be content,
grievously struck as we have been by the spirit's hoof.*                1660
*Such is the saying of a woman, if any condescend to hear it.*

AEGISTHUS   *But are these men to pelt me with the flowers of a
random tongue,*
*and to fling out such words as these, making trial of their fortune,
and miss the target of good sense, rejecting the man in power?*

CHORUS   *This would not be the way of Argives, to fawn upon an
evil fellow.*                                                           1665

AEGISTHUS   *Well, in days to come I shall still pursue you.*

CHORUS   *Not if the spirit guide Orestes to return here.*

AEGISTHUS   *I know that men in exile feed on hope.*

CHORUS   *Act, grow fat, polluting justice, since you have the
power!*

AEGISTHUS   *Know that you shall pay me the penalty for this
foolishness in time!*                                                   1670

CHORUS   *Boast in confidence, like a cock beside his hen!*

CLYTEMNESTRA   *Do not care for these idle barkings; you and I,
ruling this house, shall order all things for good.*

*Exeunt omnes.*

---

1661   CLYTEMNESTRA is surely being ironical; cf. 277, 483f., 590f., 1401f.
1668   Still another proverb.

117

# BIBLIOGRAPHY

### A. TEXT WITH COMMENTARY

Eduard Fraenkel, Oxford, 1950 (in three volumes, with a literal translation; the commentary is very detailed).

J. D. Denniston and D. L. Page Oxford, 1957 (240 pages; succinct notes).

### B. VERSE TRANSLATIONS

Louis MacNeice, London, paperback edition, 1964. Richmond Lattimore, in Grene and Lattimore, *The Complete Greek Tragedies*, Chicago, 1953– .

Robert Fagles, *Aeschylus: The Oresteia*, New York, 1975 (Penguin 1977).

### C. GENERAL

E. R. Dodds *Morals and Politics in The Oresteia* (*The Ancient Concept of Progress*, Oxford, 1973, ch. III).

Anne Lebeck *The Oresteia: a study in language and structure*, Washington, D.C., 1971.

Oliver Taplin, *Greek Tragedy in Action*, London, 1978.

# AESCHYLUS: ORESTEIA

# THE CHOEPHOROE

('The Libation Bearers')

# INTRODUCTION

Aeschylus' version of Orestes' return and revenge was not the only one extant in antiquity, and it is of some interest to compare his account with those that preceded it. In *The Odyssey*, Zeus sends his messenger Hermes to Aegisthus, when Aegisthus is plotting the murder of Agamemnon, to warn him that if he carries out his plan Orestes will one day avenge the murder. Nonetheless, Aegisthus kills Agamemnon, and in due course Orestes returns from exile and kills Aegisthus. What happens to Clytemnestra is not revealed; she dies at the same time, but we are not told that Orestes kills her. Orestes himself returns to Argos from exile in Athens. The first author to have him spend his exile at the court of Strophius, the king of Phocis, seems to have been Agias, author of the post-Homeric epic *Nostoi*, which describes the return of the chief Greek heroes from Troy. This was probably a work of the seventh or sixth century; by that time the Delphic oracle had already become important, and the change may have been dictated by the wish to make Delphi, which lay in Phocian territory, prominent in the story.

Orestes' revenge was described in the *Oresteia* of the famous sixth-century lyric poet Stesichorus of Himera in Sicily. Unfortunately we know few details of his work, but he seems to have introduced the figure of Orestes' nurse, who according to Pindar saved Orestes from death at the hands of his father's murderers, and who plays a notable part in Aeschylus' drama. Both Stesichorus and Pindar call the nurse by heroic names; Aeschylus calls her by a servile name, in harmony with his presentation of her character (see 732 with note). Stesichorus also mentions the dream that warned Clytemnestra of her approaching end:

> To her there seemed to come a snake, his crest stained with blood; and then appeared the king, the son of Pleisthenes.

In this story the snake clearly stands for Agamemnon, but in Aeschylus' version of the dream it symbolizes Orestes (526f). More important, Stesichorus was probably the first author to describe how Orestes, because of matricide, is pursued by the Erinyes, the terrible beings from the world below whose function was to punish those who murdered their own kin. In Stesichorus, as in Aeschylus, Orestes is sustained by the advice and help of Apollo, the god of the Delphic Oracle; Stesichorus told how Apollo gives Orestes a bow with which to defend himself against the Erinyes. In Aeschylus, Orestes does not have to defend himself with actual weapons, but Apollo helps him first by granting him purification and then by his advocacy at his trial.

In Aeschylus, the place of Orestes' exile must be Phocis because of its connection with the oracle. Orestes returns accompanied by Pylades, son of the king of Phocis, who according to the usual legend later marries Orestes' sister Electra. Pylades may well be regarded as the spokesman of Apollo's oracle, for his only speech in the play is an injunction not to disobey the oracle's command (see 900–901 with note). But the connection with Athens that appears in Homer is equally important to Aeschylus. In the last play of the trilogy, it is in Athens that Orestes seeks refuge from the pursuit of the Erinyes, and it is an Athenian court, presided over by Athene herself, that acquits him of the charge brought against him.

The stage is dominated by the mound that represents Agamemnon's grave; Orestes and Pylades appear before it, and Orestes calls upon the gods to help revenge his father's murder. They are interrupted by the arrival of Orestes' sister Electra, accompanied by the slave-women from the palace who form the Chorus. The figure of Electra, so important in Greek tragedy, does not appear in Homer, where Agamemnon's daughters are called Chrysothemis, Laodice, and Iphianassa. As far as we know, Electra is mentioned first by Xanthus, an obscure lyric poet belonging to the same school as the more celebrated Stesichorus. In the present play the women of the Chorus describe themselves as captives taken in war, and, indeed, slaves were commonly captives in the world of Greek epic.

Electra and the slave-women have come to the grave because Clytemnestra has given a most surprising order—they are to offer a libation at the grave of Agamemnon. What accounts for her sudden wish to placate the spirit of the husband she has long ago murdered and consigned to a dishonored grave? We learn from the Parodos, the first ode sung by the Chorus, that it is because of a dream, whose exact details we learn only later. The Chorus knows that her effort at appeasement is bound to prove futile. For although the murderers of Agamemnon are at present all-powerful, the law of Zeus—that the doer must suffer—demands that eventually they must pay the penalty for the blood they have shed.

The story of Orestes' return does not call for the same frequent glimpses into past and future as the preceding story of the deaths of Agamemnon and Cassandra. The past is often mentioned, but its details are now familiar to the audience; the future—the pursuit of Orestes by the Erinyes and his eventual escape—the poet is concerned to keep uncertain. The first half of the play concentrates on Electra's recognition of Orestes and on the preparations for the attack on the usurpers. An all-important preliminary to these preparations is the great conjuration designed to arouse the ghost of Agamemnon and to ensure its active collaboration in the destruction of the murderers. The second part of the play shows how Orestes enters the palace and carries out his task. Only during the last act do the audience suddenly become aware that the Erinyes, who as they know would have pursued Orestes had he neglected to avenge his father, will now pursue him for the murder of his mother.

The sex and station of the Chorus render it especially suited to utter the bitter lamentations for Agamemnon's fate and for the tyranny of the usurpers in the first half of the play. Likewise, in the second half the Chorus is well suited to utter the passionate prayers for the victory and for the preservation of Orestes. But like the Chorus of *Agamemnon*, it is aware throughout that in the end Zeus and Justice are bound to triumph, and this knowledge relieves even the deep melancholy of the Parodos (22f). The Chorus remembers that blood once shed cannot be recalled, and touches on a motive that recurs again and again in the course of the trilogy, that blood once shed necessitates revenge. The Chorus is a party to Electra's decision to turn against her mother the power that Clytemnestra's offerings were supposed to exert. Terrified by the warning dream, Clytemnestra had sent them to the tomb to appease her husband's ghost. Throughout the great lyric scene in which brother and sister in alternation conjure their father's spirit to rise and strike against his murderers, the Chorus spurs them on with declarations of passionate hatred against the enemy and with reminders that Zeus will never allow such crimes to go unpunished. Afterward, the Chorus, together with Electra, listens to Orestes' instructions to those who wish to help him; then in the First Stasimon (585f) it dwells on the enormity of Clytemnestra's crimes, comparing her, after the fashion of tragic choruses, with the most monstrous criminals of the past and declaring that Justice and the Erinyes must soon take their revenge on her. After Orestes has made his entry into the palace and deceived his mother with the false report of his own death, the Chorus gives him material help by telling the Nurse to ask Aegisthus to come, not with his bodyguard, as Clytemnestra has instructed her, but alone. As the decisive moment approaches, the Chorus seconds Orestes and Pylades with a prayer to the gods whose assistance they most need, followed by an injunction to Orestes to fulfill Apollo's order with utter ruthlessness (the Second Stasimon, 783f). After the double killing, the Chorus sings a great hymn of triumph to Justice and Apollo, who have brought salvation to the house of Atreus. Nowhere does it doubt the rightness of Orestes' decision to kill his mother; nowhere does it apprehend that at the very moment of his triumph, he will be menaced by the same dangers that would have overwhelmed him had he refused to obey Apollo's oracle.

Aeschylus has no interest in character for its own sake, and this fact is especially easy to perceive here. Electra, who in Sophocles and Euripides will be a dominating figure, has the conventional qualities of a princess in the heroic age. Deeply loyal to her father and brother, bitterly hostile to her father's murderers, she is not yet required to exhibit the ferocious hatred portrayed in later tragedy. Scenes in which long-separated relatives became aware of one another's identity were to become part of the regular stock-in-trade of tragedy and, later, of the New Comedy of Menander and his contemporaries; the recognition of Orestes by Electra in this play is a simple and almost primitive, but also dignified and moving, example of the type. Euripides in his *Electra* derided both Electra's recognition of a lock of hair left by Orestes on his father's tomb and, still more, her recognition of her brother's footprints. Sharing his attitude, some modern critics have declared the footprints to be an interpolation, and they are careful to delete the passage in which Euripides made fun of them as being an interpolation made to ridicule a second interpolation in that of Aeschylus. Advocates of this theory fail to recognize that the technique of tragedy in Aeschylus' time was of a simplicity utterly removed from modern naturalism. When Electra voices her love for her restored brother, she echoes the famous words in which the Homeric Andromache voices her love for her husband Hector; the archaic beauty and simplicity of the recognition scene in *The Libation Bearers* is similar in feeling to the poetry of Homer.

Critics who have labored to read into Aeschylus' characters the individualism of Elizabethan or even of Ibsenian drama have had a hard time with the central figure of the last two plays of the *Oresteia*—the character from whom the trilogy takes its name. Orestes often speaks poetry of great richness, not to mention the lyrics that he sings during the great scene of conjuration; but of individuality he shows little trace. Near the beginning of the play (269f), he describes with horrifying vividness the awful fate that Apollo has warned him he will suffer if he neglects his duty to avenge his father, and he takes it as a matter of course that he can do nothing but obey. Even if he did not trust Apollo, he continues, he must win back his father's property, and he must not allow the

Argive people to remain subject to the tyranny of the usurpers. Modern critics whose minds have been dominated by the unconscious presuppositions dictated by modern drama have tried hard to show that Orestes can kill his mother only if he is spurred by the stimulus afforded by the conjuration scene. Their attempt is not successful (see note on Conjuration Scene, 306). The poet's words make it unambiguously clear that the purpose of the conjuration is to secure the all-important assistance of Agamemnon's ghost; nowhere is there the slightest evidence that Orestes has even considered the possibility of disobeying Apollo. After the conjuration, Orestes, speaking like a commander, tells his sympathizers of the parts required of them by a well-contrived strategic plan, which he goes on to carry out.

An unfortunate result of the eagerness of modern commentators to lay stress on Aeschylus as a thinker and religious poet has been their frequent neglect to observe that *The Libation Bearers*, like *Agamemnon*, is full of suspense, action, and skillfully contrived surprise. When Orestes comes to the supreme moment of confrontation with his mother, he meets each of her pleas with what is, from Apollo's point of view, the proper answer. Despite the stilted form of dialogue in which each actor speaks one line in turn, the scene not only brings out the poignancy of the tragic dilemma, but conveys the feelings of both participants. Only at the end does Orestes hesitate, and then only for a moment; then Pylades, the neighbor of Apollo, reminds him of his duty, and he obeys. Some of the critics who have found signs of hesitation in the earlier behavior of Orestes suppose the poet to have prepared the way for the madness that comes upon him during the final scene, when the Erinyes, visible only to his eye, come to pursue him. In fact no such signs can be discerned; in his conscious mind, at least, Aeschylus conceived the madness instilled by the Erinyes as a purely external visitation.

Aegisthus makes only a brief appearance in this play; more noteworthy is the appearance of Clytemnestra. The sinister ambiguity of her opening words of welcome (668f) shows that she is still the Clytemnestra of *Agamemnon*. Must the grief she expresses when she first hears the false report of her son's death be considered totally insincere (691f)? Perhaps not; but she acknowledges that

128

she can only feel secure if the threat of her son's return is removed. The point is driven home when she assures the messenger that he will not be cheated of the reward commonly paid to the bearers of good news. Unmixed grief is shown only by Orestes' old Nurse, a humble figure who makes a brief but astonishingly vivid appearance that contrasts sharply with the stiff archaic dignity of the heroic characters. In the sculpture scenes depicting the battle of the Lapiths with the Centaurs on the west pediment of Zeus's temple at Olympia, the canons of prevailing taste did not permit the features of the heroes and heroic maidens or of the central figure of Apollo to express emotion; this was reserved for the ferocious and subhuman Centaurs. By a somewhat similar convention Aeschylus allows the Nurse a vivacious garrulity and a readiness to mention humble objects and pursuits that set her off from all other tragic characters, except the Guard in Sophocles' *Antigone*.

In its concluding words the Chorus, terrified by the sudden madness of Orestes, expresses the deepest uncertainty about the future. First came the Thyestean feast, then the death of Agamemnon. Is the house of Atreus now saved, or is it lost? At what point in time, they ask, will the might of destruction finally be lulled to sleep?

# CHARACTERS

AEGISTHUS, king of Argos

CHORUS, slave-women

CLYTEMNESTRA, queen of Argos

ELECTRA, daughter of CLYTEMNESTRA

NURSE

ORESTES, son of CLYTEMNESTRA

PYLADES, friend of ORESTES

SLAVE

# THE LIBATION BEARERS

Scene: the grave of AGAMEMNON. Enter ORESTES
and PYLADES.

ORESTES  Hermes of the earth, you who watch over your
 father's kingdom,
be my preserver and fight beside me in answer to my prayer.
For I have come to this land, returning from my exile

    • • • • • •

And on the mound of this grave I cry to my father
to give ear, to listen . . .                                         5

---

*Orestes:* pronounce *Ŏr·est′·ēs; Pylades:* pronounce *Pie′·lă·
dēs.*

1    At the beginning of the play, perhaps as many as thirty
lines are missing from the single manuscript. The first nine
lines printed in the text were preserved through quotations
by other authors. The meaning of the opening line is
disputed between Euripides and Aeschylus in Aristophanes'
*The Frogs* (1119f). Euripides thinks it means, "Hermes of
the earth, who looked upon my father's murder"; Aeschylus
thinks it means, "Hermes of the earth, who watches over
your father's [i.e., Zeus's] kingdom." Some modern scholars
say that Agamemnon is the father referred to, but there is

. . . *a lock for Inachus in payment for my nurture,*
*and this second lock in token of my mourning.*

. . . . . .

*For I was not here to bewail your death, father,*
*nor did I stretch out my hand as your corpse was borne to*
*    burial.*

. . . . . .

He sees approaching ELECTRA with the CHORUS of
slave-women, carrying libations to offer at the tomb.

*What do I see? What is this company*                    10
*of women coming in black robes*
*that meets my eye? To what event can I refer it?*
*Does some new disaster come upon the house?*

---

little doubt that the interpretation of the Aristophanic
Aeschylus is right. It is relevant that Aeschylus sometimes
speaks of Hades, god of the underworld, as "the Zeus of
the dead" (see *Agam.* 1387 with my note). Hermes in his
aspect of Chthonios, "of the earth," was the intermediary
between the world of the dead and the world of the living.
He is therefore the most suitable god for ORESTES to invoke,
for he will soon have to establish communication with his
father's spirit to obtain help against his murderers.

6–   *Inachus*: pronounce *Eye′·nẵ·khus*:

7         The Inachus was the principal river of Argos. It was customary for young men to offer a lock of hair to their country's rivers in return for the nurture the rivers were supposed
to provide. It was also customary to offer a lock to the dead.
Thus Achilles in *The Iliad* (23, 142) dedicates a lock on
Patroclus' tomb that the dead warrior would have given to
the river near his home in Thessaly, the Spercheius, had it
been his fate to survive the war and to return.

8         To take part in the obsequies of one's close kin, especially
parents, was a sacred duty not to be neglected except for
the gravest reasons.

Or shall I be right if I guess that they are bringing libations
to my father, meant to appease those below the earth?          15
It can be nothing else; yes, I seem to see advance
Electra, my sister, whose bitter grief
marks her out. O Zeus, grant that I may avenge the death   Y
of my father, and of your grace fight on my side!
Pylades, let us stand out of the way, so that I may learn       20
for certain what this supplication of the women may import.

> ORESTES and PYLADES hide;
> enter ELECTRA and the CHORUS of slave-women.

### STROPHE 1

CHORUS  *Sent from the palace have I come*
*to convey libations; my hands strike me sharp blows;*
*Crimson shows my cheek as I tear it,*
*with the furrow fresh-cut by my nails.*          25
*All my life long are lamentations my heart's food.*
*Ruining the linen texture,*

---

14  Libations to the dead consisted of three offerings in a
defined order—first honey and milk, then wine, and finally
water. Normally, they would have been offered regularly at
the tomb ever since Agamemnon's death; in fact this was
the first such offering ever made there. Agamemnon had
been denied the proper rites of burial, a fact shocking to
Greek religious sentiment (see *Agam.* 1551f).

20  ORESTES and PYLADES now hide themselves and are not
noticed by the women until ORESTES speaks at 212.

22  The prevailing meter of the Parodos is the lyric iambics so
frequent in *Agamemnon*. The CHORUS consists of slave-
women of the house, who have come there as prisoners
of war (75f); they are sympathetic to ELECTRA.

23  It was usual for Greek mourners to tear their cheeks and
beat their heads as they lamented for the dead. Passionate
mourning was thought to be particularly characteristic of
Orientals (see 423f); it is not specifically stated that these
slave-women are Trojan prisoners, but the inference is not
unnatural.

*loud in my grief resounds the rending of my robes,*
*the robes that veil my bosom; far from mirth*            30
*the disaster with which they are stricken.*

### ANTISTROPHE 1

*For shrill, making the hair to stand on end,*
*the dream-prophet of the house, in sleep breathing anger,*
*uttered a midnight shriek*
*of terror from the heart of the palace*            35
*in grievous assault upon the women's chambers.*
*And interpreters of those dreams,*
*for whose rightness the gods stand surety, cried out*
*that those below the earth make angry complaint*            40
*and harbor wrath against the killers.*

### STROPHE 2

*Such is the graceless grace to ward off harm—*
*O Mother Earth!—*
*that she has sent me to compass,*            45
*she the godless woman. But I am afraid*
*to let this word fall from my lips.*
*For what payment can atone for blood spilt upon the ground?*
*Ah, hearth of utter misery!*
*Ah, destruction of the house!*            50
*Sunless, hateful to mankind*
*is the darkness that shrouds the house*
*through the death of its master.*

---

32    The cry was, in fact, uttered by CLYTEMNESTRA (535); the "dream-prophet" is the Daimon of the house, the personified curse upon it, who has caused her dream.

37    These interpreters are the domestic prophets mentioned also in *Agam.* 409.

44    As libations were poured onto the ground, the invocation of the Earth is natural.

47    *this word:* the prayer with which the pourer would normally accompany the libation (cf. ELECTRA's words at 87f).

48    That blood once spilt can never be atoned for is a theme that recurs again and again in the *Oresteia* (cf. *Agam.* 1017).

## ANTISTROPHE 2

And the awe that once irresistible, invincible, not to be with-
    stood,                                            55
passed through the ear and mind of the people
now stands far away; and fear
is rife. Among mortals
success is a god and more than a god.              60
But the balance of justice is swift
to visit some beneath the light of day;
another fate awaits those that linger
in the twilight, a fate of woe;
and others night ineffectual enshrouds.        65

## STROPHE 3

Because of blood drained by the fostering earth
the vengeful gore stands clotted, and will not dissolve away.
Calamity, inflicting grievous pain, keeps
the guilty man forever infected with an all-destroying sick-    70
    ness.

## ANTISTROPHE 3

For him that has violated a bridal bower there is no
remedy; and though all streams flow
in one channel to cleanse the blood
from a polluted hand, they speed their course in vain.

## EPODE

But as for me—since a constraint that beset my city        75
has been laid on me by the gods; for from the house,
of my father they led me to a fate
of servitude—things just and things unjust

. . . . . .

---

61    The text is corrupt, the sense wholly uncertain. If the
        emendation I have translated could be accepted, the sense
        would presumably be that the avenging hand of Justice
        strikes some during their lifetime, others only at the very
        end of it, and others only in the underworld.

71    The sense is that just as virginity once lost cannot be
        recovered, neither can the guilt of murder be washed away.

79    The text here is hopelessly corrupt.

must I approve, mastering the bitter                                       80
repugnance that is in my mind. And I weep behind my sleeve
for the hapless fortunes of my masters,
chilled by secret grief.


ELECTRA  You servant women, who set the house in order,
since you are here in this supplication                                    85
to attend me, give me your counsel in this matter!
What am I to say while I pour these funeral offerings?
What wise words may I utter, what prayer may I make to my
        father?
Am I to say I bring them from a loving wife to a loved
husband, when I bring them from my mother?                                 90
That I dare not do; and I do not know what I can say
as I pour this libation on my father's tomb.
Shall I speak the words men are accustomed to speak,
"Grant in return equal benefits to those who send
these funeral honors"—yes, a gift deserving fair return!                   95
Or must I in silence and dishonor, even as my father
perished, pour them forth for the earth to drink,
and retrace my steps, like one who has thrown out refuse,
hurling the vessel from me with averted eyes?
Share my responsibility, dear women, in deciding this;                     100
for we share the hatred that we cherish in the house;
do not hide your counsel in your hearts through fear of any!
For the fated hour awaits both the free man
and him who is made subject by another's might.
Tell me, if you have any advice better than this!                          105

---

98   After throwing away refuse, the Greeks would turn away
     without looking around for fear that the malignant powers
     might be provoked by such an action.

103  The CHORUS, being slaves, may be unwilling to take the
     responsibility for offering advice. ELECTRA tries to overcome
     this feeling by reminding them that slave and free alike
     cannot escape their fate.

CHORUS  I revere your father's tomb as though it were
an altar;
and I will tell you, since you so order me, the thought that
comes from my heart.

ELECTRA  Tell it me, even as you have voiced your
reverence for my father's grave.

CHORUS  Speak, as you pour, words good for the loyal.

ELECTRA  And to which among my friends am I to give
that title?                                                                 110

CHORUS  First to yourself and to whoever hates
Aegisthus.

ELECTRA  Then is it for myself and you that I must say
this prayer?

CHORUS  You yourself learn the answer and then explain
it!

ELECTRA  What other, then, must I add to this company?

CHORUS  Remember Orestes, absent though he is.          115

ELECTRA  Well said! Excellently have you instructed me.

CHORUS  Then to those guilty of the murder, with
mindful heart . . .

---

106  Dialogue lines belonging to the CHORUS, like those in this
scene, were spoken by its leader, the Coryphaeus.

108  This form of dialogue, called *stichomythia*, in which each
speaker utters one or two lines at a time, is characterized by
extreme stiffness and formality. Here the Coryphaeus gradually convinces ELECTRA to accompany the libation with a
prayer very different from that which CLYTEMNESTRA would
have wished. For the original audience, who believed strongly
in the efficacy of prayer and in the power of the dead to
influence events on earth, the matter had real importance.

111  *Aegisthus*: pronounce *Ee·gis'·thus*.

ELECTRA  What shall I say? Prescribe the form, instruct
my inexperience!

CHORUS  Pray that there may come to them some god or
mortal. . .

ELECTRA  Do you mean a judge or one who does justice?  120

CHORUS  Express it plainly—one who shall take life
for life!

ELECTRA  And can I ask this of the gods without
impiety?

CHORUS  Surely you can ask them to pay back an enemy
with evil!

ELECTRA  Mightiest herald of things above and things
below                                                       165
help me, Hermes of the earth! Call upon
the deities below the earth to hear my prayers,             125
those who watch over your father's house.
And call upon the Earth herself, on her who brings forth
    all things
and when she has nurtured them receives again their
    increase.
And as I pour this lustral water for the dead

---

123  It was a truism of early Greek popular morality that one
should do good to one's friends and harm to one's enemies.
Thus the respected Solon prays, "May I taste sweet in the
mouths of my friends, bitter in those of my enemies; may I
be respected by friends and feared by foes."

165  Hermes was the patron of heralds (cf. *Agam.* 514), as well
as the intermediary between the world above and the world
below. This is line 165 in the manuscript, but is generally
believed to belong here.

126  See note on 1.

129  The sprinkling of lustral water preceded every sacrifice, including a libation (cf. *Agam.* 1037).

*I call upon my father, and say, "Take pity on me,* 130
*and kindle in our house the dear light that is Orestes!"*
*For now are we, as it were, vagrants, sold*
*by our mother, who has got in exchange as husband*
*Aegisthus, him who is guilty of your murder.* ———→ Clytemnestra actually killed
*I live the life of a slave; and from his possessions* 135
*Orestes is an exile; and they in their arrogance*
*enjoy great luxury amid the profits of your labor.*
*And that Orestes may come here with happy fortune*
*I pray to you. Do you hear me, father,*
*and for me, grant that I may be more right-minded by far* 140
*than my mother, and in my acts more innocent.*
*For us I utter this prayer; and for our enemies*
*I pray that one may appear to avenge you, father,*
*and that the killers may in justice pay with life for life.* ✗
*This I interpose in the middle of my prayer for good,* 145
*against them uttering that prayer for evil.*
*But for us convey upward good fortune,*
*by grace of the gods and earth and justice triumphant!*
*Such are my prayers, and after them I pour forth these*
*offerings.*
*And custom bids that you crown them with flowers of*
*lamentation,* 150
*giving voice to the paean for the dead.*

CHORUS *Shed a plashing tear, lost*
*for our lost master,*

---

145 This is evidently a ritual formula, designed to make it quite
clear to the deity that the evil prayed for was only for the
speaker's enemies, whereas the good was for the speaker's
friends.

151 A paean is a kind of hymn, originally sung in honor of
Apollo and having cheerful associations. Thus to speak of a
"paean for the dead" conveys a kind of paradox.

152 The CHORUS sings a short lyric stanza without strophic
responsion; the meter is iambic mixed with the dochmiacs

*upon this bulwark of evil,*
*this loathed pollution, averting what is good,*                   155
*that is the libation we have poured. Hear me, majesty!*
*Hear me, king, from your gloom-enshrouded spirit!*
*Ah, what man shall come, mighty with the spear,*                 160
*deliverer of the house,*
*brandishing in his hands the Scythian armament,*
*and in close combat wielding weapons whose haft he grasps?*

ELECTRA   Now my father has received the libations
which the earth has drunk.

ELECTRA notices a lock of hair on the tomb.

But here is news; share it with me!                              166

CHORUS   Speak; my heart is dancing with alarm.

ELECTRA   I see here upon the tomb a severed lock.

CHORUS   To what man or what deep-girdled maiden can
it belong?

ELECTRA   That is easy for anyone to guess.                      170

CHORUS   Then may my old age learn from your youth?

---

so often found in lyrics that express emotional agitation. The
rhythm of the dochmiac meter is well conveyed by Jebb's
mnemonic: "Thĕ wīse kăn-gároōs/Rĕsént lēath-ĕr shoēs."

154   The text is uncertain. If the interpretation here adopted is
correct, the CHORUS, despite ELECTRA's attempt to alter the
effect of CLYTEMNESTRA's libation by accompanying it with
her own prayer, still refers to the offering as though it were
an instrument of CLYTEMNESTRA's purpose.

162   The Scythians, who inhabited the country between the
Carpathians and the River Don, were famous archers.

168   ELECTRA notices the lock referred to by ORESTES in the
Prologue (see note on 6). Only a close relation would make
such an offering to the dead.

171   A stereotyped form of expression; it recurs at *The Suppliants*
361.

ELECTRA   There is none but I that could have shorn it.

CHORUS   Yes, for they to whom it fell to offer hair in
mourning are his enemies.

ELECTRA   Yes, to the eye it seems very like . . .

CHORUS   Like whose hair? That is what I wish to know.   175

ELECTRA   It is very like my own to look upon.

CHORUS   Can it then be a secret offering of Orestes?

ELECTRA   It seems very like his locks.

CHORUS   And how has he dared to come here?

ELECTRA   He has sent a shorn lock in honor of his father.   180

CHORUS   In your words lies yet greater cause for tears,
to think that his foot shall never more tread this soil.

ELECTRA   To my heart also rises a wave
of bitterness, and I am pierced as though an arrow had
        transfixed me;
and from my thirsty eyes there pour,                        185
uncontrollable, the drops of a stormy flood,
as I look upon this lock. For how can I suppose
that any other in the city is the owner of this hair?
Why, no, it was not his murderess who shore it,
my mother, whose heart                                      190
is all unmotherly toward her children. ———— ✗
For me to assent outright,
and say this adornment comes from the dearest
of mortals to me, Orestes . . . but hope is flattering me!

*Clytemnestra
not so
motherly, so
what about?
every'g
iphigenia
Front?*

---

181   Both the Coryphaeus and ELECTRA are saddened by the
      thought that even if the lock belonged to ORESTES, its
      presence on the tomb does not prove that he came in person
      to Argos.

185   The eyes are called "thirsty" because they are thought of as
      longing for moisture and, therefore, shedding tears.

141

Ah, if it had only sense and language, like a messenger,  195
so that I was not tossed this way and that in two minds,
but either I knew for certain that I must reject this lock,
supposing it were cut from an enemy's head,
or it was kin to me and could share my grief,
adorning this tomb and honoring my father!  200
But the gods on whom we call know well
by what tempests we, like sailors,
are buffeted; and if we are fated to find safety,
from a small seed a mighty trunk may come.

> She notices the footprints.

Yes, and here are tracks, a second indication,  205
the tracks of feet matching each other and resembling mine.
Yes, here are two outlines of feet,
his own and those of a fellow traveler.
The heels and the marks of the tendons in their measure-
    ments agree with my own prints.  210
I am in torment, and my reason is confounded!

> ORESTES and PYLADES emerge from their hiding
> place.

---

205   The recognition of the footprints is mercilessly ridiculed by
Euripides in his *Electra* (518f; see Introduction, page 127).
There is no good reason to doubt the genuineness of the footprint episode. In the *Odyssey* Menelaus remarks that the
hands and feet of Telemachus resemble those of his father
Odysseus (4, 149). Since the theory that the beauty of the
body depended on its proportions was known to Greek
sculptors as early as the first half of the fifth century, relatives might very well be thought to resemble each other in
the proportions of their hands and feet. Further, the footprints provide ELECTRA and the CHORUS with an indication
of ORESTES' presence distinctly more reliable than the lock.
A lock, as they are quick to remember, might have been sent
to Argos from abroad, but not a footprint.

ORESTES  Pray, as you make acknowledgment to the gods
that your prayers have been fulfilled, that in the future
also you may fare well!

ELECTRA  Why, what fortune now do the gods allot me?

ORESTES  You have come to the sight of what you have
long prayed to look on.                                    215

ELECTRA  And whom among men do you know that
I call for?

ORESTES  I know that you make much of the name of
Orestes.

ELECTRA  And why then have I found an answer to my
prayer?

ORESTES  I am he; look for none closer to you than I!

ELECTRA  Why, are you weaving some snare against me,
stranger?                                                  220

ORESTES  If so, I am hatching a plot against myself.

ELECTRA  Would you make sport of my misfortunes?

ORESTES  Of my own too, if I make sport of yours.

ELECTRA  Then am I to address you as Orestes?

ORESTES  Why, you see my very self, and find me hard to
recognize;                                                 225
yet when you had seen the hair I had cut off in mourning,
you were excited, and thought you saw me;
and when you were scanning the traces of my footprints

· · · · · ·

He offers her the lock.

Put the lock to the place from which I cut it,
and see how like is your brother's head to your own!       230

He offers her the garment.

Look on this piece of weaving, the work of your hand,

on the strokes of the batten, and the picture of the beasts
    upon it!
Contain yourself! Do not lose your wits for joy,
for I know that those closest to us are hateful to us.

ELECTRA  O best beloved darling of your father's house,   235
O hope, much wept for, of seed that can preserve,
trusting in your prowess you shall win back the house of
    your father.
O joy-giving presence that has four characters
for me! For I must address
you as my father, and to you falls the love   240
I should bear my mother—her I most justly hate—
and that I bore the sister who was ruthlessly smitten.
And you have been a brother true to me, you who showed
    me due regard.
Only may Power and Justice, and Zeus the third,
mightiest of all, be on your side!   245

ORESTES  Zeus, Zeus, be witness of these doings!
And look upon the orphan brood of the father eagle,

*in vain*

*orestes + Electra referred to as orphans of the father Eyle*

---

235   The word rendered by "darling" is a lover's word, found
      in high poetry but also in comedy.

237   *trusting . . . prowess:* this phrase echoes a familiar Homeric
      expression. What follows (238f) is an obvious reminiscence
      of Andromache's great speech in the sixth book of the *Iliad;*
      Andromache, who has lost her parents and brothers, says,
      "Hector, you are my father and my lady mother, you are my
      brother and you are my husband."

242   IPHIGENEIA. In Homer, Agamemnon has three daughters—
      Chrysothemis, Laodice, and Iphianassa. Of these names, only
      Chrysothemis occurs in tragedy (Sophocles' *Electra*).

244   The third libation at banquets was poured in honor of Zeus
      the Preserver, and he was sometimes referred to as "Zeus
      the Third Preserver" (cf. *Agam.* 1385, with my note; *Eum.*
      758).

247   The eagle was the bird of Zeus.

of him who perished in the coils and meshes
of a dread viper! Bereft of their father
they are oppressed by starving famine; for they are not yet
    full grown,                                          250
so as to bring a quarry like their father's to the nest.
Even thus may I and Electra here
be seen by you, children robbed of our father,
both alike exiles from our home.
Now if you cause to perish these nestlings of a father          255
who made sacrifice and did you great honor, how
shall you get the honor of rich banquets from such a hand
    as his?
If you cause the eagle's brood to perish, you will no more
be able to send signs to men that they will trust;
and if this stem of royalty becomes all withered,              260
it will no more serve your altars on the days when oxen are
    slaughtered.
Rescue and raise it from humble state to greatness,
our house, low though now it seems to lie.

    CHORUS  O children, O preservers of your father's hearth,
be silent that none may observe you                            265
and for the sake of talking report all this
to those in power; them may I one day see
perish in the pitchy ooze of the flame!

    ORESTES  Never shall I be betrayed by Loxias' mighty

*Apollo*

---

258 The eagle was also important in augury; compare the portent
    of the eagles in the Parodos of *Agam.* 110f.

264 In scenes of conspiracy the leader of the CHORUS often has
    the function of reminding the conspirators of the danger of
    discovery.

267 A fragment of Aeschylus mentions the practice of covering
    people with pitch and then burning them alive.

269 *Loxias* is a name for Apollo, given him in his aspect as a

oracle, which commands me to pass through this danger,          270
raising many a loud cry and naming
chilly plagues to freeze my warm heart,
should I not take vengeance on those guilty of the murder,
after the same fashion bidding me take life for life,
driven to fury by the grievous loss of my possessions.          275
And with my own precious life, he said, I should pay
this debt, enduring many loathsome ills.
For as he revealed to mortals the means of mollifying
malignant powers below the earth, he spoke, naming these
    plagues—
leprous ulcers that mount upon the flesh with cruel fangs,       280
eating away its primal nature;
and a white down sprouting forth upon this infection.
And he spoke of other assaults of the Erinyes,
brought about by the shedding of my father's blood.
                    . . . . . .
seeing . . . clear, though in the dark he directs his glance.    285
For the dark arrows of the infernal powers,
darted by kindred fallen who call for vengeance,

---

god of prophecy and thought to be connected with a word
meaning "crooked." It thus refers to the deviousness of his
oracles.

275 Note that both here and at 301 the need to recover his house
and property is mentioned as one of ORESTES' motives.

276 Primitive and horrifying though the passage doubtless is,
that is no reason for rejecting it as interpolated. Further, it
is essential to the play; ORESTES must at this point lay heavy
stress on the awful consequences of *not* killing his mother.
The Erinyes were thought to afflict their victims with loathsome diseases (280–83) and madness (286–90). A person
polluted by the shedding of a kinsman's blood was excluded
from religious worship and social contact with others (291–
94). The Erinyes were thought to suck their victims' blood
(295–96); at *Eum.* 264–65, they themselves threaten ORESTES
with this fate.

284 There is a gap in the text at this point; the object of the
verb "seeing" in 285 is lost.

and madness and vain midnight fears
harass and torment and drive him from the city,
his body maimed by the brazen scourge.                           290
And such men may have no part in the festal bowl
or in the pouring of drink-offering,
but are kept far from the altars by their father's unseen
wrath; and none may receive nor entertain such a one,
but he must perish at last honorless and friendless,            295
cruelly shriveled by a death that wastes him utterly away.
Such were the oracles; and must I not believe them?
Even if I lack belief, the deed must be done.
For many longings move to one end;
so do the god's command and my great sorrow for my father;  300
and moreover I am hard pressed by the want of my
      possessions,
not to leave the citizens of the most glorious city upon
      earth,
the overthrowers of Troy with noble hearts,
thus to be subject to a pair of women.
For his heart is a woman's; whether mine is, he shall soon
      know.                                                      305

CHORUS   Come, mighty Fates, by the will of Zeus

---

302   This passage recalls the protest of the Chorus of Argive
      elders against having to submit to the rule of the usurpers
      in the final scene of *Agamemnon*. 305 recalls the moment
      during that scene when the Coryphaeus addresses AEGISTHUS
      as "Woman" (1625).

306   In *Prometheus*, where the possibility of Zeus's fall from
      power exists, the will of Zeus is not necessarily identical with
      fate (515f); but as long as Zeus reigns, his will and fate are
      the same. The philosophical problem of determinism had
      not at this time presented itself to the poets, and we must
      beware of supposing that they took either a determinist
      or an antideterminist view.

306–  The lyric part of the conjuration scene is often called "The
478   Great Kommos"; *Kommos* means the "beating" of the head
      or breast by mourners and it denotes a scene in which the

CHORUS and actors sing alternate stanzas as they do here. This part of the scene is unique in tragedy, both in its form and in its content. To grasp its import it is necessary to rerr ember that the poet assumes belief in the power of the dead to influence events on earth. It is all-important for ORESTES and ELECTRA to establish contact with the departed spirit of Agamemnon and to secure its aid in taking revenge upon the murderers. This simple but central fact has not proved easy for all modern minds to grasp. Many critics, including even the great scholar Wilamowitz, have tried to show that the great conjuration takes place in order to overcome the reluctance of ORESTES to commit the awful act of matricide. In order to strengthen the case for this theory, they have conjectured that lines 434–38 have been accidentally transposed and should come after 455; they would thus constitute the last of the lyric stanzas uttered in alternation by ORESTES, ELECTRA, and the CHORUS. There is no ground for supposing anything of the sort (see note on the passage in question). Nor is there anywhere any suggestion that ORESTES, like Hamlet, needs strengthening in his resolve; his long speech at 269 shows him fully determined and explains why. The great conjuration is directed not at the living but at the dead.

The conjuration scene consists of a lyric part (306–478) and a spoken part (479–509), in which the same ground is gone over in the less emotional and more explicit fashion proper to spoken dialogue. We may compare the division of the Cassandra scene of *Agamemnon* into a lyric and a spoken part. In the lyric half ORESTES, ELECTRA, and the CHORUS sing lyric stanzas in alternation, with marching anapests by the CHORUS at regular intervals. The responsion of the lyric stanzas is unique; instead of each strophe being followed by the corresponding antistrophe, the greater part of the scene shows a curious kind of interlacing responsion between stanzas placed at intervals from each other. The pattern is as follows:

I.  306–14  Marching anapests of CHORUS
    315–22  Strophe 1 (ORESTES)
    323–31  Strophe 2 (CHORUS)

332–39 Antistrophe 1 (ELECTRA)
340–44 Marching anapests of CHORUS
345–53 Strophe 3 (ORESTES)
354–62 Antistrophe 2 (CHORUS)
363–71 Antistrophe 3 (ELECTRA)
372–79 Marching anapests of CHORUS
380–85 Strophe 4 (ORESTES)
386–93 Strophe 5 (CHORUS)
394–99 Antistrophe 4 (ELECTRA)
400–404 Marching anapests of CHORUS
405–9 Strophe 6 (ORESTES)
410–17 Antistrophe 5 (CHORUS)
418–23 Antistrophe 6 (ELECTRA)
II. 424–28 Strophe 7 (CHORUS)
429–33 Strophe 8 (ELECTRA)
434–38 Strophe 9 (ORESTES)
439–43 Antistrophe 9 (CHORUS)
444–50 Antistrophe 7 (ELECTRA)
451–55 Antistrophe 8 (CHORUS)
456–60 Strophe 10 (ORESTES, ELECTRA, CHORUS)
461–65 Antistrophe 10 (ORESTES, ELECTRA, CHORUS)
III. 466–70 Strophe 11 (CHORUS)
471–75 Antistrophe 11 (CHORUS)
476–78 Marching anapests of CHORUS

The introductory anapests serve as a transition. The first section of the lyric scene (315–423), the dirge over the tomb, consists of six strophes with their antistrophes arranged to form four triads, separated from one another by marching anapaests of the CHORUS; the meter is for the most part aeolic mixed with iambic. The second section (424–55), the conjuration proper, consists of three strophic pairs in irregular response followed by a strophe and antistrophe in which the two actors sing one line each and the CHORUS the rest. The meter of this section is iambic; it contains no marching anapests, not even at its beginning or end. The third section of the lyric scene consists of a short stanza by the CHORUS in Aeolic meter, not forming part of the Kommos proper, but containing the comment of the CHORUS on what has gone before. Marching anapests of the CHORUS of 476–78 round off the first section of the conjuration scene.

149

accomplish, even by the way
that Justice now moves to tread!
"For hateful word let hateful
word be paid"; as she demands her due                               310
loud cries the voice of Justice;
"for murderous stroke let murderous
stroke atone." "Let the doer suffer";
so goes a saying three times ancient.

### STROPHE 1

ORESTES   Father, who fathered us to woe,                          315
what word or act
can I succeed in wafting to you from above
where you lie in your resting place?
Over against the realm of darkness stands the realm of light;
yet none the less the lament                                       320
that brings them honor is a joy
for the Atreidae who lie before the palace.

### STROPHE 2

CHORUS   My son, the dead man's mind is not subdued
by the fire's ravening jaw;                                        325

---

309   The words of the CHORUS recall the terms in which the
      Chorus of *Agamemnon* warned CLYTEMNESTRA of the truth
      of this fundamental principle of Aeschylean justice (1563f).

315   Before all else ORESTES must establish communication with
      his father; this can be effected by lamenting at his tomb.
      The world of the dead is separate from the world of the
      living, but the dead take pleasure in ritual lamentation.

322   *Atreidae:* pronounce Ă·*trУ́*·*dee*.
      Agamemnon's tomb, visible in the center of the stage,
      stands before the palace, whose doors will later open. Like-
      wise, Pindar speaks of the dead kings of Cyrene as being
      buried "before the palace" (*Pythian* V. 96).

324   The doctrine here enunciated by the CHORUS is vital to the
      understanding of the whole conjuration. "The punisher"

*but late in time he shows his anger.*
*The dead is lamented,*
*and the punisher is revealed;*
*and the lament due to fathers*
*and begetters hunts down the guilty one,*       330
*when raised full loud and strong.*

### ANTISTROPHE 1

ELECTRA  *Hear now, O father, as in turn*
*we voice our grief with many tears!*
*It is your two children who bewail you*
*in a dirge over your tomb!*       335
*Your tomb has received them as suppliants*
*and as exiles alike.*
*What is there here of good? What here is free from ill?*
*Is not ruin still unconquered?*

CHORUS  *But even though things are thus, a god, if he*
    *will,*
*may yet cause us to utter cries of more auspicious note;*     340
*and instead of lamentations by the grave*
*the paean in the royal halls*
*may bring back the well-loved mixing bowl of new wine.*

---

(328) is the personified curse, or perhaps the dead man's spirit, whom the lament will arouse to vengeance.

336  Cf. 254, where ORESTES claims that he and ELECTRA are both exiles. For a Greek, exile involved the loss of one's rights, so that even though ELECTRA had not left Argos she can still be called an exile. The expression used implies that the tomb is compared to an altar, where suppliants take refuge; it has been compared to one by the CHORUS at 106, and the poet Simonides said of the heroic dead at Thermopylae, "Their tomb is an altar."

343  On the paean, see note on 151. There is probably allusion to the mixing bowl of new wine that was used at funerals or feasts.

*STROPHE 3*

*Honor or War*

ORESTES _Would that beneath Ilium_                                    345
_pierced by the spear of one of the Lycians,_
_father, you had been slain!_
_You would have left glory in your halls,_
_and for your children a life_
_that would have made men turn to view them_
_in their walks abroad;_                                              350
_and you would have occupied a high-heaped_
_tomb in a land beyond the sea,_
_a fate your house could easily have borne._

*ANTISTROPHE 2*

CHORUS _Dear to the dear ones who nobly fell at Troy,_
_preeminent below the earth_                                         355
_as a king of august majesty,_
_and minister of the mighty_
_rulers there below!_

---

346  *Lycians:* pronounce *Licé·ians.*
    The Lycians are mentioned presumably because they, under their leaders Sarpedon and Glaucus, were the bravest allies of the Trojans. ORESTES' whole speech is modeled on one made by Achilles in *The Odyssey* (24. 30f). He speaks in Hades to Agamemnon and says he wishes that Agamemnon had been killed before Troy instead of meeting his death as he did.

354  Some scholars have wanted to emend the text because it seems to imply that Agamemnon's status in Hades was affected by the manner of his death, a notion the critics finds surprising. But two passages in *The Odyssey* (11. 388; 24. 20) might be held to imply this; his ghost is described as "sorrowful," and it is surrounded by the souls, not of those who fell at Troy, but of those who fell in the ambush in which he perished. The same notion governs Virgil's portraits of the dead in the underworld (*Aeneid* 6. 479f).

*For you were a king, while you lived,*     360
*over those that fulfilled their mortal lot,*
*with your might and with your man-controlling scepter.*

### ANTISTROPHE 3

ELECTRA  *Not even beneath Troy's*
*walls, father, would I have had you perish,*
*and with the rest of the host that perished by the spear*     365
*be buried by Scamander's stream!*
*But would that first your slayers*
*had been brought low in such a fashion*
*that far off men might have learned*     370
*of their deadly fate,*
*even men with no part in these troubles!*

CHORUS  *All this is more precious than gold, my child.*
*Greater than great good fortune, even that of the blessed,*
*are the things you speak of; for it is in your power.*
*But now—for the thud of this double*     375
*scourge strikes home!—our cause has champions*
*already below the earth, and those in power,*
*these hateful ones, have hands that are not clean;*
*and it is for you, his children, to act!*

### STROPHE 4

ORESTES  *This pierces through to my ear*     380
*like an arrow!*
*Zeus, Zeus, you who send up from below*
*late-avenging ruin*
*to the ruthless and reckless violence of men,*
*nonetheless the debts due to parents shall be discharged!*     385

---

375  *double scourge:* the beating of both hands on the tomb.

376  The thought that "our cause has already its champions below the earth" is of course calculated to encourage the avengers, as is the thought that the hands of their enemies are stained with blood (cf. 66f with note).

382  The reference is to Hades, whom Aeschylus calls "the Zeus below" (see note on 1).

153

### STROPHE 5

CHORUS  May it be granted me to raise a piercing
cry of triumph when the man
is smitten and the wife
perishes! For why do I hold back
what at all events hovers here
—and before my heart's prow                              390
blows a cutting wind
of rage—my mind's rancorous hatred?

### ANTISTROPHE 4

ELECTRA  And when shall the mighty
Zeus lay his hand upon them—                             395
ah, ah, severing their heads?
Grant an assurance to our land!
Justice from the unjust I demand!
Hear me, Earth and honored powers below!

CHORUS  But it is the law that drops of blood            400
spilt on the ground demand further
bloodshed; for murder calls on the Erinys,
who from those who perished before
brings one ruin in another's wake.

### STROPHE 6

ORESTES  Alas, sovereign powers of the world below!      405
Look on us, powerful curses of the dead!
Behold the remains of the Atreidae in their helplessness
cast out in dishonor from their home! Which way
is one to turn, Zeus?

---

386  This is the first mention of the idea that CLYTEMNESTRA
must be killed.

402  *Erinys*: pronounce E·*rine'*·*is*.

408  Those who try to make the play into a modern drama by
arguing that ORESTES hesitates to decide to kill his mother
invest this rhetorical question with a perplexity that is not
really there. ORESTES' determination is shown by his calling
upon the rulers of the underworld and the curses of the
dead (sometimes identified with the Erinyes, as at *Eum.*
417); it amounts to an appeal to Zeus for aid.

### ANTISTROPHE 5

CHORUS *My heart is in turmoil once more,*      410
*as I listen to this lament.*
*And now I am bereft of hope,*
*and my mind darkens*
*at these words as I hear them;*
*but when once more valiant confidence prevails,*      415
*hope removes my pain,*
*appearing before me in her beauty.*

### ANTISTROPHE 6

ELECTRA *What must we say to find the target? Must*
    *we recount*
*the agonies we have suffered, yes, from our begetters?*
*She may try to fawn upon him, but there is no appease-*
    *ment;*      420
*for like a savage wolf, not to be cajoled*
*by my mother, is his wrath.*

### STROPHE 7

CHORUS *I beat an Arian dirge upon my breast, after*
    *the fashion*
*of a Cissian wailing woman,*
*and with clenched fists and much spattering of blood*      425

---

413   In moments of violent passion the *phrenes*, originally perhaps the lungs but believed to be the seat of thought, were
said to darken (cf. e.g., *The Iliad* 1. 103).

418   Cf. 315f; they have to establish communication with the
dead man's ghost and arouse it to indignation.

422   *Arian:* pronounce *Air'·ian.*

     Here ends the dirge at the tomb, the first section of the
lyric part of the conjuration scene.

423   *Cissian:* pronounce *Siss'·ian.*

     The CHORUS appears to be recalling its behavior during the
delivery of the Parodos (22f). "The Arians" was an old
name for the Medes, and Cissia was the district of Persia
in which lay Susa, the ancient capital; the Greeks associated
passionate lamentation with Orientals.

*could you have seen once more and yet once more my arms*
    *stretched forth*
*from above, from on high, and while the ringing blows re-*
    *sounded*
*upon my battered, miserable head.*

### STROPHE 8

ELECTRA  *Ah, ah, cruel,*
*reckless mother, in a cruel burial*                           430
*a king without his people,*
*without his due of mourning*
*a husband you had the heart to bury unlamented!*

### STROPHE 9

ORESTES  *All without honor he was, as you tell it.*
*But for my father's dishonoring she shall pay,*             435
*by the action of the gods,*
*and by the action of my hands.*
*Then may I perish, once I have slain her!*

### ANTISTROPHE 9

CHORUS  *He was mutilated; I must tell you this;*
*and the doer was she who gave him this funeral,*           440
*striving to make his death*
*a burden on your life.*

---

429  CLYTEMNESTRA had denied Agamemnon's body a proper burial (cf. *Agam.* 1551f).

434  This stanza is transposed to follow 455 by those who think the conjuration takes place to give ORESTES the strength to decide to kill his mother. They have mistaken the sense of 438, which they take to mean that once he has killed his mother, ORESTES no longer wishes to live. But in Greek poetry it is common to say, "May I die, once I have killed X," meaning simply that one would do anything if one could only kill X; the expression is of the type discussed in my note on *Agam.* 539 (cf. also *Agam.* 550). These words of ORESTES give no ground for supposing that he hesitates to obey Apollo's command.

439  Murderers used to mutilate the corpses of their victims to prevent their ghosts from pursuing them; they cut off the

*Now you know the woes your father suffered, all without
honor.*

### ANTISTROPHE 7

ELECTRA    *You tell of my father's end; but I was far
away,*
*dishonored, I that deserved a better fate!*                    445
*Shut away in my chamber like a savage dog*
*I gave forth watery drops more readily than laughter,*
*as in my prison I poured out a lament of many tears.*
*Hear this and write it in your mind, father!*                    450

### ANTISTROPHE 8

CHORUS    *Write it; and let our words pass through
your ears*
*with tranquil mind.*
*For these things are as we say;*
*yourself be passionate to hear the rest!*
*With wrath inflexible must you enter the struggle!*               455

### STROPHE 10

ORESTES    *On you I call! Be with your dear ones, father!*

ELECTRA    *I join my voice to his, bathed in tears.*

CHORUS    *And this whole company echoes the call.*
*Come to the light, and hear us!*
*Be with us against our enemies!*                                  460

### ANTISTROPHE 10

ORESTES    *Might shall clash with might, Justice with
Justice.*                                                          ✕

ELECTRA    *O ye gods, fulfill my prayer as Justice demands.*

CHORUS    *A shudder creeps over me as I hear the prayer!*
*Doom has long since been waiting;*
*and may it come to us as we pray for it!*                         465

---

hands and feet of the victim, strung them on a rope, put
the rope round his neck, and drew it under his armpits.

461    CLYTEMNESTRA, as avenger of Iphigeneia, and AEGISTHUS, as
avenger of his brothers and sisters, each had a certain meas-

### STROPHE 11

*Ah, sorrow inbred in the race,*
*and bloody stroke*
*of ruin discordant!*
*Ah, woes lamentable, unbearable!*
*Ah, pain not to be quelled!* 470

### ANTISTROPHE 11

*The house has a remedy for this,*
*a remedy of suppuration; not from others,*
*without, but from its own children*
*must it come, by means of cruel, bloody strife.*
*To the gods beneath the earth this hymn is sung!* 475

*Come, give ear, blessed ones below the earth,*
*to this prayer, and send help*
*readily to his children, so that they triumph!*

ORESTES  *Father, who perished in unkingly fashion,*
*grant my prayer for the lordship of your house!* 480

---

ure of justice on their side when they slew Agamemnon; so of course has ORESTES when he comes to avenge his father.

466  This concluding strophe and antistrophe are not part of the conjuration, which ends at 465, but comprise a brief comment by the CHORUS.

471  A suppurating wound was treated by the application of "tents" or "pledgets" designed to catch the pus, a remedy that was used only in desperate cases. In this case the "treatment" consists in the successive murders.

475  Hymns were normally sung to the Olympian gods of heaven, so that the idea of a hymn to the gods of the underworld conveys something of the grim travesty of a "paean of the Erinyes" at *Agam.* 645.

476  The CHORUS rounds off the lyric part of the conjuration scene with a final prayer for victory to the gods below.

479  ORESTES and ELECTRA now make their appeal to the ghost in more explicit and less emotional fashion, using dialogue instead of lyric meter and speaking instead of singing.

ELECTRA  I, too, have a like request for you—
that I may escape after having laid utter ruin on Aegisthus.

ORESTES  For thus you may get the banquets that are
    men's custom;
but if we fail, while others feast richly you shall go without
your due honor at the savory banquet of burnt offerings.    485

ELECTRA  And I shall bring you libations from my rich
    store,
wedding libations from my paternal home;
and first of all I shall do honor to this tomb.

ORESTES  O Earth, send up my father to survey the
    battle!

ELECTRA  O Persephassa, grant him beauteous victory!    490

ORESTES  Remember the bath in which you were
    murdered, father!

ELECTRA  Remember the new sort of covering they
    devised!

ORESTES  You were caught in fetters of no smith's
    working, father!

ELECTRA  And in the shroud of a vile plot!

ORESTES  Do these shameful words not rouse you,
    father?    495

ELECTRA  Do you not raise erect your beloved head?

ORESTES  Either send Justice to fight by your dear ones'
    side,

---

483  Compare this appeal to the simple self-interest of the ghost
    with the appeal to the self-interest of Zeus at 255f.

490  Persephassa is another name for Persephone.

491  ELECTRA echoes ORESTES' opening word, "remember"; this
    reinforces the effect of exact symmetry between the utter-
    ances of the two speakers that persists throughout this scene.

or grant that we in turn get a like grip on them,
if it is your will to atone for your defeat by victory.

ELECTRA   Hear also this last cry, father!                        500
Look upon your nestlings here at your tomb,
and pity alike my woman's and his man's cry!

ORESTES   Do not wipe out this race of the Pelopidae!
For if we live you are not dead, even in death.
For children preserve a man's fame                                505
after his death; like corks they hold up the net,
retaining the cord of flax that reaches up from the deep.

ELECTRA   Listen! It is for your sake that such laments
      are uttered,
and you yourself are preserved if you do honor to our words.

They retire from before the grave.

CHORUS   Indeed, there has been no fault in this your
      lengthy utterance;                                          510
making atonement to the tomb for the lament that was
      denied it;
and for the rest, since you are resolved to act,
do now the deed and make trial of your fortune.

---

503   Pelops was an ancestor of Agamemnon.
505–  These lines are attributed to Sophocles by an author who
507   quotes them; without them ORESTES and ELECTRA would
      deliver speeches of exactly equal length down to 509. They
      may well have been interpolated, as passages of sententious
      reflection often were.
510   The word translated "without flaw" implies that ORESTES
      and ELECTRA have correctly discharged the ritual in the
      invocation of the ghost.
512   These words have been misconstrued to imply that without
      the conjuration ORESTES would have been unable to sum-
      mon the resolve to kill his mother; in fact they imply noth-
      ing of the sort.

ORESTES  *It shall be so; but we are not deflected from*
    *our course if we inquire*
*why she sent libations, what calculation led her*      515
*to offer too late atonement for a hurt past cure.*
*But to the unconscious dead it was a poor solace*
*that she sent! I do not know to what to liken these*
*her gifts, but they are less than her offense.*
*For though a man pour out all he has in atonement for one*   520
*life taken—in vain is his labor; thus goes the saying.*
*If you know what I ask, tell it me; I wish to learn it.*

CHORUS  *I know, my son, for I was there; by dreams*
*and fears that send men wandering in the night she was*
    *shaken,*
*so that she sent these libations, the godless woman.*     525

ORESTES  *Do you know the nature of the dream, so that*
    *you can truly tell it?*

CHORUS  *She thought she brought forth a snake,*
    *according to her own account.*

ORESTES  *And where ends her story and where lies its*
    *consummation?*

CHORUS  *She laid it to rest in swaddling clothes, as*
    *though it were a child.*

ORESTES  *What food did it desire, the newborn*
*monster?*     530

---

520  Again the constantly repeated motive of the irrevocability
    of bloodshed (cf. 71f, etc.).

525  *the godless woman:* what the CHORUS called CLYTEMNESTRA
    in the Parodos (46).

527  In the *Oresteia* of the early lyric poet Stesichorus, Clytem-
    nestra dreamed of a snake. But it seems that there the
    snake symbolized, not ORESTES, but Agamemnon (see Intro-
    duction, page 124).

CHORUS  She herself offered it her breast in the dream.

ORESTES  And how did her teat remain unwounded by
the hateful creature?

CHORUS  It did not, but with the milk it sucked a curd
of blood.

ORESTES  It is a vision of a man, no empty one.

CHORUS  And in her sleep she screamed in terror.      535
And many lamps that darkness had made blind
were kindled in the palace for the mistress' sake.
And then she sent these funeral libations,
hoping for a cure to cut away her distress.

ORESTES  Well, I pray to the earth here and to my
father's tomb                                         540
that this dream may be fulfilled for me;
and see, I interpret it so as to tally at all points.
For if the snake came from the same place as I
and lay among my swaddling clothes,
and opened its mouth about the breast that fed me,    545
and mingled the kindly milk with a curd of blood,
and she in terror cried out at the event,
it must come about, I say, that even as she fed the monstrous
portent,
so must she die by violence, and it is I that turn into a snake
and slay her, as this dream announces.                550

CHORUS  I choose your reading of this prodigy.
May it be so! But expound the rest to your friends,
bidding some take measures, and others refrain from action.

ORESTES  Simple is the telling. Electra must go inside;

---

539  Cautery and excision were the two main methods of ancient
chirurgery; the metaphor is from the latter (cf. *Agam.* 849–
50).

551  Like the speech of the Coryphaeus at 510–13, this serves
to dismiss one topic and pass on to the next.

and I bid you keep secret this covenant with me,                                      555
so that they who by cunning slew an honored hero
may be taken by cunning, perishing
in the same snare, as Loxias has declared,

*God demands*

the lord Apollo, a prophet never proved false in the past.
In the guise of a stranger, fully equipped,                                           560
I shall come with this man to the gate of the courtyard,
with Pylades, a stranger and a spear-friend to the house.
And we will both speak the dialect of Parnassus,
copying the sound of the Phocian tongue.
Suppose none of the doorkeepers with welcome in his mind       565
receives us (for indeed a spirit is visiting the house with
        evil):
we shall wait so that someone may put two and two together,
as he passes by the house, and say this:
"Why does Aegisthus shut out the suppliant at the gates,
if he is at home and knows the man is there?"                                          570
Well, if I cross the threshold of the courtyard gates

---

556   According to the usual story, told also by Sophocles in his
      *Electra* (35f), Apollo had told ORESTES that he must kill
      Agamemnon's murderers by guile, just as they had killed
      their victim.

560   ORESTES can call himself a stranger because he has been
      away so long.

562   *Spear-friend:* a term for "ally," the spear being for the
      Greeks, as the sword was for us, the weapon *par excellence;*
      but ORESTES uses the term because he will presently use
      violence against his enemies.

563   This means PYLADES' home country, where ORESTES spent
      his exile.

569   Hospitality to strangers and "suppliants" was a religious
      duty whose neglect might bring punishment from Zeus
      Xenios, Zeus the Lord of Host and Guest.

571   In accordance with the usual technique of tragedy, the poet

163

and find him on my father's throne,
or if he returns and then comes face to face with me,
be assured, before he can cast down his eyes,
before he can say, "Where does the stranger come from?" I
    shall strike him                                                                575
dead, spitting him on my swift-moving weapon.
And the Erinys that has had no stint of blood
shall drink unmixed gore in a third potation.
So now, Electra, keep good watch inside the house;
that this may turn out just as we wish;                                              580
and you women I charge to be discreet in speech,
to be silent where it is needful and to say what fits the time.
And for the rest I pray my father here to look upon us,
making the battle with the sword go right for me.

     EXEUNT ORESTES, PYLADES and ELECTRA.
           STROPHE 1

CHORUS  *Many are the terrors bred of earth,*                               585

---

is deliberately leading his audience to expect things that
will not happen. According to one version of the story,
familiar from vase paintings, AEGISTHUS was surprised by
ORESTES while seated on his father's throne and killed in-
stantly.

573  The text is uncertain.

581  The request to the CHORUS for silence is common in tragic
      scenes of conspiracy.

585  The pattern, "There are many formidable things, but this is
      the most formidable" recalls the famous First Stasimon of
      Sophocles' *Antigone*, "Many things are formidable, and most
      of all is Man." Further, the stasimon conforms to a standard
      type of choral ode in which the situation in the play is
      compared with other situations in the mythological past.
      When Antigone is sentenced to be buried alive, the Chorus
      compares her fate with those of three imprisoned persons
      in the past (944f); when Medea in Euripides' play is about
      to kill her children, the Chorus compares her with Ino, who
      in madness killed her offspring (1282f). This stasimon is
      corrupt in places, and in some of these it is very hard to

dread and woeful,
and the embraces of the ocean teem
with monsters inimical to mortals;
and between earth and heaven there come into being
lights that shine by day;                                590
and winged things and things that walk the earth can tell
also of the stormy wrath of whirlwinds.

### ANTISTROPHE 1

But of the reckless pride
of a man who can tell,                                   595
or of the desperate passions
of women without scruple, fellows
of the spirits that wreak ruin among mortals?

Unions in wedlock
are perverted by the victory of shameless passion, mastering
        the female,                                      600
among beasts and men.

### STROPHE 2

Let any know this whose wits are not
unstable, having learned
of the plot which the killer of her son
Thestius' reckless daughter

---

understand. It begins in trochaic meter, which later changes
to iambic.

"Earth, sea and sky have bred many formidable creatures; but what is more formidable than men's pride and
woman's passion?" (594f).

590  *lights that shine by day:* lightning and, perhaps, meteors.
604  *Thestius:* pronounce *Thess´·ti·us.*

Alythaea, daughter of Thestius, was wife of Oeneus, king of
Calydon, and mother of the great hero Meleager. Soon after
Meleager's birth it was predicted that he would not survive
longer than a brand then burning on the fire, and Althaea
seized the brand and kept it carefully. After Meleager with

*accomplished*                                                    605
*a plot of burning in the fire,*
*she who consumed in flames the charred brand assigned to*
*    her son,*
*that was his fellow in age, from the cry*
*he uttered when he left his mother's womb,*
*and remained coeval throughout life*                            610
*to the day determined by fate!*

### ANTISTROPHE 2

*And there is another woman in legend fit for abomination,*
*the murderous Scylla,*
*who at the behest of enemies*
*did to death one dear to her,*                                  615
*lured by the Cretan*
*necklace wrought of gold,*
*the gift of Minos;*
*deliberately she deprived*
*Nisus of his lock of immortality,*
*she the shameless one, as he drew breath in sleep;*            620
*and Hermes overtook him.*

---

other heroes had slain the great boar sent by Artemis to
ravage the crops of Calydon, he gave the spoils to the virgin
huntress Atalanta; in consequence a quarrel started in which
Meleager killed his mother's two brothers. Althaea in fury
took the brand and hurled it on the fire, and Meleager's death
followed. This story is the subject of Swinburne's *Atalanta
in Calydon*.

612– *Scylla*: pronounce *Sil' · la*.

620      Nisus, king of Megara, had a purple lock; while he kept this
         lock, he could not die. Minos, king of Crete, attacked
         Megara with a fleet; Scylla, daughter of Nisus, persuaded
         by the gift of a necklace (or, according to one version, she
         fell in love with Minos), cut off the lock. Megara fell
         to the Cretans, and Scylla was changed into the sea-monster
         who figures in *The Odyssey* (see note on *Agam.* 1233).

618   *Minos*: pronounce *Mie' · nos.*

622   *Hermes*: pronounce *Herm' · ēs.*

Turning toward the palace.

### STROPHE 3

*And since I have called to mind pitiless*
*afflictions, I add the tale of the hateful*
*marriage, an abomination for the house,*          625
*and the daring deeds plotted by a woman's mind.*
*Against your warrior husband,*
*against your husband like an enemy did you go,*
*honoring the hearth of the house that lacked warmth*
*the cowardly spear of a man that was no man.*       630

### ANTISTROPHE 3

*And first among crimes comes that of Lemnos*
*in story, and the people lament for it*
*with execration; and each new horror*
*men liken to the woes of Lemnos.*
*And in pollution hateful to the gods*          635
*the race of men has vanished with dishonor.*
*For none reveres what the gods detest.*
*Which of these tales have I unjustly cited?*

*old Bad Blood* [handwritten annotation]

### STROPHE 4

*And near the lungs the sword*
*drives sharply home a piercing stroke*         640
*by the action of Justice, who in defiance of the right*
*has been trampled underfoot,*

---

Hermes, the conductor of spirits to Hades, overtook Nisus, who had hoped to remain immortal.

629   This refers to AEGISTHUS. A hearth that had only a man like AEGISTHUS to light it (see *Agam.* 1435–36) lacked proper warmth; the spear of AEGISTHUS was cowardly, for he was no proper man (cf. *Agam.* 1625).

631   *Lemnos:* pronounce *Lemn'·nos.*

    Moved by jealousy of some women captives from Thrace, the women of Lemnos massacred all the men on the island, except the king Thoas, who was smuggled to safety by his daughter Hypsipyle.

*striking those who have transgressed against the whole*
  *majesty of Zeus,*
*in defiance of the right.*                                      645

### ANTISTROPHE 4

*The anvil of justice is planted firm;*
*and fate the swordsmith fashions in advance her weapon.*
*But the child is brought to the house*
*of ancient murders,*
*to atone at last for the pollution brought by the famed,*       650
*the deep-designing Erinys.*

> The CHORUS retires; ORESTES with PYLADES goes up to the
> gateway.

ORESTES  Boy, boy! Hear my knocking at the courtyard
  gate!
Who is inside? Boy, boy, I say once more, who is at home?
A third time I call for someone to cross the house,            655
if Aegisthus permits that it give hospitality.

> SLAVE  All right, I can hear you. From what land is the
> stranger? From what place?

---

646  For a similar metaphor, compare *Agam.* 1535.

648  "The child of ancient murders" refers not to ORESTES but
  to the new murder that will soon take place; for the metaphor, compare 806 below.

651  The telling word "Erinys" is held back until the end of
  the stanza; compare *Agam.* 59, 749.

653  ORESTES has already told ELECTRA and the CHORUS (571f)
  that he will immediately attack if he finds AEGISTHUS at
  the door; the moment when he approaches the door is
  therefore one of high dramatic tension. But, as usual, the
  poet has led the audience to expect things that actually
  turn out differently.

657  The SLAVE's words echo the traditional Homeric question to
  a stranger.

168

ORESTES  Announce me to the masters of the house,
to whom I come bringing news;
and make haste, for Night's dusky chariot                    660
is speeding on, and already it is time for travelers to drop
anchor in the hospitable houses of their hosts.
Let there come from the house some person in authority,
a lady, mistress of the place . . . but it would be fitter that
    a man should come.
For the respect one owes a woman in conversation obscures    665
one's words; a man can speak with confidence
to a man and make his meaning clear.

    Enter CLYTEMNESTRA (with attendants).

CLYTEMNESTRA  Strangers, say if there is anything you
    need! For we have
all that is fitting for this house;
hot baths, and bedding that charms away                      670
fatigue, and the presence of honest eyes.
But if there is need for action that requires more counsel,
this is work for men, to whom we will impart it.

ORESTES  I am a foreigner from Daulis among the
    Phocians
and as I traveled carrying my own pack                       675
toward Argos—it is here that I have ended my journey—
a stranger met me and spoke to me,

---

664  ORESTES would naturally prefer to settle with AEGISTHUS
    before being confronted with his mother.

668  *Clytemnestra:* pronounce *Klīt·em·nes'·tra.*

670  The sinister irony of these lines is manifest; the mention
    of "hot baths" can hardly be an accident. Naturally this
    irony is the poet's, directed toward the audience, not that
    of CLYTEMNESTRA herself.

672  Compare *Agam.* 1608–9, 1614; AEGISTHUS planned the mur-
    der.

674  *Daulis:* pronounce *Dor'·lis; Phocians:* pronounce *Fo'·shuns.*

after asking me my errand and telling me his,
Strophius the Phocian; for as we talked I learned his name.
"Since in any case, stranger, you are going to Argos,                680
remember in all honesty, and tell his parents
that Orestes is dead; by no means forget.
To bring him home—if this is the prevailing wish of his own
     people
or to bury him in the land of his exile, an alien guest for all
     time—
these are the instructions you must convey back to us.         685
For now the sides of an urn of bronze
enclose the ashes of a man we have well bewailed."
So much I hear and I have told you. And if I happen
to be addressing those in authority, to whom it pertains,
I do not know; but it is proper that his parent know the
     truth.                                                                       690

CLYTEMNESTRA   Ah me! Your tale is of our utter ruin!
O curse upon this house, that we wrestle with in vain,
how far your vision ranges! Even what was well bestowed out
     of the way
you with your well-aimed arrows from afar bring down,
and strip me, in my misery, bare of friends!                        695
And now—for Orestes kept good counsel,
keeping his foot outside the mire of ruin
now the hope that existed in the house as medicine

---

679   Father of PYLADES; compare *Agam.* 880f.

691   It is not safe to assume that the emotion CLYTEMNESTRA
expresses is wholly false. But it is clear from her answer to
ORESTES at 707f that her sorrow at the report of his death
is greatly lessened by the thought that now she and
AEGISTHUS are safe; the speech of the NURSE (734) with
its spontaneous expression of unmixed grief throws this fact
into strong relief.

698   When criminals were condemned to death in Athens, they
were entered in the register as "present" or as "absent"

against the evil revelry you must write down as present and
    awaiting death.

ORESTES  For my part, my hosts being so prosperous        700
I should have wished it were on account of good news
that I had become known to them and had been entertained;
    for where
is good will greater than between host and guest?
But piety made it seem wrong to me
not to fulfill such an office for Orestes' friends,        705
when I had given my promise and become your guest.

CLYTEMNESTRA  I say that nonetheless you shall receive
    your due,
nor shall you be the less a friend to the house;
another might as well have come to bring this news.
But it is time that strangers who have spent the day        710
on a long journey should get their proper entertainment!
Take him to the house's guest-chambers for men
and also these followers and fellow travelers,
and there let them have the treatment that befits this house;
and I charge you to act as one who will be held to strict
    account.        715
But we shall impart this to the ruler of the house
and we shall have no lack of friends
when we take counsel touching this event.

---

because only if they were present could the sentence be
carried out. If the interpretation I have adopted is correct,
the passage alludes to this fact; but this explanation is not
certain.

700  Messengers who brought good news commonly received a
rich reward, and tragic messenger scenes frequently contain
allusions to this fact.

713  ORESTES and PYLADES will have been accompanied by silent
slaves carrying their baggage.

716  Compare 672–73 with note.

171

Exit CLYTEMNESTRA followed by the others.

CHORUS *So be it, loyal handmaids of the house;*
*when shall we display*      720
*the strength of our voices in honor of Orestes?*
*O sovereign Earth and sovereign mound*
*of the barrow that now lies*
*over the body of the master of the fleet, the king,*
*now give ear to us, now give us aid!*      725
*For now it is the time for guileful Persuasion*
*to enter the arena on his side, and for Hermes of the Earth*
*and of the Night to watch over this*
*contest of the deadly sword!*

The stranger, it seems, is working some mischief!      730

------

719    The scene is separated from the next one by a brief passage of marching anapests chanted by the CHORUS; for this use of marching anapests, compare *Agam.* 783f, 1331f; also above, 306f.

727    For Hermes of the Earth, compare 1 with note; Hermes is also the god of thieves, who traditionally operate at night, and by Apollo's command ORESTES is employing guile to carry out his act of vengeance.

731f   (See Introduction, page 129.) The NURSE, with her chatter about infants and their habits, affords the sharpest contrast to the dignity of all other Aeschylean characters. The only other humble character in Greek tragedy whose talk is characteristic of his station is the Guard in Sophocles' *Antigone*; no Euripidean nurse or slave is like this. Not that the NURSE's language is in any way like that of comedy; it is not its colloquialism but its reference to familiar and untragic matters that is surprising. In *The Iliad* (9. 490–91) Achilles' old tutor, Phoenix, refers similarly to the infantile habits of his former charge, and in *The Odyssey* (19. 363) Odysseus' old nurse, Eurycleia, laments similarly over her troubled life. The unfeigned sorrow of the talkative old woman supplies an effective contrast to the way in which CLYTEMNESTRA has received the news of her son's death.

Enter the NURSE.

But I see here Orestes' nurse in tears.
Where are you on your way to, Cilissa, that, that you are at
    the gate of the house?
grief is your unhired fellow traveler.

NURSE   The mistress bids me summon Aegisthus for the
    strangers
with all speed, so that unmistakably,               735
as man from man, he may come and learn
this story they have just reported. To the servants
she assumed a look of sorrow, hiding inside her eyes
the mirth she felt at work accomplished well
for her—but for this house things are altogether ill,     740
made so by the message which the strangers have rendered
    clearly.
Indeed his heart will be gladdened by the hearing,
once he learns the news. O woe is me!
For the ancient woes blended together
in this house of Atreus were hard to bear,           745

---

Also, by an effective stroke of tragic irony, the harmless
NURSE has a decisive effect upon the action, for the Coryph-
aeus makes her disobey CLYTEMNESTRA's orders and tell
AEGISTHUS to come without his bodyguard.

730f   This speech is in trimeters and is spoken by the Coryphaeus,
     like the rest of the dialogue with the NURSE. The Coryphaeus
     infers that ORESTES is already getting to work.

732   Cilissa: pronounce Sy·liss′·sa: "Cilician woman." Many
     slaves in Greece bore names that expressed their racial
     origins; thus in the New Comedy "Getas" and "Syrus" are
     common names for slaves. Stesichorus and Pindar (see In-
     troduction, p. 124) had given the Nurse the heroic names
     Laodameia and Arsinoe.

733   For the mode of expression, compare Agam. 979.

744   For the metaphor, compare Agam. 1395–98.

745   Atreus: pronounce Ayt′·ruse.

and afflicted the heart within my breast;
but never have I endured such agony as this!
For my other sorrows I bore patiently;
but my dear Orestes, for whom I wore away my life,
whom I reared up after I received him from his mother          750

. . . . . .

and of loud commands that set me moving in the night,
and I bore many labors without profit to myself—
for the unreasoning thing has to be nursed
as though it were an animal—how else?—according to its
        humor.
For a child still in swaddling clothes does not tell you          755
whether it is hungry, or maybe thirsty, or wants to make
        water;
and the infant stomach must have its own way.
To guess at these needs I had to be a prophet, and often, I
        know,
did my prophecy prove false, I who washed the child's swad-
        dling clothes;
and the offices of washerwoman and nurse were combined.     760
These two handicrafts were mine
when I received Orestes for his father;
and now, alas, they tell me of his death,
and I go to fetch that man who is the ruin
of this house, and gladly will he learn this story.          765

CHORUS   How then does she bid him come attended?

NURSE   What do you mean by "how"? Speak again, so
    that I can understand you better.

CHORUS   I mean, does she say with his guards or alone?

NURSE   She bids him bring the spearmen who attend
    him.

---

750   Something is certainly missing after 750; how much is quite
    uncertain. Line 750 implies that the NURSE cared for him
    from the moment he came into the world, as we can see
    from *Odyssey* 19. 353, whose language is plainly echoed here.

CHORUS  Then do not yourself give the news to our
    detested ruler;                           770
but tell him to come alone, to hear without fear the news
as soon as possible, and with rejoicing heart;
it rests with the messenger to put a crooked statement
    straight.

NURSE  But are you sane? After the message they have
    brought?

CHORUS  But suppose Zeus should some day make to
    change the wind                       775
that blows us ill?

NURSE  What do you mean? Orestes, the hope of the
    house, is gone.

CHORUS  Not yet; even a poor prophet could guess
    that.

NURSE  What are you saying? Have you some knowl-
    edge beyond
what has been told?

CHORUS  Go, take the message, do as you are ordered!
The gods are caring for whatever is their care.      780

NURSE  Well, I will go and do as you say in this;
and with the gods' granting may all turn out as well as maybe!

Exit NURSE.
*STROPHE 1*

CHORUS  *Now in answer to my prayer, Zeus,*
*father of the Olympian gods,*

---

780  Compare *Agam.* 974.

783  This ode is one of the most difficult in all Greek tragedy;
    its text is exceedingly corrupt, and in several places it cannot
    be restored with any real certainty. It consists of three
    strophes and antistrophes, whose prevailing meter is trochaic;
    between each strophe and its antistrophe is interposed a
    stanza outside the strophic responsion, termed a mesode,
    whose prevailing meter is ionic ( $\smile\smile--$ ). The first strophic

grant good fortune to the house's                                785
rulers, who long to see
the rule of order!
For the sake of Justice has my every word been uttered;
Zeus, be her protector!

### MESODE 1

Ah! Set him before his foes
that are inside the palace,                                       790
Zeus, for if you exalt him to greatness,
twofold and threefold shall be
your reward at your pleasure!

### ANTISTROPHE 1

And know that the orphaned colt of a sire dear to you
is harnessed in the chariot                                      795
of calamity; do you regulate
his running, and give it
the rhythm of those that come home safely,
so that over this course we see straining forward
a gallop that reaches the goal!

### STROPHE 2

And do you who within the house inhabit                          800
the inner chamber whose wealth gives joy,
give ear, gods that feel with us!
Come! . . .
redeem the blood of deeds done long ago
by a new act of justice!                                         805

---

pair with mesode (783–99) contains a final prayer for success to Zeus; the second (800–19) contains successive prayers
to the household gods of Agamemnon's palace, to Apollo,
and to Hermes; the third (820–37) exhorts ORESTES to carry
out with resolution the awful duty that awaits him.

791    Again the prayer appeals to the deity's self-interest; compare
255f with note.

800    This prayer is addressed to such household deities as Zeus
Ktesios, god of the storeroom (see *Agam.* 1038 with note);
Hestia, goddess of the hearth (see *Agam.* 1056 with note),
etc.

*May ancient murder no longer bear its offspring in the house!* ✗ *But that could continue*

### MESODE 2

*And do you who dwell in the mighty cavern, fair built,*
*grant that our hero's house may in prosperity look up once*
     *more,*
*and that the light of freedom*
*may look on him with friendly*                               810
*eyes, out of her veil!*

### ANTISTROPHE 2

*And may Maia's son in all justice give him help,*
*for he has greatest power*
*to waft, if he will, the action to success;*
*and much that lies in darkness he shall illumine, if he will.*   815
*I utter a mysterious word:*
*by night he sets darkness before men's eyes,*
*and by day he is no plainer to the view.*

### STROPHE 3

*And then at last, glorious,*
*bringing release from fear,*                                820
*shrill, showing that the breeze is fair,*
*sung high by charmers of the winds,*
*shall the song be on our lips: "Our ship goes well!"*

---

806   For the notion that one murder may beget another, com-
      pare *Agam.* 753; above 648; etc.

807   The god addressed is Apollo, Lord of Delphi. Before
      Apollo's coming, the oracle had belonged to the earth-
      goddess; the ancients believed that beneath the temple there
      was a chasm through which the divine influence came up
      from the earth to be communicated to the prophetess (see
      Dodds, *The Greeks and the Irrational,* Chap. III).

812   *Maia*: pronounce *My'·a.*
      Once again Hermes is prayed to; see note on 727 above.

818   Hermes can make himself invisible night or day by virtue
      of the "cap of Hades," the Greek equivalent of the Tarnhelm
      stolen by Wotan and Loge from Alberich.

For me, for me profit is now augmented, and destruction      825
stands far from those I love.

### MESODE 3

And do you with courage, when there comes
the time for you to act, when she cries
to you, "My child!" utter your father's name,
your father's, and accomplish      830
an act of horror none can blame!

### ANTISTROPHE 3

Maintain in your breast
the heart of a Perseus
and for your dear ones below the earth
and above, assume instead of love
a grim temper, and inside the house      835
work bloody ruin, and destroy
him who is guilty of murder.

Enter AEGISTHUS.

AEGISTHUS  I have come not unsummoned, but at a
    messenger's request;
and I hear that certain strangers have come
bringing news in no way welcome,      840
news of Orestes' death. This too will be for the house
a blood-dripping burden, still festering
and galled as it is by the bloodshed before.
How am I to suppose this tale is true and real?

---

832  *Perseus:* pronounce Pers′·yuse: Perseus was sent to kill the
Gorgon Medusa, whose face none could see without being
turned to stone; Athene therefore lent him her shield, so that
he could see the Gorgon's reflection on its surface as he
aimed his stroke.

840  Even AEGISTHUS as a kinsman pretends to feel sorrow at
the news of ORESTES' death. His extreme eagerness to question the messenger in person, however, betrays his hope that
the news may prove true, besides having the unfortunate
consequence of causing him to hurry into the trap.

Is this a story born of women's terror 845
that darts upward and perishes in vain?
What can you tell me of these things that will make the
matter clear to my mind?

CHORUS We have heard the story, but question the
strangers
when you have gone inside! What messengers can do is
nothing
compared with questions put by man to man. 850

AEGISTHUS I wish to see the messenger and to
question him with care;
was he himself nearby when Orestes died,
or did he learn from vague report what he has told us?
He can by no means deceive a mind whose eyes are open.

Exit AEGISTHUS.

CHORUS Zeus, Zeus, what can I say, where can I begin 855
my prayer and invocation of the gods?
In my loyalty
how can I find words to match the need?
For now blood shall stain
the edges of the blades that slaughter men; 860
these will either bring disaster complete
on Agamemnon's house,
or else, kindling a torch to win freedom
and power to rule the city
Orestes shall possess the great wealth of his fathers. 865
Such is the bout which as sole antagonist of two
godlike Orestes is about to join;
and may it lead to triumph!

---

845 The metaphor is from sparks flying upward from a bonfire.
854 The metaphor of the "mind's eye" is not uncommon in
Greek poetry.
855 The interval between the exit of AEGISTHUS and his death
is filled in by a short choral passage of marching anapaests
(compare note on 719). This time the only god invoked is
Zeus.

The death-cry of AEGISTHUS is heard from inside.

CHORUS  Aha!                                                              870
*How do things stand? How is the issue determined for the*
*house?*

*Let us stand aside while the affair is being settled,*
*that we may seem guiltless in this trouble;*
*for now has the issue of the battle been decided.*

Enter SLAVE.

SLAVE  *Woe! Utter woe! The master is struck down!*        875
*Woe yet again for the third time I cry!*
*Aegisthus is no more! Come, open up*
*as quickly as you can, unbar the doors*
*of the women's rooms! We need a right strong arm—*
*not to help him who is already dead; what need?*              880

He shouts.

*My shout falls on deaf ears; to folk that lie in ineffective*
*sleep*
*I utter futile words. Where is Clytemnestra? What is she at?*
*Now, it seems, near her consort*
*shall her head in turn fall, smitten by the stroke of justice.*

Enter CLYTEMNESTRA.

CLYTEMNESTRA  *What is the matter? Why do you raise*
*the alarm in the house?*                                          885

---

870  These lines are in lyric iambics, the lyric meter closest to
     the iambics of dialogue and therefore usually chosen for
     isolated lyric utterances similar to ordinary dialogue.

879  The strong man is needed to open the doors at once, as a
     parallel passage in the *Odyssey* (23. 187) helps to show;
     with grim irony the SLAVE goes on to make it clear that he
     is not calling for a strong man in order to save AEGISTHUS.

883  This line contains a textual crux; the translation adopts a
     possible emendation.

SLAVE   A living man, I say, is slain by the dead.

CLYTEMNESTRA   Ah woe! I understand your words, despite the riddle!
By guile shall we perish, just as we slew by guile!
In all speed give me a man-slaying axe! ✗
Let us know if we are the victors or the vanquished;   890
yes, so far along the path of catastrophe have I come!

Exit Slave; ORESTES and PYLADES become visible.

ORESTES   You are the one I seek; this man has had
enough.

CLYTEMNESTRA   Oh woe! You are dead, dearest one,
mighty Aegisthus!

ORESTES   Do you hold the man dear? Then in the
same tomb
you shall lie, and in death shall you never lose him.   895

---

886   This alludes to the false report of ORESTES' death.

889   Several vase paintings not far removed in date from the
Oresteia show CLYTEMNESTRA using an axe in this scene; an
axe might be at hand even in a house expecting no attack.
This may be the origin of the story used by Sophocles in his
Electra and by Euripides in several plays that Agamemnon
was killed with an axe. In Aeschylus there is a notable imprecision about the weapon Agamemnon was killed with,
perhaps because Aeschylus wanted to focus on the fatal
garment that was thrown over him; perhaps it was a sword
(see note on Agam. page 103). ORESTES and PYLADES, together with the body, came into view probably by means of
the device known as the ekkyklema, a kind of platform
which could be wheeled or pushed forward to disclose the
scene behind the stage door. (Compare note on Agam.
1372f.)

CLYTEMNESTRA   Hold, my son, and have respect, my
    child,
for this breast, at which many a time in slumber
have you sucked with your gums the milk that nourished
    you!

ORESTES   Pylades, what am I to do? Shall I respect my
    mother, and not kill her?

PYLADES   Where henceforth shall be the oracles of
    Loxias                                                     900
declared at Pytho, and the covenant you pledged on oath?
Count all man your enemies rather than the gods!

ORESTES   I judge you the victor, and your advice is
    good.

To CLYTEMNESTRA.

Come this way! I wish to kill you by his very side!
For in life you preferred him to my father.               905
Sleep by his side in death, since you love
this man, while him you should have loved you hate!

---

896   The word translated "respect" here and at 899 is *aidos*, which
      basically means the respect or consideration one owes to
      any person because of his status; it is often used of those
      who give in to the entreaties of a suppliant, and hence in
      some contexts it is not far from meaning "pity." It is espe-
      cially applicable to the respect owed to parents. According to
      a well-known story, Helen, when recaptured by Menelaus
      during the sack of Troy, moved him to spare her life by
      showing him her bare breast.

900   These are the only words spoken by PYLADES. As the son of
      the king of Phocis and a neighbor of the Delphic god, he
      is well qualified to be his spokesman here; his name suggests
      Pylai, the meeting place of the Amphictyonic League, which
      protected Delphi.

901   *Pytho:* pronounce *Pie' · tho.*

CLYTEMNESTRA  It was I who reared you, and I would grow old with you.

ORESTES  What! Shall you, my father's killer, share my home?

CLYTEMNESTRA  Fate, my son, must share the blame for this.

910

ORESTES  Then this your doom also has been sent by Fate.

CLYTEMNESTRA  Have you no awe of a parent's curse, my son?

ORESTES  No, for you gave me birth and yet cast me out into misfortune.

CLYTEMNESTRA  I did not cast you out when I sent you to the house of an ally.

ORESTES  Vilely was I sold, though born of a free father.  915

CLYTEMNESTRA  Then where is the price I got for you?

ORESTES  I am ashamed to taunt you outright with that.

CLYTEMNESTRA  Name also the follies of your father!

ORESTES  Do not reproach him who labored, you who sat at home!

CLYTEMNESTRA  It is a cruel thing for wives to be separated from a husband, my son.

920

---

908  These lines are in the standard form of dialogue called *stichomythia*; see note on 108.

915  For the notion that ORESTES has been sold by his mother, compare 132f; the price was of course her relationship with AEGISTHUS.

918  The reference is to Chryseis (see the first book of *The Iliad*), Cassandra, and others.

ORESTES   Yes, but the husband's toil supports them while they sit inside.

CLYTEMNESTRA   It seems, my child, that you will kill your mother.

ORESTES   You yourself, I say, not I will be your slayer.

CLYTEMNESTRA   Take care, beware your mother's wrathful hounds!

ORESTES   And how shall I escape my father's, if I neglect this duty?                                                                        925

CLYTEMNESTRA   I am like one who, still alive, laments to her own grave in vain.

ORESTES   Yes, for it is my father's fate sends you this doom.

CLYTEMNESTRA   Ah woe, that I bore and reared this serpent!

ORESTES   In truth the fear your dream inspired was prophetic!

---

921   Hesiod in the *Theogony* (398f) had compared women with drones, who sit in the hive and live off the production of the working bees. ORESTES' language in this passage echoes much misogynistic matter in early Greek poetry.

924   The Erinyes are often called "hounds," and in *The Eumenides* they are depicted as picking up a scent and pursuing their quarry just as hounds do (see *Eum.* 131f, 246f).

925   It must be remembered that if ORESTES had not killed his mother, the Erinyes would have pursued him for failing to avenge his father; in that event he would not have had the protection of Apollo; compare 276f.

926   CLYTEMNESTRA calls ORESTES "a tomb" because of his insensibility; there was a proverb that "pleading with a stupid man is like pleading with a tomb." But ORESTES makes her words apply not to himself but to his father.

928   CLYTEMNESTRA remembers her warning dream (see 526f).

Wrong was the murder that you did, wrong is the fate that
   now you suffer!                                930

   Exit ORESTES with CLYTEMNESTRA.


   CHORUS   Even for these I lament in their twofold disaster;
yet since sorely tried Orestes has mounted to the peak
of many deeds of blood, we choose rather to have it thus,
so that the eye of the house may not be utterly extinguished. X

### STROPHE 1

There came Justice in time to the sons of Priam,      935
there came a heavy retribution;
and there has come to the house of Agamemnon
twice a lion, twice a god of war!
Altogether he has got his inheritance,
he, the exile prompted by Pytho,              940
well sped on his course by the counsels of the gods!

### MESODE

Cry out in triumph at the escape of our master's palace

---

930  In accordance with the normal rules of Attic drama, the
     killing probably took place off stage.

934  The eye was accounted the most precious part of the body,
     and the most precious part of anything might therefore be
     referred to as its "eye."

935  The CHORUS sings an ode of triumph, entirely in the
     dochmiac meter. For the basic rhythm of dochmiacs, see the
     note on 152–63; they are regularly used to express agitation
     or excitement. As in the Second Stasimon, a mesode stands
     between each strophe and its antistrophe (942–45, 962–64).

935  Once again, as so often in Agamemnon, a parallel is drawn
     between the just punishment of the house of Priam and the
     just punishment of the house of Atreus; only here CLYTEM-
     NESTRA and AEGISTHUS are in question.

938  ORESTES and PYLADES are probably referred to.

*from evil and the wasting of its substance*
*beneath the rule of two polluters,*
*a grievous fortune!* 945

### ANTISTROPHE 1

*And there has come one who directs war by stealth,*
*the crafty Hermes;*
*and there guided his hand in the battle the trueborn*
*daughter of Zeus—Justice is the name*
*we mortals give her, hitting the mark—* 950
*breathing upon her foes her deadly wrath.*

### STROPHE 2

*Even this did Loxias, he who occupies*
*the mighty cavern of the land of Parnassus,*
*loudly proclaim; with guileless guile* 955
*does he visit mischief grown inveterate;*
*and ever somehow does the divine prevail,*
*so that we do not serve the wicked;*
*it is right to reverence the power that has the mastery of*
*heaven.* 960

---

946   In this stanza—if the text I have adopted is right—Hermes, Zeus, and Zeus together with his daughter Justice are praised for their part in the revenge; Apollo is praised in the following stanza (953f). Zeus, Apollo, and Hermes are all prayed to in the two opening strophic pairs of the Second Stasimon (783f with notes).

948   The name of Justice—in Attic Greek *Dike*, but in the dialect of choral lyric *Dika*—is here derived from *Dios kora*, "daughter of Zeus." In terms of modern scientific etymology the derivation is absurd; but in early Greece belief in the magical significance of names was widespread (compare, e.g., *Agam.* 681f), and many etymologies that cannot possibly be valid were taken seriously. In his dialogue *Cratylus*, Plato discusses many etymologies of this kind; just how seriously he took them is not easy to determine.

953   See 807f above. Parnassus is the mountain on whose slopes the Delphic temple stands; for the name "Loxias," see note on 558.

### MESODE

*Now can we see the light, and the great curb*
*has been lifted from the household.*
*Arise, O house! For all too long*
*have you lain prostrate.*

### ANTISTROPHE 2

*And soon shall all-accomplishing time pass*          965
*the portals of the palace, when from its hearth*
*all pollution shall be driven*
*by means of a cleansing which expels destruction.*
*In the light of a fortune fair to look on can we see*
*the whole, as we cry out,*          970
*"The tenants of the house shall be cast out."*
*Now we can see the light!*

*Hoping for the end to the curse*

> Enter ORESTES; some believe that a crowd of
> Argive citizens, admitted to the palace by order
> of ORESTES to hear his speech, enters the stage.
> The fatal garment used in the murder of
> AGAMEMNON is displayed near the dead bodies of
> CLYTEMNESTRA and AEGISTHUS.

ORESTES   Look upon the two tyrants of the land,
the spoilers of my house who killed my father!
Majestic were they then, seated upon their thrones,          975
and dear to each other even now, as we may read by the fate

---

965   To us this personification of time seems strangely artificial,
but in Greek it is not uncommon; compare those examples at
*Agam.* 894, 985.

971   The "tenants of the house" are the Erinyes, who have so long
beset it; compare *Agam.* 1186f.

973   In this scene the bodies remain visible, and the fatal garment
in which Agamemnon was entangled is displayed. It is a
reasonable surmise that the stage is occupied not only by
the CHORUS but by others representing the people of Argos
summoned to the palace by ORESTES. Each of ORESTES'
opening speeches (973–1006, 1010–17) is followed by a brief
utterance by the CHORUS in marching anapests, the two
anapestic passages being exactly symmetrical.

*they have suffered; and their covenant abides by its sworn
    terms.
Together they swore death for my unhappy father,
and together they swore to die; and they have kept their oath.*


*Look also, you who take cognizance of this sad work,*     980
*on the device they used, to bind my unhappy father,
their manacles for his hands and fetters for his feet!
Spread it out! Stand by in a circle,
and display her covering for her husband, that the father
    may behold
—not my father, but he who looks upon this whole world,*     985
*the Sun!—may behold my mother's unholy work,
so that he may bear me witness on the day of judgment
    when it comes
that it was with justice that I pursued this killing—*

---

977    i.e., "they abide by the sworn terms of their covenant."

978    (See note on 434.) ORESTES imagines his mother and her
lover as having said, "May we die, if only we can kill Agamemnon!" Since they did indeed conspire together to kill
him, and a conspiracy according to ancient ways of thought
involves an oath, he can speak of them as having *sworn* to
kill Agamemnon and to die together, and as having kept
their oath.

980    The word translated "take cognizance" has legal connota-
tions; ORESTES is formally calling his audience to witness the
guilt of the people he has put to death, displaying as his
evidence the instrument of murder.

985    From Homer's time onwards it was common to call upon
the all-seeing Sun to witness actions that had taken place
within its view.

987    What possible occasion does ORESTES have in mind? He is
aware that he may have to give an account of his action;
later he has to justify it before the Areopagus with the
Erinyes as his prosecutors.

that of my mother (for Aegisthus' death I count for nothing;
he has suffered the adulterer's penalty, as is the law).    990
What name am I to give this thing, speak I never so fair?    997
A trap for a wild beast, or, draped over the dead man's feet,
the draping of a coffin? No, a net,
a hunting-net, you might call it, or a robe to entangle a man's
    feet.    1000
Such a possession might some brigand set,
a cheater of travelers who plays a robber's trade, ╳
and with this cunning snare
might he slay many a man and much delight his heart
    thereby.    1004
But she who devised this hateful deed against her hus-
    band,    991
whose children she had borne beneath her girdle,
a burden once dear, but now of deadly hatred, as the sight
    of her reveals,
what think you of her? Had she been a sea-snake or a viper,
would not her very touch have had power to rot another
    yet unbitten,    995
such was her shamelessness and evil pride!

---

989    According to fifth-century Athenian law, a man might law-
fully put to death the seducer of his wife; the first speech
of the orator Lysias is a defense of a man who had done
so.

997    The transposition adopted in the text was suggested only
during the present century, but it removes more than one
serious difficulty better than other suggested expedients.

998    The word used for "coffin" originally meant "bath," and
the phrase is obviously meant to suggest the bath in which
Agamemnon was murdered. The words, indeed, mean "the
curtain of a bath," and they are thus a doubly apt description
of the object in question.

1001    ORESTES imagines that an object like the robe might be a
suitable device for some atrocious brigand like Procrustes,
Sciron, or the other criminals punished by Theseus.

May I never have such a mate to share 1005
my house! Sooner than that, may the gods make me perish
    childless!

    CHORUS  *Alas, alas, for woeful work!*
*Hateful the death by which you were undone!*
*Alas, alas!*
*And for him that survives suffering now ripens to the full.*

    ORESTES  Did she do the deed or not? This robe 1010
is my witness, as to how Aegisthus' sword dyed it.
And the blood that gushed forth was time's partner
in spoiling the many dyes applied to the embroidery.
Now do I speak his eulogy, now am I here to render him
    due lamentation;
and as I call upon this web that slew my father 1015
I grieve for what was done and what was suffered and for all
    our race,
bearing as I do the unenviable pollution of this victory.

-----

1005   Childlessness for an ancient Greek was one of the worst
      possible disasters, so that the final words are more emphatic
      than they might seem.

1007   These are marching anapests; see note at the beginning of
      the scene.

1010   Again ORESTES uses legal language.

1011   This does not necessarily imply that CLYTEMNESTRA bor-
      rowed a sword from AEGISTHUS with which to murder
      Agamemnon. We know that the body was mutilated after
      death, and it was a common practice in the ancient world
      to stab again and again the dead body of a hated enemy,
      as the Greeks did that of Hector (*Iliad* 22. 371).

1014   CLYTEMNESTRA had outraged her dead husband by de-
      priving him of the rite of lamentation by his nearest kin
      (*Agam.* 1548–59 with notes); now ORESTES is here to
      discharge the duty that he could not perform then.

1017   For the Greeks the essence of victory was that it should

CHORUS  None among mortals shall pass his whole life
    free from suffering,
enjoying honor to the end.
Alas, alas!
One sorrow comes today, another shall come tomorrow.    1020

*unending*

ORESTES  But I would have you know—for I do not know
    how it will end—
I am like a man in a chariot driving my team
far from the course; for my wits are hard to govern
and carry me away, losing the battle; and close to my heart
fear is ready to sing, and my heart to dance in anger to its
    tune.    1025
And while I am still sane, I make proclamation to my
    friends,
and I declare that not without justice did I slay my mother,
the polluted murderess of my father and an object loathed
    of heaven.
And among the promptings that urged me to the deed, I
    give first place
to the prophet of Pytho, Loxias, whose oracle told me    1030
that if I did this thing I should be free
of guilt, but if I did not—I will not name the penalty;
for no man's arrow shall reach that height of woe.

*Loxias*

---

be enviable, so that the expression used here is a kind of
bitter paradox. An untranslatable particle in 1016 indicates that although ORESTES laments for all that has happened, he would not change what he has just done.

1018    These are again marching anapests, symmetrical with those
at 1007–9; for the commonplace that they express, compare *Agam.* 1341–42.

1021    The metaphor of "going off the course" is used to describe
the onset of madness, not only here, but in *Prometheus*
when Io goes mad (883–84).

1033    The sense appears to be that if all the troubles were piled

And now behold me, and see how, armed
with this branch and wreath, I shall approach as sup-
    pliant                                       1035
the dwelling at earth's navel, the domain of Loxias,
and the light of the fire called everlasting,
an exile for the shedding of this kindred blood; for to no
    other hearth
did Loxias order me to turn.
This command I lay upon all men of Argos, as time goes
    on                                           1040
to remember how the evil was brought about,
and to bear me witness, when Menelaus shall come.
But I, a wanderer, an exile from this land,
in life and death leaving this report of me . . .

. . . . . .

CHORUS  Why, your act was noble! Let not evil
    slander
gag your mouth, do not speak any ill-omened words!     1045

---

        on one another you could not shoot an arrow high enough
        to reach the top.

1035    Suppliants approaching the altar of a god carried boughs
        and wore garlands.

1036    Delphi was believed to be at the center of the earth.

1037    Many Greek altars had fires burning on them which were
        supposed never to go out. If they were put out (as happened,
        for example, when the temples of Athens were destroyed in
        480 B.C. by the Persians under Xerxes), they had to be
        renewed from Delphi.

1041    *Menelaus:* pronounce *Men·e·lay'·us.*

        In the manuscript two lines have been made into one by
    mistake; the text has been conjecturally restored. The
    satyr-play that accompanied the *Oresteia, Proteus,* re-
    counted the adventures of Menelaus after he had been
    separated from Agamemnon's ship by the storm described
    at *Agam.* 636f.

You have liberated the whole state of Argos,
lopping the heads of two serpents with dexterous stroke.

ORESTES   Ah, ah!
Here are ghastly women, like Gorgons,
with dark raiment and thick-clustered snakes
for tresses! I cannot stay!                                          1050

CHORUS   What are these fancies, O truest of all men to
        your father,
that vex you? Stay, do not be afraid for your victory is great!

ORESTES   Fancies have no part in these troubles for me;
for I know that these are my mother's wrathful hounds.

CHORUS   Yes, for the blood is still fresh upon your
        hands.                                                       1055
It is that makes turmoil come upon your mind.

ORESTES   O lord Apollo, see, they multiply;
and they drip from their eyes a hateful stream.

CHORUS   There is but one way of cleansing; Loxias by
        his touch
will free you from these troubles.                                  1060

ORESTES   You do not see these, but I see them!
They hound me on, I cannot stay!

        Exit ORESTES.

CHORUS   Good luck go with you, and may the god
        watch over you
and guard you in his kindness, so that your fortune prospers!

Now upon the royal house                                            1065

---

1048   Only ORESTES can see the Erinyes; but in the last play of
       the trilogy, *The Eumenides*, they are visible to everyone be-
       cause they form the Chorus.

1054   See note on 924 above.

1065   The CHORUS finishes with marching anapests, listing the

*for yet a third time has the tempest*
*blown and proved grievous!*
*First came the eating of children's flesh,*
*the cruel woes of Thyestes;*
*Then were the sorrows of the king, the husband,*　　　1070
*when slaughtered in his bath there fell*
*the war lord of the Achaeans;*
*and now thirdly has there come from somewhere a*
　　　　*deliverer—*
*or shall I say a doom?*
*What shall be the decision, what the end*　　　1075
*of the might of destruction, lulled at last to rest?*

---

three successive visitations of the curse upon the family and inquiring what is to be the family's future.

1069 *Thyestes:* pronounce *Thi·ess′·tēs.*
1072 *Achaeans:* pronounce *A·kee′·ans.*
1073 There is an allusion to "Zeus the Preserver who comes third," a title that derives from the pouring of the third libation at a banquet in honor of Zeus the Preserver (cf. *Agam.* 245f, 1385–86).
1076 The play ends with the ominous word *ate,* "destruction."

# BIBLIOGRAPHY

### A. TEXT WITH COMMENTARY.

No adequate commentary on *The Choephoroe* exists in English; A. Sidgwick's school edition (*Aeschylus, Choephori*: London: Oxford University Press, 2nd ed., 1902) is useful. Dr. A. F. Garvie is preparing a text with commentary.

### B. VERSE TRANSLATIONS.

Richmond Lattimore in Grene and Lattimore, *The Complete Greek Tragedies*, Chicago, 1953–
Robert Fagles, *Aeschylus: The Oresteia*, New York, 1975 (Penguin, 1977)

### C. GENERAL.

E. R. Dodds, *Morals and Politics in The Oresteia* (=*The Ancient Concept of Progress*, Oxford, 1973, ch. III)
Anne Lebeck, *The Oresteia: a study in language and structure*, Washington, D.C., 1971

# AESCHYLUS: ORESTEIA

# EUMENIDES

## ('The Kindly Ones')

# INTRODUCTION

From long before the time of Homer, certain categories of crime were punished by the terrifying powers of the underworld—the Erinyes. Although they primarily avenged crimes committed by offspring against parents, even if such crimes fell short of parricide or matricide, they also punished people who had failed to keep their oaths, as they did in Hesiod.

The Erinyes were probably personified curses; Aeschylus has them say that they are called Curses below the earth (*Eum.* 417). From early times, they seem to have been regarded as the defenders of the natural order of things. Before the word *Dike* came to mean "Justice," it meant "the proper order of nature" or "custom." Early in the fifth century B.C., the Ephesian philosopher Heraclitus said that if the sun exceeded the measure appointed it, the Erinyes, the assistants of Dike, would check it; thus he saw them as the maintainers of the proper order of the universe.

In *The Iliad* (19. 407f) Hera allows Xanthus, the immortal horse of Achilles, to warn his master of approaching death; it is the Erinyes who stop him from speaking. In Hesiod the Erinyes are daughters of Earth, whereas in Aeschylus they are daughters of Night; in either case they belong to the ancient gods, who were mighty long before the birth of Zeus, the present ruler of the universe. Although the cult of the Erinyes was never widely diffused, they were worshiped at several places, particularly in Athens. Despite their terrifying aspect as the punishers of crime, they resembled other underworld divinities in having the power to bestow fertility, and hence prosperity and happiness. Worshipers often referred to them euphemistically as "The Venerable Ones" (Semnai) or "The Kindly Ones" (Eumenides). When Aeschylus has them accept Athene's offer of a home in Athens, he is taking advantage of a long-existing cult and a long-recognized aspect of their character.

Throughout the *Oresteia*, the Erinyes exert a powerful influence on the fortunes of the house of Atreus. They punish Troy for Paris's offense against the laws of hospitality (*Agam.* 59, 749); later Cassandra sees them besieging the house of the Atreidae (*Agam.* 1117, 1190f); and it is to them, together with Dike and Ate, that Clytemnestra claims to have sacrificed her husband. In *The Libation Bearers* we are reminded three times that Agamemnon's murderers must pay the penalty to the Erinyes (402, 651, 577), and we are told that if Orestes should fail to avenge his father, it is they who would inevitably punish him (269f). Yet they will also punish him for the murder of his mother, and in the last scene, visible only to the eyes of Orestes, they appear to hound him from his home. Unlike Agamemnon, Clytemnestra and Aegisthus have no human heirs left to avenge them. Thus in the third play the Erinyes, hitherto seen only by Orestes, must themselves appear to carry out their duty, and they themselves form the Chorus of the play. As in *The Suppliants*, where the daughters of Danaus, the main actors in the story, form the Chorus, here too the Chorus is more than usually involved in the events depicted.

Orestes is confronted with a problem to which there is no satisfactory answer; he should neither kill his mother nor fail to avenge his father. He turns to an institution that at least since the end of the eighth century B.C. exercised a powerful influence on Greek religion and politics—to Apollo's oracle at Delphi. The story that Orestes spent his exile, not as *The Odyssey* claims in Athens, but in Phocis, near Delphi, occurs first in the post-Homeric epic called *Nostoi*, "The Return of the Heroes from Troy" (see note on 841 of *The Libation Bearers*). Stesichorus in the sixth century B.C., a century after *Nostoi*, used it in his *Oresteia*, and also has Apollo protect Orestes against the Erinyes by giving the boy a bow with which to keep them off. During Aeschylus' lifetime, when the oracle gave comfort to the Persian invaders, the influence of the oracle suffered a blow from which it never quite recovered, but even after this, it continued to be very great. Delphi was the acknowledged arbiter on questions of sacral law, religious ritual, and the ceremonies of purification by which the Greeks sought to remove the "pollution" attached to those guilty of certain crimes, especially murder of kindred. According to the usual story, deliberately altered by Aeschylus to save Apollo from the reproach of having used violence (see note on 5), the oracle had first belonged to the primeval earth-goddess. She had been a central figure of Greek religion before the Olympians, and Apollo had conquered the oracle by slaying her sacred snake, the Python. Afterwards, he had undergone a ceremony of purification; and in many cities, including Athens, it was customary for those guilty of involuntary homicide to undergo such a ceremony.

In Aeschylus' play Apollo purifies Orestes by washing him in pig's blood, and after this ceremony, Orestes no longer considers himself polluted. This, however, does not free him from the attentions of the Erinyes, who flatly reject Apollo's order that they should henceforth leave Orestes alone. Strictly speaking, they are within their rights; it is their duty to destroy anyone who has shed his kindred's blood—"his own blood," as the Greeks considered it to be—and to them the plea of extenuating circumstances is irrelevant. Apollo treats Orestes' crime as a case of justifiable homicide and thus grants purification, but the Erinyes bitterly denounce him for having infringed upon their time-honored prerogative. As in *Prometheus*, there is a clash between gods who belong to different generations—the Erinyes, who as daughters of Night are counted among the ancient gods, and Apollo, who is the son of Zeus. This conflict ends, not in the defeat of the representatives of the old order, but in a settlement in which their claims are fully recognized; far from abandoning their ancient functions, they are exalted and dignified with new honors. The play that has begun by horrifying its audience with the gruesome appearance and bloodthirsty threats of the Erinyes ends by honoring them with solemn panegyrics, claiming that they are among the greatest benefactors of mankind.

201

After Orestes, at Apollo's order, has fled from Delphi to Athens, both sides are persuaded by Athene, the patron goddess of Athens, to let her handle the conflict. She chooses to refer it to a group of leading Athenian citizens composing a tribunal over which she herself presides on this occasion. The tribunal takes its seat upon the Hill of Ares, or Areopagus, where in fact the famous Court of Areopagus held its sessions, a court destined to last for centuries and to be the audience for St. Paul's famous sermon (Acts 17:22–31). (For further discussion of the allusions to the Court of the Areopagus and to the Argive alliance, the reader is referred to the Appendix.) The Erinyes are the prosecutors, and Apollo is the advocate of Orestes. Before the votes are cast, Athene announces that if they prove equal she will cast her deciding vote in favor of acquittal, and it is by this vote that Orestes is acquitted.

Some critics have found Athene's reason for voting for Orestes insufferably frivolous, and others have tried to invest it with a wholly imaginary profundity. She says that she had no mother, having sprung fully armed from the head of Zeus, and therefore cannot sympathize with a mother's point of view. In fact Athene, who is the sister of Apollo and the daughter of Zeus, from whom the authority of Apollo's oracles is derived, is likely to sympathize with the plea of extenuating circumstances against the Erinyes' irrational insistence on the letter of the law. But to say so would run the risk of the Erinyes' immediately carrying out their threat to take vengeance on Athens if they lose their case. Instead Athene must regard the situation as a stalemate that can be resolved only by her personal decision; the motive of this decision is less likely to be offensive to the Erinyes if it is personal to the presiding judge.

Orestes takes his leave, with thanks to Athene and promises to her city; his case is settled. It remains for Athene, however, to restrain the Erinyes from carrying out their fearsome threats of destruction against Athens. By a judicious mixture of threats and promises, conveyed with all possible dignity and tact, Athene succeeds in this difficult task. If she wished, she could deal with the Erinyes by force; the younger generation of gods now rules the universe, and she could borrow Zeus's thunder and treat her adversaries as the Titans and the Giants had been treated. But she has no need to do so; by offering them the consolation of a special cult in Athens, she can not only appease their wrath but also win for her city the many blessings that they have the power to give. Nowhere is there any hint that from this time forth the Erinyes are to renounce their cherished functions; on the contrary, Athens' homicide law in Aeschylus' time acknowledged their importance. If the play reflects the transition from the blood-feud to the rule of law, it reflects a transition to a law that explicitly recognized the duty of obtaining redress.

At the beginning of the play, the Erinyes appear as figures of unspeakable horror. When the door of the temple opens to reveal the terrifying beings who, so far unseen, have dominated the action of the two previous plays, the dignified priestess of Apollo, the Pythia, is reduced to panic by their hideous aspect. When the ghost of Clytemnestra rises to wake the sleeping Erinyes with a clamor for revenge, their utterance proves no less frightful than their looks. Apollo denounces them as figures of outmoded horror; they have no place in Hellas, he declares, but in eastern countries, whose barbarous peoples practice torture and mutilation. Yet, at the end of the play these same monstrous and uncanny beings are honored by Apollo's own sister, the tutelary goddess of Athens.

The turning point is the Second Stasimon (490f), the song in which the Erinyes first offer a rational statement of the nature of their office and the reasons for its existence. Were they to cease punishing the killers of kindred, the social order would dissolve. They are the protectors of Dike, goddess of Justice, dear to Zeus; through them Zeus gives to men the "grace that comes by violence" (*Agam.* 182). Far from being primitive relics of a vanished order, as Apollo has maintained, they are pillars of every government, including that of Apollo's own father, Zeus. In the great charge that she delivers to the Areopagus just before the votes are cast (681f), Athene unmistakably echoes the words of the Erinyes in the Second Stasimon. She speaks not of the Erinyes' function in the government of the universe, but of the function of the Areopagus in the government of Athens; her deliberate echoing of their words, therefore, clearly indicates an analogy between the two. By her whole conduct toward the Erinyes, both before and during the trial and during the great conciliation scene following the announcement of the verdict, Athene shows that she recognizes the value and im-

203

portance of their task. The trilogy ends with their triumph, and·
by the light of flaming torches they are escorted to the shrine where
from now on they are to be worshiped with special reverence.

We can thus see how the moral and theological principles
implicit in the history of the house of Atreus are connected with
the political doctrines shown in the last play of the trilogy. We
have witnessed the stern reciprocal justice of Zeus: he who, like
Paris or Atreus, commits an outrage against another shall himself
(or his descendants) suffer outrage in return. The doer shall suffer
and thereby learn the folly of breaking Zeus's law. Profiting from
his example, men shall receive the "grace that comes by violence."
The Erinyes, serving Zeus's purpose, are there to teach men this
legend.

The dreadful action of Atreus sets in motion a chain of successive crimes. In strict logic, there is no reason why it should end
before the family has been annihilated. Yet when Orestes, faced
with a choice between intolerable decisions, consults Apollo, the
god supports him against the Erinyes. Apollo and the Erinyes refer
their dispute to the arbitration of a third party, and an issue that
admits of no real resolution is arbitrarily resolved by a personal
decision. Although the Erinyes lose their victim, they are not defeated or disgraced; on the contrary, they are appeased by the grant
of new honors, and the importance of their functions is empha-
sized. In the city, as in the universe, anarchy and despotism must
both equally be avoided; freedom can survive only if it is balanced
by the existence of a force that can punish crime. From the history
of the house of Atreus, men may learn wisdom. Likewise, the
citizens of Athens must learn wisdom in the course of time (1000);
they must never expel from their city the force capable of inspiring
terror and in whose absence freedom might degenerate into anarchy.

See the Appendix (pp. 273–75).

# CHARACTERS

APOLLO, son of Zeus

ATHENE, patron goddess of Athens

CHORUS, the Erinyes

THE GHOST OF CLYTEMNESTRA, slain mother of ORESTES

ESCORT, torch-bearers

ORESTES, son of Agamemnon

PYTHIA, priestess of Apollo

# THE EUMENIDES

Enter PYTHIA.

PYTHIA  *First among the gods in this prayer I honor*
*the first prophet, Earth; and after her Themis,*
*she who was the second to take her seat*
*in this place of prophecy, as a tradition tells; and third*

---

1f PYTHIA: Pronounce *Pié-thi-a.*
  The opening scene takes place in what was, together with the
sanctuary of Zeus at Olympia, the greatest of Greek shrines—
the temple of APOLLO at Delphi. Before APOLLO came to
Greece, the Delphic oracle had belonged to the great earth-
goddess who played an important part in the Minoan and
Mycenaean religions. This fact is clearly reflected in the tradi-
tions of the Greeks about the oracle's early history. Our
earliest account of the oracle's beginnings is contained in the
Homeric "Hymn to Apollo," a work hardly later than the
seventh century B.C. Indeed the hymn does not allude to an
oracle before APOLLO's time; but it tells how, in order to
win the site for his own, APOLLO had to fight and kill the
great serpent, the Python. Euripides, in a choral ode in his
play *Iphigeneia in Tauris* (1249f), says that before the oracle

belonged to APOLLO it was owned by Themis, goddess of right-eousness. Themis, the mother of the Titan Prometheus according to one story, belonged to the earlier generation of gods, before the time of Zeus and his son APOLLO. She was often identified with Ge or Gaia, the earth-goddess. According to Euripides, and this was undoubtedy the oldest story, APOLLO forcibly dispossessed her. The snake in Greek religion is often associated with subterranean powers, and the Python must have been the sacred guardian snake of the earth-goddess; indeed, in the oldest version of the legend he may have been identical with her. The belief that Delphi was the center of the earth probably goes back to the oracle's earliest period. The ancient stone known as the omphalos (navel), supposedly marking the earth's center, may date from this time. The earth was supposed to send up messages from below (see *The Libation Bearers*. 807f with note).

In Hesiod's poem, *Theogony*, which gave an authoritative account of the genealogy of the gods, Gaia (Earth) was the consort of Ouranos (Heaven), the first ruler of the universe. Themis was their daughter and the sister of their son Kronos, who succeeded Ouranos upon his throne and was finally ousted by his son Zeus. Clearly Gaia's time as the possessor of the oracle was meant to coincide with the reign of Ouranos and Themis' time, to coincide with the reign of Kronos; when Zeus overthrew Kronos, APOLLO, Zeus's son, could replace Themis as the god of Delphi. Aeschylus, however, was eager to avoid the story that APOLLO violently dispossessed his venerable relative. This is why Aeschylus makes Themis voluntarily hand over the oracle to her sister Phoebe. Phoebe was the mother of APOLLO's mother Leto, and APOLLO's name, "Phoebus," is the masculine form of her name. It was therefore easy for Aeschylus to have APOLLO acquire the oracle as a birthday present from his own grandmother.

Aeschylus liked to begin a play with a momentous word or phrase, often a divine name occurring in a prayer. Thus *The Suppliants* begins with "Zeus" and *Agamemnon* with "To the gods I pray"; *The Libation Bearers* begins with the prayer of Orestes to Hermes; and a lost play, probably the first of

*in succession, with the consent of Themis, and with no vio-*
 *lence done to any,*       5
*another Titaness, a child of Earth, took her seat here,*
*Phoebe. And she gave it as a birthday gift*
*to Phoebus; and he bears a name taken from hers.*
*Leaving the lake and ridge of Delos,*
*sailing to the ship-frequented coasts of Pallas,*    10
*he came to this land and to his seat upon Parnassus.*
*He was escorted on his way with solemn reverence*
*by sons of Hephaestus, the road-makers who made tame*
*the land before untamed.*
*And when he came he had great honor from the people,*   15

---

Aeschylus' trilogy about Achilles and the death of Hector, begins "To Zeus's majesty I first do reverence" (frag. 283 in the Loeb edition, vol. ii).

5 *Themis:* pronounce *Themm-is.*

  Stress is laid on the voluntary nature of the transfer because the story that APOLLO took the oracle by force was so well known.

9 *Delos:* pronounce *Deé-los.*

  APOLLO's other famous shrine at Delos, his birthplace, was older than the one at Delphi. Excavation, however, has now confirmed that his mother Leto and his sister Artemis (originally identical with the earth-goddess and her daughter) were established on Delos before he was. The lake and Mount Cynthus are the two most conspicuous features of the holy island.

10 The coasts of Pallas are the coasts of Athens, Pallas being another name of ATHENE, the patron goddess of Athens.

11 Delphi stands on a slope of Mount Parnassus; above it tower the twin peaks of the great mountain, the Phaedriades, and below it the cliffs drop sheer to the gorge of the river Pleistos.

12f *Hephaestus:* pronounce *He-feé-stus.*

  The Athenians are called "children of Hephaestus" because of the story that their legendary ancestor, Erichthonius, was the son of Hephaestus and the earth-goddess.

and from Delphus, the king seated at the tiller of the land.
And Zeus made his mind inspired with the diviner's art
and set him up as the fourth prophet on this throne:
Loxias is the spokesman of his father Zeus.
These are the gods I place in the forefront of my prayer;      20
and in my speech I honor Pallas who dwells before the
     temple;
and I revere the nymphs, who live in the Corycian cave,
hollow, dear to birds, the haunt of gods.
And Bromios has dwelt in the region, nor do I forget him,

---

16   The Delphians traced their descent from a mythical Delphus,
     supposed to be descended from the earth-goddess and her con-
     sort.

19   The word translated "spokesman" is *prophetes*, the Greek
     word from which "prophet" is derived. Originally it simply
     meant "spokesman"; the notion that the prefix *pro-* meant
     "before" and that *prophetes* meant "one who foretells the
     future" arose only later. "Loxias" is the name of APOLLO in
     his capacity as an oracular god, and it supposedly derived from
     the deviousness of his oracles (*loxos* means "crooked").

21   The shrine of Athene Pronaia (before the temple) lies a
     good way east of the temple of APOLLO, near the cleft of
     Castalia. Very likely this was the original site of the cult; ex-
     cavations have shown that worship continued there from
     prehellenic times, long before the foundation of the classical
     sanctuary of APOLLO.

22   *Corycian:* pronounce *Kore-iss-ian*. The Corycian cave, which has
     the same name as another famous cave at Corycus in Cilicia, is
     high up near the summit of Parnassus (about 8,200 feet high);
     the visit takes two days and a night. Like other mountain caves,
     it was thought to be a haunt of Pan and the nymphs.

24– From at least as early as the seventh century B.C., Dionysus
26   —Bromios is one of his names—had been accepted at
     Delphi. The brothers were even said to share the place,
     Dionysus being at home there in the winter months, while

ever *since the host of Bacchants had the god for leader,*          25
*and he contrived for Pentheus the death of a hunted hare.*
*On the waters of Pleistos and on Poseidon's might*
*do I call, and on Zeus the Fulfiller, the Most High;*
*and so I take my seat as prophetess.*
*And now may they grant me far better fortune than in my*
      *goings in*                                                   30

---

APOLLO was away in the land of his favorite people, the Hyperboreans, in the remote north. Festivals held every two years at Delphi, at which women danced during the night to the light of torches in honor of Dionysus, are mentioned by the poets (e.g., Sophocles, *Antigone* 1126f) and continued well into historical times. In this passage, Aeschylus dates Dionysus' establishment at Delphi from the time of the god's legendary conquest of Greece. In a lost play called the *Xantriai* Aeschylus told, or at least mentioned, the story of how Dionysus punished his cousin Pentheus (pronounce *Penth'-yuse*), king of Thebes, for denying his divinity. Dionysus inspired Pentheus' mother and aunts with frenzy, making them tear Pentheus to pieces; the story is handled by Euripides in his extant play *The Bacchants*.

27 *Pleistos*: pronounce *Plicé-tos; Poseidon*: pronounce *Pos-eyé-don.*
    For a comment on the Pleistos, the river of Delphi, see note on 11 above. In classical religion Poseidon figures as brother of Zeus and lord of the sea, but he had originally been the consort of the Minoan-Mycenaean earth-goddess. He had therefore been honored at Delphi from an early time; in historic times he had an altar inside APOLLO's temple. There was a story that he originally owned Delphi but exchanged it with APOLLO for another shrine.

28 "The Fulfiller" and "the Most High" were both cult-titles of Zeus; for the former compare *Agam.* 973 and *The Suppliants* 525; and for the latter *Agam.* 55, 509.

30 In primitive prayers the worshiper regularly asked the god to grant him favor greater than he ever had before.

*in time past; and if any of the Greeks are present,*
*let them enter in order of the lot, as is the custom;*
*for I prophesy as the god may lead me.*

> She opens the door of the temple and goes in,
> but comes out almost immediately.

*Dread to tell of and dread for the eyes to see*
*is the thing that has sent me back from the house of Loxias,*        35
*so that I have no strength left and cannot hold myself up-*
      *right,*
*I run with the aid of my hands, not with swift feet;*
*for an old woman afraid is nothing, no better than a child.*
*I was on my way to the inner chamber with its many chaplets,*
*and I saw upon the navel-stone a man polluted in the sight of*
      *the gods,*        40
*seated there as a suppliant;*

---

31   The oracle was originally for the Greeks, and they were
     supposed to have precedence over foreigners. Originally the
     order of consultation was determined by lot, as here, though
     later the Delphians awarded special precedence to particular
     states and individuals.

37   The ancient commentary on the play interprets this as mean-
     ing that Pythia is on all fours. But it may mean that her
     hands are trembling.

39   The inner shrine, like the omphalos or "navel-stone" (40),
     was hung with garlands to mark its sacred character.

41   The blood is presumably the pig's blood used by Apollo to
     purify Orestes from the pollution caused by murder (see
     280–83 below). Purification from blood-guilt was an important
     idea in Delphic religion as early as the seventh century B.C.
     In this play Orestes is regarded as being freed by his purifica-
     tion from the provisions of the interdict against speaking to a
     polluted person, allowing him to enter one's house, or taking
     part in worship (see 443f); but it does not cause the Erinyes
     (pronounce *I'-rin-ē-ez*) to give up their pursuit.

his hands and newly drawn sword were dripping with blood,
and he held a branch of olive grown on high,
a branch wreathed in reverent fashion with a great tuft of
    wool,
a silvery fleece (for so I shall describe it clearly).       45
And in front of this man slept a wondrous troop
of women, seated upon chairs.
Not women, but Gorgons I call them;
no, not even to the shape of Gorgons can I compare them.
I have seen before now paintings of those that carried off   50
the feast of Phineus; but these appear wingless,
black, altogether hateful in their ways;
and they snore with a blast unapproachable,
and from their eyes they drip a loathsome liquid.
And their attire is such as one should not bring       55
near to the statues of the gods nor into the houses of men.
I have not seen the tribe this company belongs to,
nor the land that can boast to breed this race
unscathed, and not repent of its labor.
The outcome now must be the care of the master     60
of this house, the mighty Loxias himself.
He is both healer-seer and prophet,
and can purify the halls of others.

    Exit PYTHIA; the central door now opens reveal-

---

43 An olive branch was customarily carried by suppliants. Such branches had chaplets made of wool hanging upon them (e.g., *Iliad* 1. 14f).

48 The obvious point of resemblance to Gorgons was their having snakes for hair.

51 *Phineus*: pronounce *Fine'-yuse*. Phineus was persecuted by the bird-women known as Harpies, who flew down and seized his food before he could eat it.

54 Their eyes dripped blood (cf. *The Libation Bearers* 1058).

55– They wore long black robes (cf. *The Libation Bearers* 1049);
56 these seem to have been dirty and ragged.

ing APOLLO and ORESTES inside the temple.

APOLLO  I will not abandon you; but I will guard you to
    the end,
whether by your side or far removed,                              65
and I will not grow gentle to your enemies.
And now you see these mad ones overcome;
the despicable creatures have fallen in sleep, gray
virgins, ancient maidens, with whom no god
nor any among men nor any beast has intercourse.                 70
For the sake of evil they came into being, since evil
darkness and Tartarus below the earth is their portion,
loathed as they are by men and by Olympian gods.
Nonetheless fly from them, and do not grow faint!
For they will drive you over all the wide mainland,              75
striding ever over the earth you tread in your wanderings,
and beyond the sea and seagirt cities.
Do not grow weary as you struggle to cope with this
ordeal; but go to the city of Pallas
and sit there, taking her ancient image in your arms.            80
And there shall we have judges of your cause, and words
to charm them, and shall discover means
to release you forever from this distress;
for it was I who persuaded you to slay your mother.

ORESTES  Lord Apollo, you know how to be righteous;             85

---

64  APOLLO's language recalls the formulas used in prayers ad-
    dressed to the gods for such protection.

67  The manner of the transition suggests that the sleep of the
    Erinyes is due to a charm cast upon them by APOLLO, who
    would have wanted no disturbance during the rite of purifica-
    tion he had just performed.

79  Athens, where there was an ancient wooden image of ATHENE.

85f Athenian law distinguished between criminal offenses and

but since you have that skill, learn also not to be neglectful!
But your strength renders sure your power for good.

  APOLLO  Remember, let not fear overcome your mind.
And you, my brother, son of the same father,
Hermes, guard him; true altogether to your title,                  90
be his escort, as you protect this my suppliant.
Zeus, I say, respects this sanctity of outlaws                *young + old*
that is sent to men with auspicious guidance.

>    Exeunt APOLLO and ORESTES; CLYTEMNESTRA'S
>    GHOST appears. The GHOST addresses the ERINYES
>    inside the temple who are still invisible to the
>    audience.

  CLYTEMNESTRA  Sleep on! Aha! And what is the use of you
      asleep?
And I, thus dishonored at your hands                               95
among the other dead—the reproach
of the deeds of blood I did still lives on among the departed,
as in indignity I wander; I declare to you

---

86  offenses due to negligence, and the wording here suggests that
    the poet has this distinction in mind.

89  APOLLO's address to Hermes does not prove that Hermes is
    present on the stage; a god may be addressed whether he is
    present or not.

91  The words allude to a well-known cult-title of Hermes, "The
    Escorter."

92  "Outlaws" here means "suppliants," who were traditionally
    under the special protection of Zeus.

94  The GHOST's indignation that the Erinyes can sleep at such a
    time and its injunction to them to take action that will
    remedy its own plight in Hades recall the words of the ghost
    of Patroclus to the sleeping Achilles in The Iliad (23. 69f);
    but CLYTEMNESTRA's indignation is more bitter, as suits her
    character and the circumstances.

that they level a most grievous charge at me
who suffered so sorely at the hands of my nearest kin—       100
none among the divinities is angry on my account,
slaughtered as I was by matricidal hands.
See these wounds in your heart!       103
Full many an offering of mine have you lapped up;       106
libations without wine, sober appeasements,
and solemn feasts by night upon the hearth that housed the
    fire
I burned, at an hour not shared by any of the gods.
And all this I see trampled under foot;       110
and he is gone, he has escaped you swiftly as a fawn;
he has leapt easily, from the middle of your net,
mightily mocking you.
Listen, for on my plea depends
my whole existence. Take heed, goddesses below the earth,       115
for as a shadow I, Clytemnestra, now invoke you!

    The ERINYES in their sleep are heard to utter
    whining sounds.

---

103   This line is followed in the manuscripts by two lines that
     mean:

      For in sleep your mind has eyes that shine brightly;
      but by day the fate of mortals cannot be foreseen
      [or, possibly, "mortals can see ahead"].

     The first of these lines could make sense in the context; the
     second, whichever of several different possible interpretations
     is adopted, seems to make none, and it is probably interpolated.
     Although the first line might be genuine, I am inclined to
     think that it came from the same context as the second and
     that both were jotted down in the margin by some reader as a
     parallel passage, then included in the text by mistake.

107   Wine was never offered to the Erinyes, who preferred water
     and honey. Like other gods who lived below the earth, they
     received sacrifices at night.

109   *gods:* probably used in the sense of "Olympian gods," as at
     *Agam.* 637.

CLYTEMNESTRA  Whine if you will, but the man is gone
  far off in flight;
for suppliants are not without friends.

  Again the whining sound.                                    120

CLYTEMNESTRA  You are all too drowsy; you have no pity
  for my suffering;
and Orestes, killer of me, his mother, is gone.

  The Erinyes make a moaning sound.

CLYTEMNESTRA  You moan, you are drowsy; up, up, quick,
  get up!
What task has fate assigned to you but to wreak trouble?      125

  Again the moaning.

CLYTEMNESTRA  Sleep and weariness, powerful conspirators,
have reduced to nothing the dread serpent's power.

  The Erinyes twice make a shrill, whining sound.

CHORUS  Seize him! Seize him! Seize him! Seize him! Mark!     130

CLYTEMNESTRA  In a dream you pursue your beast, and you
  bay like
a hound that never ceases to think of the chase!
What are you at? Up, do not be overcome by weariness!
Do not be ignorant of my pain, made soft by sleep!
Let my just reproaches sting your heart!                      135
For to the righteous these are goads.
Waft your bloody breath upon him!
Dry him up with its vapor, your womb's fire!
After him, shrivel him up in a renewed pursuit!
  The GHOST vanishes

---

129  *serpent*: the Erinyes who were often portrayed in snake form.
137  The Erinyes are repeatedly said to shrivel their victims by
  sucking up all their blood; they themselves drip blood from
  their eyes as well as breathing it out.

Now the ERINYES become visible to the audience.

CHORUS   *Wake up and then wake your neighbor as I wake*
*you!*                                                                    140
*Do you sleep? Up, cast away sleep,*
*and let us see if in this prelude there is any fault!*

They rise and move into the orchestra.

### STROPHE 1

*Ho, ho! Out upon it! We have suffered, dear ones—*
*much have I suffered, and all in vain!—*
*we have suffered a grievous blow, alas,*                                145
*a hurt unbearable.*
*Slipped from the net and vanished is the beast:*
*Vanquished by sleep, I have lost my prey.*

### ANTISTROPHE 1

*Ah, son of Zeus! You are a thief!*
*Young as you are, you have ridden us down, aged divinities—*   150

---

142   *prelude:* refers to the ghost dream that the Erinyes have just
had.

143   The meter of the parodos is dochmiac ( ◡ –– ◡ – ) mixed
with iambic; the dochmiacs, as usual expressive of violent
emotion (see *The Libation Bearers*, 152f), easily prevail. The
second strophe (155–61) and its antistrophe (162–68) are
marked by an especially close symmetry; 159 and its antistrophic
line, 165, each consist of a preposition governing a noun and
then the same preposition governing a second noun:

hypŏ phrĕnăs, hypŏ lŏbōn        pĕrī pŏdă, pĕrī kărā
Each is followed by a sentence beginning with the same main
verb *paresti*, here rendered "it is mine."

144   This line (like its antistrophic line 150, and also 147 ~ 154,
155 ~ 162, 169 ~ 174) is an iambic trimeter, just like the
iambic trimeters that are the usual meter of dialogue. But like
the rest of the ode, these trimeters will be sung and not spoken.

150   The motif of a conflict between older and younger genera-

*respecting the suppliant, a godless man,*
*hateful to parents.*
You have stolen away the matricide, god that you are!
What is there in this that any shall say is just?

### STROPHE 2

To me in my dreams there came reproach,                          155
and smote me like a charioteer
with goad grasped in the middle,
under my heart, under my vitals.
It is mine to feel cruel, most cruel,                            160
the sting of the public scourger's cruel lash!

### ANTISTROPHE 2

Such are the actions of the younger gods,
whose might goes altogether beyond justice.
The throne drips blood,
about its foot, about its head!                                  165
It is ours to see earth's navel-stone stained
with a grim pollution it has got from deeds of blood.

### STROPHE 3

With defilement at the hearth, seer that he is,
he has stained his own sanctuary by his own impulse, his own

*Is that what Aeschylus thinks?*

        summons,                                                 170

---

tions of the gods is important in this play, as it is in *Prometheus.* In *Prometheus* the hero, as a Titan and a son of Earth,
belongs to a generation older than that of his enemy Zeus. In
*The Eumenides* the Erinyes, as daughters of Night, also belong
to the older generation of gods (cf. 162f).

*honoring things mortal beyond what the gods' law permits,*
*and destroying the ancient dispensations of the fates.*

ANTISTROPHE 3

*To me too he is hateful, and that man shall be never free;*
*though he flee beneath the earth, he shall never gain his*
    *liberty.*                  175
*He shall come stained with the guilt of murder*
*to where he shall get upon his head another to pollute him.*

    Enter APOLLO.

APOLLO  Out of this house with all speed, I command you!
Be off, leave my prophetic chambers,          180
for fear you get a winged, glistening snake,
sped from my bowstring wrought of gold,
and disgorge in agony a dark froth from humans,
as you vomit up clots of the blood that you have sucked!
It is not fitting you should come to this house;     185
your place is where sentence is given to lop off heads and
    gouge out eyes,
where murders are, and by destruction of the seed

---

172  The Erinyes mean that APOLLO is preventing them from
     fulfilling the functions allotted to them by an ancient dispensa-
     tion.

176–  *He*: ORESTES who is himself a cause of pollution. When the
177  Erinyes threaten that he will get another to pollute him, they
     mean that he will become a victim of the Alastor, the per-
     sonified family curse, to which this description can also be
     applied. The Erinyes are often said to leap upon the heads of
     their victims.

186  APOLLO means that the Erinyes do not belong in Greece but
     in some country inhabited by barbarians. All the practices re-
     ferred to in this passage were in vogue among the Persians
     and could be illustrated from the account given of them by
     Herodotus.

the manhood of the young is ruined, and there are mutilations
and stoning, and men moan in long lament,
impaled beneath the spine. Do you not hear                    190
what sort of feast it is that you so love
that the gods detest you? The whole fashion of your form
suggests it. The den of a blood-lapping lion
should be the habitation of such creatures; you should not in
        this place
of oracle rub off contagion on those near you.                195
Be off, a flock without a shepherd!
Such a herd is loved by none among the gods.

CHORUS  Lord Apollo, hear in turn our answer!
You yourself are no mere abettor of this deed;
but in all things you have so acted that the blame is yours
        alone.                                                200

APOLLO  How so? Extend your speech just far enough to
tell me.

CHORUS  Your oracle told the stranger to kill his mother.

APOLLO  Yes, it did, thereby ordaining vengeance for his
father. Why not?

CHORUS  And then you promised to receive him, with
blood fresh on his hands.

APOLLO  Yes, and I told him to come as suppliant to this
house.                                                        205

CHORUS  And then do you revile us for acting as his escort?

APOLLO  Yes; you are not fit to approach this house.

CHORUS  But this is the task assigned to us. . . .

APOLLO  What privilege do you speak of? Proudly tell of
your noble prerogative!

---

194– The notion that pollution could be "rubbed off onto" others
195  occurs even in a speech by the late fifth-century orator
     Antiphon.

221

CHORUS  We drive from their homes the killers of their
mothers.                                                                              210

APOLLO   And what of a woman who has slain her
husband?

CHORUS   That would not be the
shedding of one's own blood with one's own hand.

APOLLO   Indeed you dishonor and reduce to nothing
the pledges of Hera the Fulfiller and of Zeus,
and the Cyprian is cast aside in dishonor by your plea,          215
she from whom comes to mortals what they hold most dear.
For the marriage bed, granted by fate to man and woman,
is mightier than an oath, if Justice is its guardian.
So if you allow to those that kill their partners
such license that you do not requite them nor visit them with
    your wrath,                                                                      220
I say that your pursuit of Orestes is not just.
For the one crime I see that you greatly take to heart,
while in the other matter you are manifestly milder.
But the goddess Pallas shall review this case.

CHORUS   I shall never leave that man!                                  225

APOLLO   Well, pursue him, and give yourself more trouble.

CHORUS   Do not speak as though you would curtail my
    privileges!

---

212   Blood relations were thought of as having the same
      blood. Thus in Sophocles' *Oedipus the King* Oedipus can
      speak of having shed *his own* blood when referring to his killing
      of his father (1400).

214   Hera is called "The Fulfiller" (*Teleia*) in her capacity as god-
      dess of marriage; Zeus the Fulfiller was associated with her
      in this cult, and their marriage was the archetype of all mar-
      riages.

215   *the Cyprian:* a name of Aphrodite.

224   APOLLO has already told ORESTES to go to Athens (79–80).

APOLLO  Even if your privileges were offered me, I would refuse them.

CHORUS  Yes, for in any case you are accounted great by Zeus's throne.
But, since a mother's blood drives me on, with my charge          230
I will pursue this man and hunt him down.

APOLLO  And I will protect him and will guard the suppliant.
For dread among mortals and among the gods
is the wrath of him who has implored mercy, if one willingly
betrays him.

The scene changes to Athens; enter ORESTES.

ORESTES  Queen Athene, I have come at Loxias' bidding.          235
Graciously receive a wretched man,
not needing to be purified nor with unclean hands,
but with his guilt's edge already blunted and worn off
against other habitations and traveled ways of men.
Crossing over land and sea alike,                               240
and keeping the oracular commands of Loxias,
I come to your house; your image, goddess,
will I guard here as I await the issue of the trial.

Enter the ERINYES.

---

235  Changes of scene are rare in tragedy (see Oliver Taplin, *The Stagecraft of Aeschylus*, 1977, p.375f.). Aeschylus' play *The Women of Etna* seems to have had no less than four, as we have learned from a papyrus published in 1952 (see frag. 287 in the Loeb edition). The scene has changed to the ancient temple of ATHENE on the Acropolis.

237  See note on 41.

242  APOLLO has told ORESTES to clasp the image of the goddess (80); this image is presumably visible on the stage, for the Erinyes mention at 259 that ORESTES is holding it.

223

CHORUS  *Just so! Here can the man's trail be clearly seen!*
*Follow the guidance of the voiceless informer!*                      245
*Yes, like a hound after a wounded fawn*
*by the drops of blood do we track him down.*
*My many labors, deadly to men, leave my breast panting;*
*for I have ranged through every place on earth*
*and beyond the sea in wingless flight*
*I have come pursuing, not slower than a ship.*
*And now he must be cowering somewhere here;*
*the scent of human blood, so familiar, greets me!*

*Look, look again!*
*Scan every spot,*                                                    255
*that the killer of his mother may not escape us in flight,*
    *unpunished.*

They catch sight of ORESTES.

*Here he is! Once more he has protection,*
*and with arms twined about the image of the immortal goddess*
*seeks to stand trial for the debt he owes.*                          260
*But that may not be. His mother's blood upon the ground*
*is hard to gather up. Faugh!*
*Gone, spilt on the ground, is the liquid!*
*No, in atonement while you still live you must let us swill*
*the rich, red offering from your limbs; from you*                    265
*may I win myself a meal—a cruel drink!*

---

244  "Epiparodos" means a second entry of the CHORUS, a rare oc-
     currence in tragedy. The change of scene has required the
     CHORUS, contrary to custom, to leave the stage (231); they
     now return. First, the Coryphaeus speaks in dialogue meter
     (244–53); then, the CHORUS sings (254–75). The meter is
     dochmiac, but iambic trimeters occur sporadically (261, 264,
     267, 269, 272–73); it is very like the meter of the Parodos, but
     lacks strophic responsion.

261  See note on *The Libation Bearers* 49.

*Still living I shall dry you up and hale you down below,*
*so that in requital you may pay with sorrow for your*
    *mother's murder.*
*And if any other mortal who has wronged*
*a god or a stranger,*                          270
*with impious action, or his dear parents,*
*you shall see how each has the reward Justice ordains.*
*For Hades is mighty in holding mortals to account*
*below the earth,*
*and with mind that records them in its tablets he surveys*
    *all things.*                                   275

    ORESTES   *Schooled by misery, I know well*
*many ways of purifying, and I know where speech is proper*
*and where silence; and in this instance*
*it is a wise teacher who has ordered me to speak.*
*For the blood upon my hand grows drowsy and fades,*     280
*and the pollution of my mother's killing can be washed away;*
*while still fresh at the hearth of the god*
*it was expelled through Phoebus' cleansing by means of*
    *slaughtered swine.*

---

273   Aeschylus in *The Suppliants* 230f speaks of a Zeus below the
     earth trying the dead for their crimes. (There and at 158 of the
     same play he calls Hades "the second Zeus," echoing Homer,
     *The Iliad* 9. 457.) The metaphor of writing in a book recalls a
     passage from an unknown lost play of Aeschylus preserved in a
     papyrus (see frag. 282 in the Loeb edition), in which the
     goddess of Justice herself describes to the CHORUS how she
     enters men's crimes in the book of Zeus.

277–  The knowledge of when to speak and when to keep silent may
278   be classed among the means of preserving ritual purity, for
     abstention from ill-omened utterance (*euphemia*) formed a
     regular part of most religious rituals. In this case it is of
     course essential that ATHENE and the inhabitants of Athens
     know that ORESTES has been purified by APOLLO.

283   *Phoebus:* pronounce *Fee'-bus.*

It would take long to tell the tale from the beginning,
to how many I have come without my company proving
    baneful;                                  285
Time purifies all things as it grows old with them.
And now with pure lips I call in pious accents
on this country's queen, Athene,
to come to help me; and without the spear she shall acquire
me and my country and the Argive people          290
as an ally to be trusted truly and forever.
But whether in the region of the Libyan land

---

284–  Since it was probably believed that the presence of an ac-
285  cursed person could bring disaster upon innocent people who
were in his company, ORESTES can offer the absence of such a
disaster as proof of his freedom from pollution. Similarly, the
client for whom Antiphon wrote one of his speeches points to
the safe arrival of a ship on which he has traveled as proof of
his innocence of the charge of murder.

286  This line seems otiose to modern taste, and it may well be
a parallel passage written in the margin by a reader and later
copied by mistake into the text; but it is not quite safe to
assume that this is so since the ancients often allowed such
generalizing comments in places where no modern writer would
insert them.

287  The whole speech so far has been uttered in order to justify
the claim now made.

288  ATHENE: pronounce *Ath-een'-ee.*

289  This is the first of the passages in the play that seem to refer
to the alliance between Athens and Argos existing at the time
of the first production (see Appendix, p. 274).

290  *Argive:* pronounce *Ar-gyve* [hard "g"].

292  In early times those who invoked a god begged him to come
from wherever he happened to be, specifying each of his
favorite haunts to be sure of being heard (see for one example among many the prayer to Apollo at *Iliad* 16. 514f).

In historical times ATHENE's Homeric epithet of Tritogeneia

about *the stream of Triton, river of her birth,*
*she plants her leg erect or covered,*
*bringing succor to her friends, or makes the Phlegrean plain,*    295
*like a bold commander, the object of her survey,*
*may she come—for she hears me even from afar, goddess that*
    *she is—*
*that she may grant me release from this my plight!*

CHORUS   *Not Apollo, I say, or mighty Athene*
*shall save you from going all neglected*    300
*down to ruin, not knowing where in your mind joy can dwell,*
*a bloodless shadow, food for spirits.*
*Do you not deign to answer? Do you reject my words,*
*you who have been fattened up for me and consecrated to me?*

---

was connected with Lake Tritonis in Libya, not far from Cyrene, which was said to be her birthplace. Thus it is not unnatural for Lake Tritonis to be mentioned as one of the places where ATHENE may happen to be. Still, the poet may have in mind the presence in Egypt, at the time of the production of this play, of an Athenian force despatched to help a local prince, Inaros, in his revolt against the Persians.

293   *Triton:* pronounce *Trý-ton; Phlegrean:* pronounce *fleg-ree'-an.*

294   This is simply a highly metaphorical way of saying "is walking or sitting"; either the leg (Greek says "foot") is erect or it is covered, as she sits, by her robes.

295   The Phlegrean plain, on Pallene (now Kassandra), one of the three prongs of Chalcidice, in Macedonia, was the traditional site of the Battle of the Gods and Giants, in which ATHENE took a leading part. Those who are eager to find an allusion to the Athenian expedition to Egypt in the passage immediately preceding this have suggested that there may have been fighting in this region at the time of the first production; but there is no independent evidence for this.

304   The Erinyes compare ORESTES to a sacrificial beast, which is especially fattened for sacrifice to a god. In his case, however, no sacrifice at an altar is intended; the Erinyes plan to suck his blood while he is still alive.

*I shall feast on you alive, not after sacrifice by an altar;*　　305
*and you shall hear this song to bind you fast!*

*Come and let us join hands in the dance,*
*for it is our purpose*
*to display our grim minstrelsy,*
*and to tell how our company discharges*　　310
*its office among men!*
*We claim to walk straight in the path of justice.*

---

306　Spells intended to bind the victim have survived in large numbers and are usually inscribed on leaden tablets. They contain such formulas as "I bind and have bound your hands and feet and tongue and soul" or (in a charm designed to influence the result of a race) "Bind the horses' legs and check their power to start and leap and run." Most of the examples date from as late as the Roman Empire, but they are mentioned by Plato and must have existed long before his time.

307　Like a number of Aeschylean parodoi and stasima, the Binding Song is preceded by a prelude in marching anapaests. In this prelude the Erinyes insist on the essential justness of the manner in which they carry out their duties. This theme is elaborated not only in the ode that follows (321f) but even more explicitly in the Second Stasimon (490f).

312ff　The connection of the Erinyes with Justice is stressed in the Second Stasimon (see especially 511–25).

　　The meter of the first strophe and antistrophe (321–27 and 333–40), like that of the ephymnium that follows each of them (328–34 and 341–46), is mostly trochaic; frequent resolutions cause a slow and solemn effect. Then with the second strophe and antistrophe (349–59 and 360–66), the Erinyes change to a wholly different meter, long dactylic lines, the first period being rounded off by the pherecratean (xx –⌣⌣– x: 351–62) and the second by a kind of trochaic verse that occurs frequently in the first part of the ode. The second strophe is followed by another trochaic stanza; it is possible, though not certain, that it should be inserted after the second antistrophe

Upon him whose hands are clean in act
comes no wrath from us;
he lives out his life unscathed.                                    315
But if any man, like this one, transgresses
and tries to hide his bloody hands,
as truthful witnesses by the dead
we stand, and as avengers of blood
to him with full power are we made manifest.                        320

STROPHE 1

Mother who bore me,
mother Night, to be a punishment for those in darkness
and for those who see the light
hear me! For Leto's son
is trying to rob me of my honor
by taking from me this                                              325
cowering hare, one rightly consecrated
to the appeasement of his mother's blood.

*(handwritten marginal note)* quoted to / referred / to as here

---

also (after 356), as is done in the Oxford text. The third
strophic pair resembles the second; again dactyls are rounded
off by a trochaic line (371 ~ 80), and again the strophe, and
perhaps the antistrophe also, is followed by a trochaic stanza
(372–76), as in the Oxford text. The fourth strophe and
antistrophe are prevailingly iambic. The iambic meter (x –
⌣ – ) has an obvious affinity with the trochaic ( _ ⌣ _ x,
and the transition is an easy one. These iambics have an effect
of special solemnity, heightened by the substitution in two
places (at the end of 383 ~ 391 and 387 ~ 394) of a spondee
(– –) for the regular iambic metron (x – ⌣ –).

321  In the *Theogony* of Hesiod, Night was a daughter of the
primeval Chaos; she thus suggests immemorial antiquity as
well as darkness. Hesiod makes her the mother of the Fates,
but Earth the mother of the Erinyes. In Aeschylus, as in
Sophocles, the Fates as well as the Erinyes are children of
Night.

### REFRAIN 1

Over our victim
we sing this song, maddening the brain,
carrying away the sense, destroying the mind,                    330
a hymn that comes from the Erinyes,
fettering the mind, sung
without the lyre, withering to mortals.

### ANTISTROPHE 1

For this is the office that Fate
with her piercing stroke has ordained
that I should hold fast:                                         335
that after mortals to whom has come
wanton murder of their own,
I should follow, until
they descend below the earth; and after death
no wide liberty is theirs.                                       340

### REFRAIN 1

Over our victim
we sing this song, maddening the brain,
carrying away the sense, destroying the mind,
a hymn that comes from the Erinyes,
fettering the mind, sung                                         345
without the lyre, withering to mortals.

---

328   The word translated as "victim" is a passive participle, im-
      plying that ORESTES has already been sacrificed.

329   The Erinyes traditionally madden their victims; ORESTES goes
      mad when they first appear in the last scene of *The Libation
      Bearers*.

332   The lyre was associated with happy occasions (compare *Agam.*
      990). The Binding Song was no doubt accompanied on the
      aulos, a pipe somewhat like a clarinet.

### STROPHE 2

At our birth, I say, the grant of this office was ordained;
but we must keep our hands off the immortals, nor is
    there any                                         350
that shares the feasts of both alike;
and in white robes I have no lot or share

• • • • • •

### REFRAIN 2

For I have chosen the ruin
of households; when violence                        355
nurtured in the home strikes a dear one down
after it in pursuit we go,
and mighty though the killer be,
we put him in darkness through the fresh blood on his hands.

### ANTISTROPHE 2

Eager to exempt some one of the gods from this concern,    360
denying to our prayers fulfillment

---

349   The Erinyes continually stress the antiquity of their powers
which have been given them by their sisters, the Fates (cf.
172, 333f, etc.).

350   The worship of the subterranean gods was kept wholly apart
from that of the Olympians. Black was the characteristic
color of the immortals below the earth.

360–  The text is altogether uncertain at this point. If the version
366   I have translated is correct, the sense seems to be that Zeus
has decreed that the Erinyes shall have nothing to do with
the Olympian gods in order to save one of the Olympians
from being pursued by them. The god in question may have
been Ares, who according to a well-known story was arraigned
before the Areopagus at Athens for the killing of Halirrhothius,
son of Poseidon; but we hear nowhere that he was pursued
by the Erinyes.

and forbidding us to make inquiry,
Zeus has held our bloodstained, hateful race          365
unworthy of his converse.


### STROPHE 3

But the glories of men, for all their splendor beneath the
    light of day,
wither away and vanish below the earth, dishonored,
before the onslaught of our black raiment and the dancing     370
of our feet, instinct with malice.

For in truth leaping
from on high, with heavy fall
I bring down my foot;
my legs trip the runner,                              375
swift though he be, with an irresistible doom.


### ANTISTROPHE 3

And as he falls he knows it not, by reason of the blight that
    drives him mad;
such is the darkness of pollution that hovers over a man;
and a murky mist spreads over his house, as is proclaimed
by rumor, bringing many a sigh.                        380


### STROPHE 4

For the ordinance abides; skilled in contrivance
and strong to accomplish evil

---

370  Like other odes sung by tragic choruses, this was accompanied
by dances executed by the CHORUS. The mention of leaping
probably gives some notion of what kind of dance accompanied the words at this point.

*and mindful of it are we, awesome*
*and inexorable to men;*
*unhonored and unesteemed is the office*      385
*we pursue, apart from the gods*
*in the sunless slime;*
*it makes rough the path of the seeing*
*and of the blind alike.*

*ANTISTROPHE 4*

*Who then among mortals*
*feels not awe and dread,*      390
*hearing from me the covenant*
*ordained by fate and granted by the gods*
*so that it is valid? Still for me*
*remains my ancient privilege, nor*
*do I lack honor,*
*though it is beneath the ground that I have my station,*      395
*inhabiting the sunless gloom.*

     Enter ATHENE.

     ATHENE  From far off I heard the sound of your summons,
from the Scamander, while I was taking possession of the land

---

383   The word translated "awesome" is *semnai*, sometimes used as
     a euphemism for the Erinyes, "the dread ones," themselves.
     Here its effect is enhanced by substituting its two long syllables
     for the iambic metron (x – ‿ –).

387   Slime is a regular feature of ancient descriptions of the under-
     world.

388   *the seeing . . . blind:* "the living and the dead"; the latter
     live in the darkness of the underworld (cf. 322).

391   The word translated by "covenant" is the solemn word
     *thesmos*, which responds metrically with *semnai* and carries
     the same strong metrical emphasis.

398   *Scamander*: pronounce *Skam-and'-er*.
     In Homer an Athenian called Menestheus is said to have

which the chiefs and leaders of the Achaeans
—a great share of the spoils their spears had won—                    400
assigned me to be mine utterly and forever,
a choice gift for the sons of Theseus.
From there I have come, speeding onward my unwearied foot,
without the aid of wings, making my billowing aegis rustle,
harnessing this car to young and vigorous steeds.                     405
And as I look on this company, new to the land,
I feel no fear, but wonder sits upon my eyes.
Who are you? I address all of you together—
this stranger also who sits here by my image—
you who are like to no race of those begotten,                        410
whom the gods see not among the goddesses,
nor are you like the forms of mortals. . . .
But to speak ill of others who are free of blame
is far from Justice, and Right will have none of it.
    CHORUS   You shall learn all briefly, daughter of Zeus;        415

---

fought at Troy. According to a tradition that is later than
Homer but was well established before the time of Aeschylus,
Demophon and Acamas, the sons of the great legendary
Athenian hero Theseus, took part in the campaign. The notion of Athens being awarded part of the Trojan territory at
this date might acquire a degree of plausibility from the
existence of these stories describing their participation. Yet,
it may well have been invented to justify the Athenian claim
to Sigeum in the Troad; which had been the subject of a
dispute with Lesbos toward the end of the seventh century
(Herodotus 5. 94; see D. L. Page, *Sappho and Alcaeus*, Oxford, 1955, p. 152, for details).

402   *Theseus:* pronounce *Thees'-yuse.*

404   The Aegis appears in early Greek art, not as a shield, but as
a kind of collar or cloak regularly worn by ATHENE and carrying upon it the face of the Gorgon killed by Perseus. If the
text is right, the "steeds" will be the winds, sometimes depicted as or even called horses; "this car" will be the Aegis.

for we are the eternal children of Night,
and Curses is our name in our home below the earth.

ATHENE   Your lineage and the names you are called by I know.

CHORUS   My privileges also you shall soon learn.

ATHENE   I shall learn them, if a clear account is given.     420

CHORUS   The killers of their kin we drive from their homes.

ATHENE   And what is the limit of the killer's flight?

CHORUS   The place where joy has no existence.

ATHENE   Is that the exile toward which your screeching would drive him?

CHORUS   Yes; he thought it right to become his mother's murderer.     425

ATHENE   Was there no other constraint that made him go in fear of wrath?

CHORUS   Why, what spur is there so keen as to drive to matricide?

ATHENE   Two parties are present, and we have heard half the case.

CHORUS   But he will not take an oath, he will not give one!

---

417   In Homer Althaea calls upon the Erinyes to punish her son Meleager, and we are told that "the gods accomplished her curses" (*Iliad* 9. 454f). In Aeschylus' *The Seven Against Thebes*, the curse of a father is identified with the Erinys (70); the Erinyes were probably first thought of as personified curses.

429   According to a very ancient mode of legal procedure, which left traces in Athenian law of the fifth century, the accused was asked to swear that he was innocent, calling upon the gods to destroy him if he swore falsely. ORESTES could not have

ATHENE  You wish to be thought to act justly rather than
to do so.                                                    430

CHORUS  How so? Explain it; for you are not poor in
wisdom.

ATHENE  I say you must not try to win by oaths an unjust
victory.

CHORUS  Why, put him to the question, and pronounce
a righteous judgment.

ATHENE  Would you commit to me the settlement of the
charge?

CHORUS  Surely; we reverence you as worthy and of worthy
parentage.                                                   435

ATHENE  Stranger, what answer do you wish to make in
your turn?
Tell me what are your country and your family and your
fortunes,
and then try to rebut this accusation,
if it is with confidence in justice that you sit
clutching my image near my altar,                            440
a suppliant to be revered after Ixion's fashion.

---

denied having killed his mother; and once he had admitted
this, the Erinyes would have regarded their case as won. But
since ORESTES' defense will rest upon a plea of justification,
this request is unfair, as ATHENE points out (430, 432).

441  Ixion: pronounce Ix-eye'-on. The Thessalian hero Ixion was the
first murderer and the first suppliant, and therefore set a prece-
dent. He killed his father-in-law after a dispute over his wife's
dowry, but was purified of the murder by Zeus himself, who even
entertained him on Olympus. Ixion rewarded his hospitality by
making love to Hera. Zeus allowed him to believe he was to enjoy her favors, but the god substituted a cloud in Hera's likeness;
the result of this union was the Centaurs. Aeschylus dealt with

*To all these charges return an answer I can understand!*

ORESTES  Queen Athene, your last words contain
a great cause of anxiety that I will first remove.
I am no suppliant in need of purifying, nor was it with pollu-
tion                                                                                     445
upon my hand that I took my seat near your image.
And I will tell you of a powerful proof of this.
It is the custom for the killer to be silent,
till by the action of a purifier of blood-guilt
the slaughter of a suckling victim shall have shed blood upon
him.                                                                                       450
Long since I have been thus purified at other
houses, both by victims and by flowing streams.
This cause for anxiety I thus dispel;
and what is my lineage you shall soon know.
I am an Argive; and my father you know well,                                455
Agamemnon, who marshaled the men of the fleet,
with whom you made Ilium's city a city no more.
He perished by no honorable death, when he came
home; my black-hearted mother
slew him, when she had wrapped him                                           460
in a crafty snare, one that bore witness to his murder in the
bath.
And I returned, having been before in exile,
and killed my mother—I will not deny it—
exacting the penalty of death in return for my dear father.
And together with me Loxias is answerable;                                    465
for he warned me of pains that would pierce my heart,
if I should fail to act against those who bore the guilt of this.
Whether I acted justly or unjustly, you decide the case!
For however I may fare, I shall rest content with your decision.

---

this subject in a trilogy, of which we have only small fragments. In view of the light which this work might throw on
Aeschylus' conception of Zeus, its loss is greatly to be regretted.

452  River water as well as pigs' blood was used in purification.

ATHENE   *The matter is harder than any mortal thinks*   470
*to judge of; it is not right even for me*
*to decide a trial for murder that brings down fierce wrath;*
*all the more since, disciplined as you have been,*
*you have come a suppliant pure and harmless to my house,*
*and in spite of all, the city has no reproach against you, and I*
  *adopt you.*   475

Turning to the CHORUS.

*But these have an office that cannot lightly be dismissed,*
*and if they are cheated of victory in this matter . . .*
*in time to come their anger will drop venom*
*that will fall upon the ground and become an unbearable,*
  *grievous pestilence.*
*So stands the case; either course, that you should stay*   480
*or that I should send you away is disastrous, and perplexes me.*
*But since this matter has devolved on me . . .*
    . . . . . .
*judges . . . of murder, respecting the covenant*
*of their oaths, which I shall establish for all time.*
*Do you summon witnesses and proofs,*   485
*sworn evidence to assist justice.*
*I will select the best among my citizens,*
*and will return, to decide this issue in all sincerity.*

All leave the stage, except the CHORUS and ORESTES.

---

482   The number of lines that are missing is uncertain. ATHENE
now announces her intention of founding a new court to sit
upon the Hill of Ares and try the case. In 483 the text is
uncertain, all the more so because we do not know what came
before it. A line that runs, "never transgressing their oaths,
so as to do injustice" (?), and which appears after 488, where
it makes no possible sense, probably belongs somewhere in
the gap after 482.

STROPHE 1

CHORUS   Now is the ruin of the new                    490
covenant, if the injurious plea
of this killer of his mother
is to prevail!
All mortals from now on will this act
knit fast to readiness of hand;                        495
and many the wounds, dealt in truth
by their children, that await parents
yet again in time to come.

ANTISTROPHE 1

For from us who keep watch on mortals
and send madness shall no wrath                        500
at these their deeds come upon them;
I shall let loose doom in every form.

And one shall ask of another, while he proclaims
his neighbors' ills,
when shall tribulation subside and cease;              505
and in vain does the poor wretch
offer as consolation cures that are not sure.

---

490   The first two strophic pairs in the Second Stasimon (490–
525) are in a trochaic meter similar to that of the first strophic
pair in the First Stasimon. The third strophe opens in the
same meter (526–29 ~ 538–40); then comes a run of dactyls,
recalling those of the second and third stropic pairs in the
First Stasimon (530–35 ~ 541–46); finally there is a concluding period in iambics that recalls the iambics of the fourth
strophic pair in the First Stasimon. Meter, as well as sense
throughout, serves to link the First and Second Stasimon.

490–   the new covenant: the institution of the Areopagus; 483–84
496    above are echoed.

### STROPHE 2

*And let no man call out,*
*smitten by disaster,*
*voicing these words:*  510
*"O Justice!*
*O thrones of the Erinyes!"*
*Thus, I think, shall a father*
*or a mother newly smitten*
*make lament, because*
*the house of Justice is falling.*  515

### ANTISTROPHE 2

*There is a place where what is terrible is good*
*and must abide, seated there*
*to keep watch upon men's minds;*
*it is good for them*  520
*to learn wisdom under constraint.*
*And what city or what man*
*that in the light of the heart*
*fostered no dread could have the same*
*reverence for Justice?*  525

---

517  This passage, in which the Erinyes solemnly insist upon the good done to mankind by the execution of their duties, is later echoed closely by ATHENE in her charge to the Court of Areopagus (681f, especially 696–99). The stress here laid on the necessity of punishment is wholly in harmony with the law of Zeus as it is described in the Hymn to Zeus in the Parodos of *Agamemnon* (160f).

520  Compare *Agam.* 180–81: "Wisdom comes to men against their will; and the gods who sit upon the august bench of the ruler give a grace that comes by violence."

521  The text here is uncertain, but the general sense is fortunately not in doubt. Like the strophe (516), the antistrophe ends with the name of Justice (Dike).

*Neither a life of anarchy*
*nor a life under a despot*
*should you praise.*
*To all that lies in the middle has a god given excellence,*  530
*but he surveys different realms in different ways.*
*I utter a word to fit the case:*
*impiety's child, in all truth, is insolence;*
*but from the good health*  535
*of the mind comes what is dear to all—*
*that which is much prayed for—happiness.*

*In all things, I tell you,*
*must you reverence the altar of Justice.*
*Dishonor it not,*  540
*at a glimpse of profit kicking it with impious foot;*

---

526  In this context the sense of these words must be that Zeus governs the universe, including the world of men, in a way that is neither lawless nor dictatorial; he steers a middle course between these extremes, delegating different responsibilities to different agents. Among these agents are the Erinyes, who play an important part in the administration of his law of justice.

533  Lack of reverence for the gods and for the divine law leads to the brutal insolence (*hybris*) that brings a man or his descendants to disaster; we recognize the doctrine whose fullest statement is at *Agam.* 750–81. Note in particular how one impious deed is said to "beget" others in its own likeness (*Agam.* 758–62) and how old *hybris* is said to give birth to new *hybris* (*Agam.* 763f).

534  For the content, compare *Agam.* 761–62; the descendants of the righteous enjoy prosperity. For the metaphor of physical health, compare *Agam.* 1001f.

*for a penalty shall be exacted;*
*a sovereign power awaits you.*
*In face of this, let a man rightly put first the respect he owes*
  *his parents,*                                                      545
*and let him reverence*
*the freedom of the house*
*whereby a guest and host honor each other.*

### STROPHE 4

*And so without constraint shall he be just*                          550
*and shall not lack for happiness;*
*and he shall never come to utter ruin.*
*But he who dares transgress in bold defiance*
*heaping all things together and carrying them off unjustly*
*by violence, he, I say, in time shall strike*                        555
*his sail, when the storm of trouble comes upon him*
*and his yardarm splinters.*

### ANTISTROPHE 4

*And those he calls on shall not hear him as he struggles*
*in vain amid the whirling waters;*
*the god's laughter mocks the reckless man,*                          560
*as he sees him, who thought that this should never be,*
*now enfeebled by irresistible sorrows and failing to round the*
  *point.*
*He has run aground on the reef of Justice*
*the vessel of his former happiness;*
*he is lost forever,*
*unwept for and unseen.*                                              565

Enter ATHENE, APOLLO, and ORESTES.

---

553   For the metaphor of a ship compare *Agam.* 1005f; there too
      the offender is said to strike a hidden reef (1006; *Eum.* 564).

ATHENE   Make proclamation, herald, and bid the people to
   their places!
And let the shrill Tyrrhenian trumpet
filled with human breath
show to the people its high-pitched note!
For as this court is filled,                                              570
it is proper that silence be kept, and that my ordinances be
   learned
both by the whole city for time everlasting

---

566   The scene includes ATHENE, the presiding judge; ORESTES, the
   defendant; APOLLO, his advocate; and the CHORUS, who are the
   prosecutors. The Areopagites, who form the jury, and possibly
   a number of other mutes designed to represent the audience
   must also be present. How many Areopagites appeared is not
   stated; the number must be even, since the judge will give a
   deciding vote, and twelve (the number of an Aeschylean chorus)
   is a reasonable guess. We may imagine ATHENE standing or
   seated in the center of the stage, APOLLO and ORESTES on her
   right, perhaps nearer to the audience, and the Erinyes on her
   left; most of the CHORUS will have been in the orchestra, but the
   leader of the CHORUS was probably on the stage facing APOLLO
   and ORESTES. The scene of the trial is the Aeropagus, the Hill
   of Ares, as ATHENE says at 685. There is no difficulty in supposing that after the Second Stasimon, the scene changes from
   the temple of ATHENE on the Acropolis to the Areopagus. The
   places are not far apart, and the technique of early tragedy
   allowed the poet to treat them as though they were still nearer.
   So in *The Persians* the scene changes from council chamber to
   the tomb of Darius, and then, probably, to a place near the
   city gate. Some scholars believe that the trial scene has suffered
   serious mutilation (see Taplin, *Stagecraft*, 395f.).

567   *Tyrrhenian:* pronounce *Tirr-een'-ian:* the Tyrrhenians were the
   Etruscans, with whom the Greeks had been in contact since
   the eighth century B.C.; they were supposed to be the inventors
   of the trumpet.

571f   Something is missing after one of these lines, probably after

243

*and by . . .*
*that just decision be duly made of their case who stand here.*

> There is a pause; the herald blows his trumpet,
> the jurors take their places, and other mutes rep-
> resenting the audience áppear. APOLLO enters, and
> takes up his position near ORESTES.

CHORUS   Lord Apollo, exercise your sway over what is your
own!
*Declare what share you have in this affair!*                          575

APOLLO   *I have come both to bear witness—for according*
*to custom*
*this man is a suppliant and has sat by the hearth*
*of my house, and I have cleansed him of blood—*
*and to plead for him myself; and I am responsible*
*for his mother's killing.*                                             580

> Turning to ATHENE.

*Do you bring on the case,*
*and decide as you know how to!*

---

the latter; supposing only one line is lost, it may have run
"and by the judges and by the advocates."

574   The leader of the CHORUS is in effect telling APOLLO to mind
his own business—a prelude to challenging him to prove his
right to take part in the proceedings.

580–  The word translated "bring on" is a technical term used to
581   denote the duty that in historical times fell to the King
Archon. He no doubt inherited the duty of presiding over
the Areopagus, as he did other duties, from the kings who
had ruled Attica in the beginning. It is sometimes inferred
that the absence of an Athenian king from this play is proof
of Aeschylus' antimonarchical sentiment. It suits Aeschylus'
purpose, however, to have the goddess herself preside; no
Athenian, however democratic, ever tried to deny the existence
of Theseus, the most famous legendary king of Athens. He
is mentioned at 402, 686, and 1026; his father Aegeus, at 683.

ATHENE  (addressing the CHORUS) *It is for you to speak,*
    *for I bring on the case.*
*For the prosecutor should first tell all from the beginning*
*and should rightly explain the matter.*

CHORUS  *We are many, but we shall speak briefly;*      585
*and you answer speech for speech in turn.*
*Say first whether you are the killer of your mother!*

ORESTES  *I killed her; there is no denying that.*

CHORUS  *There already is the first of the three falls!*

ORESTES  *The enemy over whom you utter this boast is not*
    *yet down!*      590

---

583  It was normal for the prosecutor to speak first and establish
his case. But instead of the leader of the CHORUS making a
long speech, which would be against the normal technique
of Aeschylean tragedy, the Erinyes begin with an interrogation
of the defendant; from 587 to 606, this takes the form of
stichomythia.

585  This line has led some scholars to think that each member
of the CHORUS asked a question in turn. Between 587 and
608 there are eleven speeches by the CHORUS; if these scholars
are right, 585–86 would have to be spoken by the Coryphaeus
and then one line by each of the other members of the
CHORUS. The scene in *Agamemnon* (1348–71) in which each
member of the CHORUS speaks two lines while Agamemnon is
being murdered might be thought to favor this notion; but
there is no positive evidence that Aeschylus here departed from
the usual rule that dialogue trimeters of the CHORUS were
spoken by the Coryphaeus.

587  For the CHORUS, the mere fact that ORESTES has killed his
mother is in itself decisive (cf. 429f with note).

589  In Greek wrestling the loser of three falls lost the bout (compare *Agam.* 171–72 and *The Libation Bearers* 339 for a metaphor
derived from this fact). What are the two remaining falls?

CHORUS  But you must tell us how you slew her.

ORESTES  I will; with sword in hand I struck her in the throat.

CHORUS  And who persuaded you? On whose counsel did you act?

ORESTES  Upon Apollo's oracles; he is my witness.

CHORUS  Did the prophet instruct you to kill your mother?  595

ORESTES  Yes, and up to this moment I find no fault with what befell.

CHORUS  Well, if the vote lays hold on you, you will soon change your tune.

ORESTES  I have confidence; my father is sending help from his grave.

CHORUS  Put your confidence in corpses, you who have killed your mother!

ORESTES  Yes, for she bore the mark of a double pollution.  600

CHORUS  How so? Explain this to the judges!

ORESTES  In slaying her husband she slew my father.

CHORUS  Well, then, you still live, but she by her death has been freed of guilt.

---

The CHORUS will also have to prove that the killing was deliberate (hence their questions at 591 and 593); and it is a fair surmise that they will also have to establish that it was unjust. ORESTES admits the deed and says that it was deliberate, but he contends that it was justified. The prosecution insists that matricide must be punished, whatever the extenuating circumstances.

595  The word rendered by "instruct" is one used specifically of the kind of instruction in ritual or in religious matters customarily given by the Delphic Oracle. Its use, therefore, like that of the word "prophet," has an ironic effect.

ORESTES  But why did you not harry her, while she still
lived?

CHORUS  She had not the same blood as the man she killed.  605

ORESTES  And have I the same blood as my mother?

CHORUS  How else did she nourish you beneath her girdle,
murderer?
Do you disown your mother's dearest blood?

ORESTES  You now give your testimony, and expound the
law to me,
Apollo, whether I had Justice with me when I slew her.  610
For the deed—I did it—I cannot deny;
but pronounce upon this deed of blood, whether you think
I acted justly or unjustly, that I may prove it to the court.

APOLLO  I shall say to all of you, to this high tribunal
of Athens, that he acted justly, and as a prophet I shall not
speak falsely.  615
Never have I spoken on my mantic throne
words touching a man or a woman or a city
which had not been ordained me by Zeus, father of the
Olympians.
I bid you understand how mighty is this righteous plea,
and comply with the design of my father;  620
for an oath has not greater power than Zeus.

---

609  The word translated by "expound the law" is the same as that
referred to in the note on 595; its use reminds us of APOLLO's
special authority.

616  Compare the words of PYTHIA at 19 above. The dependence
of APOLLO's oracle on Zeus was the received doctrine; we find
it stated in the Homeric Hymn to APOLLO (see note on 1).

621  The oath referred to is presumably the jurors' oath; APOLLO
means that even if the jurors think the Erinyes have right on
their side, they cannot condemn ORESTES in defiance of the
will of Zeus.

CHORUS  Was it Zeus, you tell us, gave you this oracle,
to tell Orestes here to avenge his father's murder
and to account nowhere the respect he owed his mother?

APOLLO  Yes, for it is not the same—the death of a noble
    man,                                                          625
honored by the Zeus-given scepter,
and by a woman's hands at that, not by martial
far-darting arrows, as of an Amazon,
but even as I shall tell you, Pallas, and you too who sit here
to decide this matter by your vote.                              630
When he returned from the campaign, having managed
for the most part well, she received him with kindly . . .
        . . . . . .
as he was stepping from the bath, at its edge
she curtained him with a cloak, and in the maze
of an embroidered robe entangled him and struck him.            635
I have told you how he perished, the man
revered by all, the marshal of the fleet.
I have spoken as I have spoken, that the people may be stung
    to anger,
the people that has the task of deciding this trial.

CHORUS  It is the father's fate of which Zeus reckons most,
    by your account;                                             640
yet he himself bound his aged father, Kronos.

---

622–  The Erinyes evidently find it incredible that Zeus, the cham-
624   pion of justice, should defend a cause which to them seems
      patently unjust.

625   The argument based on the doctrine of the superiority of the
      male over the female, on which APOLLO is thrown back, is
      one that few among the play's original audience are likely to
      have questioned.

628   For the Amazons, see note on 685.

632   Probably not more than one line is missing here; line 633 is
      barely grammatical and may be corrupt, but the general sense
      is clear enough.

641   Kronos: pronounce Kronn'-os.

*Does not this argument of yours fit ill with that?*
*I call upon you judges to witness this!*

APOLLO  *All-hateful beasts, abominations to the gods,*
*fetters can be loosed; for such hurt there is a remedy,*  645
*and abundant means of undoing it.*
*But when once a man is dead, and the earth*
*has sucked up his blood, there is no way to raise him up.*
*For against this my father has furnished no spell,*
*though all other things he turns up and down*  650
*and disposes without effort by his might.*

CHORUS  *Why, mark the manner of your plea for his*
*acquittal!*
*Shall he who has spilt his mother's kindred blood upon the*
*ground*
*then live in Argos in his father's house?*
*What altars of public worship shall he use?*  655
*And what sacred water of the phratries shall receive him?*

APOLLO  *This too I will tell you; mark the truth of what I*
*say!*

---

The *argumentum ad hominem* employed by the Erinyes is calculated to disturb those who think that Aeschylean theology always occupies the loftiest heights of abstract speculation. According to the usual story, probably first related in Hesiod's *Theogony*, Zeus overthrew his father Kronos and imprisoned him in Tartarus. Later, according to one version, Kronos (Saturn) was released and allowed to preside over the Isles of the Blessed. This version of the story is told by Pindar in his Second Olympian Ode and probably by Aeschylus in the lost part of his trilogy about Prometheus.

655–  The touch of a polluted person would contaminate the altars,
656  which is why such people were excluded from communal worship. It would also contaminate the lustral water used at the communal sacrifices of the clan. The word "phratry" (cf. *frater*, the Latin word for brother) denotes a kind of clan that in historical times had its own religious services. The occurrence of the word in a single passage of Homer, where

She who is called the child's mother is not
its begetter, but the nurse of the newly sown conception.
The begetter is the male, and she as a stranger for a stranger    660
preserves the offspring, if no god blights its birth;
and I shall offer you a proof of what I say.
There can be a father without a mother; near at hand
is the witness, the child of Olympian Zeus . . .

. . . . . .

and she was not nurtured in the darkness of the womb,    665
but is such an offspring as no goddess might bear.
And for my part, Pallas, in other things I will do all I can
to make your city and your people great,
just as I sent this man to the hearth of your house

---

its exact significance is uncertain, may have encouraged Aeschylus to suppose that phratries like those of Athens in his own time existed during the heroic age.

659   The word rendered by "begetter" is one whose plural is not uncommonly used to mean "parents." Thus, by a play on words, APOLLO is suggesting that a mother is not in the strict sense a parent. He is not actually denying that the mother nurtures the embryo with her blood, as the leader of the CHORUS has pointed out at 607–8.

663   According to an ancient story, Zeus and Hera challenged each other to produce a child without the help of another parent. Hera produced Hephaestus, the lame god of smiths and craftsmen; Zeus produced ATHENE. According to a story, Hephaestus or Prometheus, the smiths among the gods, split the head of Zeus with a hammer and ATHENE leaped out. The evidence of vase-paintings shows this story to have been well known at Athens in the time of Aeschylus.

664   After this line, probably not more than one line is missing.

667f   The offer of a bribe is less surprising in the light of fifth-century Athenian legal practice than it would be in our own day. Athenian advocates often seem less concerned to establish the innocence of their client than to show that his acquittal will be in the interest of the people of Athens; by "the

that he might be true for all time 670
and that you might gain him as an ally, goddess,
him and those after him, and that this covenant might abide
    forever
for these men's progeny to revere.

ATHENE   Am I now to tell these in sincerity to give
their righteous vote, since enough has been said? 675

CHORUS   We for our part have now shot every arrow;
but I wait to hear how the issue shall be decided.

ATHENE   Well, then, how must I dispose to escape your
    censure?

APOLLO   (addressing the judges) You have heard what you
    have heard; in your hearts
respect your oath as you cast your votes, O hosts! 680

ATHENE   Hear now my ordinance, people of Attica,
you who are trying your first trial for the shedding of blood.
In future time also there shall remain for the people of Aegeus
forever this council of judges.
And this hill of Ares, where the Amazons had their seat 685

---

people" they mean the supporters of the prevailing democratic
constitution.

670   Another reference to the Argive alliance (see 28f with note).

681–   According to a well-known story, the Court of Areopagus was
682   first assembled to try Ares for the murder of Poseidon's son
    Halirrhothius (cf. note on 360). It is possible that Aeschylus
    was the first poet to say that the Court was originally as-
    sembled to try ORESTES.

683   Aegeus: pronounce Ee-gyuse [hard "g"]. Aegeus was a legendary
    king of Athens and father of the more famous Theseus.

685   Ares: pronounce Air'-es.
    The Amazons were the race of warlike women who usually
    lived near the River Thermodon in Asia Minor. They were

*and pitched their tents, when they came in hatred of Theseus*
*with an army, and over against the city*
*raised this new city with high walls—*
*so they sacrificed to Ares, thus giving a name*
*to the rock and hill of Ares. In this place shall the awe*      690
*of the citizens and their inborn dread restrain*
*injustice, both by day and night alike,*
*so long as the citizens themselves do not pervert the laws*
*by means of evil influxes; for by polluting clear water*

---

supposed to have marched to Athens to punish Theseus for having helped Heracles carry off the girdle of their queen, Hippolyte. Hippolytus was said to be the son of Theseus either by Hippolyte herself or by another Amazon, Antiope. As daughters of Ares, they would naturally have offered sacrifice to him (688).

687   In early times "the city" did not extend beyond the Acropolis, and even in historical times Athenians used to refer to the Acropolis as "the city."

690   "Where there is fear, there is reverence" was probably already a proverb when it occurred in the pre-Homeric epic called *The Cypria*, a work of the seventh century B.C. From this point on it is necessary to compare ATHENE's words carefully with those uttered by the CHORUS at 517f. There the Erinyes are maintaining that fear plays a necessary part in Zeus's government of the universe. In strikingly similar language, ATHENE is maintaining that fear must play a necessary part in the government of Athens. In the government of the universe, the formidable element is supplied by the Erinyes; in that of Athens, it is to be supplied by the Court of Areopagus.

693f   The word translated as "pervert" is corrupt, and the number of words that would make sense by a comparatively slight emendation is embarrassingly large. Fortunately the corruption does not much matter, because it is clear from the general sense that whatever word stood here had a pejorative sense. But it is by no means clear what is meant by "evil influxes." Those who think Aeschylus sympathized with the re-

*with mud you will never find good drinking.*                                    695
*Neither anarchy nor tyranny shall the citizens defend and re-*
      *spect, if they follow my counsel;*
*and they shall not cast out altogether from the city what is to*
      *be feared.*
*For who among mortals that fears nothing is just?*
*Such is the object of awe that you must justly dread,*                          700
*and so you shall have a bulwark of the land and a protector*
*of the city such as none of human kind possesses,*

---

cent reforms of the Areopagus carried through by Ephialtes
(see Appendix, p. 273) argue that the "evil influxes" must
refer to the functions of which the reformers had deprived the
court. Those who think that Aeschylus regretted the reforms
argue that they referred to the reforms themselves; others hold
that he meant the words to be ambiguous. All three parties
commonly assume that "the laws" in 693 refers to the laws
regulating the composition of the Court of Areopagus. This is
possible but hardly certain. If "the laws" here simply mean
the laws in general, the warning against changing them is presumably connected with the fact that the most important function the Areopagus lost was that of protecting the constitution
by vetoing legislation that might transform its character. To
suppose that "the laws" at 693 simply mean the laws of Athens
as a whole happens to be the simplest and most natural way
of taking it, and I believe this interpretation is correct.

696–   Compare 526–29 with 696–97; compare 517–19 with 698–99.
699   In both the government of the universe and of Athens, a
middle course between despotism and anarchy must be taken,
and the element of government that inspires fear must not
be excluded. Zeus is no tyrant; he allows men a measure of
free will, while maintaining the rule of Justice among them.
To secure respect for Justice, he makes use of the Erinyes.
Similarly, Athens is neither a tyranny nor an anarchic state;
the laws must be guarded by an element of the constitution
that can inspire fear, and that element is the Areopagus.

neither among the Scythians nor in the domains of Pelops.
Proof against thoughts of profit is this council,
august, quick to anger, wakeful on behalf                                     705
of sleepers is the guard-post of the land that I establish.
This long exhortation I have addressed
to my citizens to heed in time to come; but you must rise
and take your ballots and decide the case,
in reverence for your oath. My speech is ended.                               710

CHORUS   But mark well! Our company might prove grievous for your land.
I advise you in no way to dishonor us.

APOLLO   And I bid you respect my oracles
and those of Zeus, and do not deprive them of fulfillment.

CHORUS   You concern yourself with deeds of blood, though
they are not your portion;                                                    715
no longer shall the oracles that you dispense be pure.

---

703 *Scythians*: pronounce *Sith-ians*; *Pelops*: pronounce *Pee'-lops*.
    The Scythians inhabited what is now South Russia, bordering
    on the Black Sea. Like the Spartans, who are the natives of
    the Peloponnese alluded to in this passage, they were noted in
    ancient times for their *eunomia*, a quality that included both
    having good laws and being willing to abide by them. The
    comparison of all people with Scythians and Peloponnesians
    shows that ATHENE is here especially concerned with the laws
    of Athens and their defense against harmful innovation. It
    was precisely the powers enabling the Court of Areopagus to
    protect the laws that had been taken from it by the reforms
    of Ephialtes. Afterwards, it retained few functions except
    that of trying cases of murder. The language of ATHENE's
    speech, especially when considered in close conjunction with
    that of the CHORUS at 517f, hardly suggests that Aeschylus is
    content to have the Areopagus concern itself only with the
    repression of homicide and give up its duty of acting as the
    guardian of the constitution.

APOLLO  Was my father too mistaken in his purposes,
when Ixion, he who was the first to kill, made supplication?

CHORUS  You say it! If I do not get justice,
my company shall prove grievous to this land in time to come.  720

APOLLO  But among the young gods and the old
you are without honor; the victory shall be mine!

CHORUS  Such were your actions in the house of Pheres also!
You persuaded the Fates to make men immortal.

APOLLO  Then is it not just to do a kindness to him who
        treats one with respect,                                    725
especially in his hour of need?

CHORUS  It was you who violated the ancient dispensations
and with wine beguiled the primeval goddesses.

APOLLO  It is you that shall soon fail to win victory in your
        suit
and shall spew out your venom with no harm to your enemies!  730

---

719  *You say it!*: for the idiom illustrated by these words compare
     Matthew 27:11, where Pilate says, "Art thou the King of the
     Jews?" and Christ replies, "Thou sayest [it]." The formula is
     regularly used by those who wish to assent to the other's words
     without taking responsibility for the statement.

723–  APOLLO had received many kindnesses from Admetus, son of
724   Pheres, a Thessalian hero. In return the god persuaded the Fates
     to allow Admetus to escape the early death that was his destiny
     if another person was willing to die in his place. The sub-
     stitute was his wife Alcestis, who was rescued from the clutches
     of death by Heracles. The subject is handled in the
     *Alcestis* of Euripides, who does not mention the story that
     APOLLO made the Fates drunk (*Eum.* 728); it had also been
     treated by Aeschylus' older contemporary Phrynichus in a
     play that has not survived.

729–  These are Apollo's last words. The rest as it stands gives no
30    indication as to when he leaves, and this may be due to muti-
     lation (Taplin, *op. cit.*, 403f.).

CHORUS   Since your youth is riding down my venerable age,
I wait to hear justice given in this case,
being still in doubt whether to visit my anger on the city.

ATHENE   It is now my office to give final judgment;
and I shall give my vote to Orestes.                                    735
For there is no mother who bore me;
and I approve the male in all things, short of accepting
        marriage,
with all my heart, and I belong altogether to my father.
Therefore I shall not give greater weight to the death of a
        woman,
one who slew her husband, the watcher of the house;          740
Orestes is the winner, even should the votes be equal.
Throw out in all speed from the urns the lots,
you among the judges to whom this duty is assigned!

ORESTES   Phoebus Apollo, how shall the issue be decided?

---

734   Why does ATHENE announce at this point that if the votes
        prove equal she will give her casting vote for acquittal? At
        some stage this has to be made clear; if she had done so only
        after the counting of the votes, the Erinyes might have been
        even more indignant. At the actual trials conducted by the
        Areopagus, if the votes were equal the defendant was acquitted
        by means of the so-called "vote of ATHENE," which was al-
        ways on the side of mercy.

736   The reason ATHENE gives for voting for acquittal has always
        been embarrassing to those who wish to portray Aeschylus as
        an "advanced" thinker. In a case in which the arguments on
        both sides seem to carry equal weight, there must be a decision
        of some kind; ATHENE must decide for acquittal. Yet, she
        cannot risk offending the powerful Erinyes by openly proclaim-
        ing that as the sister of APOLLO and the daughter of Zeus, who
        inspires his oracles, she is on the side of the younger genera-
        tion of the gods. Before she can calm the fury of the defeated
        Erinyes, she has to use all her persuasive power and back it
        with a handsome offer.

CHORUS  Black Night, my mother, do you look upon this
scene?                                                                    745

ORESTES  Now I must perish by the noose, or else see the
light!

CHORUS  So must we fall to ruin, or maintain our honors
in time to come.

APOLLO  Count fairly, friends, the pebbles now thrown out,
respecting justice in the sorting!
In the lack of judgment, great harm may be done;            750
but when judgment is present, a single vote can set right a
house.

ATHENE  This man stands acquitted on the charge of murder;
for the number of the votes is equal!

ORESTES  O Pallas, you who have preserved my house,
I was deprived of my native land, and it is you                755
who have brought me home! And the Greeks shall say,
"The man is once more an Argive, and lives
among the possessions of his father, by the grace
of Pallas and of Loxias, and of him who determines all things,
the third Preserver"; yes, it is he who had regard to the manner of my father's death                                           760
and has preserved me, in the face of these my mother's advocates.
And for my part, to your country and your people
I swear an oath that in future for all time shall prevail,
before departing now for home:

---

760  Zeus, in his aspect as Zeus the Preserver, received the third
libation at banquets (see *Agam.* 1386–87 and *The Libation
Bearers* 1073 with notes).

764  Compare 289f and 670f for what are apparently allusions to
the alliance of Athens and Argos that was in force at the
time of the play's first production (see Appendix).

257

that no ruler of my country shall come here 765
to bear against them the embattled spear!
For I myself, who shall then be in my tomb,
shall visit those that transgress the oath that I now swear
with misfortunes that shall reduce them to perplexity,
making their goings dispirited and their paths ill-omened, 770
so that they repent them of their trouble.
But if all goes well, and if they always honor
this city of Pallas with the spear of allies,
then they shall have more favor from myself.
All hail, both to yourself and to the people of the city! 775
May yours be a grip no enemy can escape,
one that preserves you and brings you victory in war!

    Exit ORESTES. A new act begins here.

CHORUS   *Ah, you younger gods, the ancient laws*

---

767   The belief that a dead hero could influence events on earth
must have been firmly held by Aeschylus' original audience.
It plays an essential part, as we have seen, in the plot of
*The Libation Bearers,* and it is equally important in other tragedies, such as Sophocles' *Oedipus at Colonus* and Euripides'
*The Heraclidae.* But it also played a part in fifth-century history,
as we see from the importance attached by the Spartans to the
recovery of ORESTES' bones from Tegea and by the Athenians
to the recovery of Theseus' bones from Scyros; the latter occurred at a date not far removed from the first production of
the *Oresteia.*

778   The Erinyes give vent to their indignation at the result of the
trial in two stanzas, both prevailingly dochmiac, although the
first has iambic and trochaic elements and the meter of one
part of the second is uncertain. Each of these stanzas is repeated (778–92 ~ 808–22; 837–46 ~ 870–80); each of the four
stanzas is answered by a speech of ATHENE in trimeters, the
speeches being of unequal lengths. After the fourth of these
speeches, the CHORUS for the first time shows interest in the
offer with which ATHENE is trying to soothe their wrath (892).
The question they ask there initiates a stichomythia in which
ATHENE and the Coryphaeus each speak one line at a time.

*you have ridden down, and snatched them from my grasp!*
*I am bereft of honor, unhappy one! And with grievous wrath*     780
*against this land, alack,*
*venom, venom in requital for my grief from my heart shall*
    *I discharge,*
*a distillation for the land*
*intolerable; and after that*
*a canker, blasting leaves and children—Ah, Justice!—*     785
*speeding over the ground*
*shall cast upon the land infections that destroy its people.*
*I lament! What can I do?*
*I am mocked! Grievous, I say,*     790
*is the fate of the hapless daughters*
*of Night, who mourn, robbed of their honor!*

    ATHENE  Be ruled by me, and bear it not with grievous
      lamentation!
*For you are not defeated, but in equal votes the trial*     795
*resulted in all truth, bringing you no dishonor.*
*Why, clear testimony from Zeus was there,*

---

This continues until 902 and contains the actual surrender of
the Erinyes. ATHENE answers with a speech indicating what
kind of blessings she hopes the Erinyes will confer upon her
city. This rounds off the dialogue, affording an easy transition
to the Third Stasimon, in which the Erinyes comply with her
request.

    The Erinyes echo their own words to APOLLO at 731. The
theme of a clash between the two different generations of
gods is prominent in this scene. In the ancient world, old age
was generally thought to confer a special title to respect (cf.
882f).

780  The word usually rendered by "honor" (*timē*) and its com-
    pounds is less abstract than our word "honor" because it also
    connotes "status," "rights," "privileges"; a man exiled from
    his city lost his *timē*. Achilles' quarrel with Agamemnon
    (*Iliad* 1) is provoked by what he regards as the deprivation of
    *timē*.

and he who had given the oracle himself bore witness,
so that Orestes could escape destruction for his deed,
and shall you spew forth grievous wrath upon this land?          800
Take thought, do not be angry, and do not cause
blight, dropping discharges supernatural,
cruel spears that will consume the seed.
For in all justice I promise you shall have
a seat and a cavern in this righteous land,                     805
sitting on gleaming thrones hard by your altars,
honored by these my citizens.

CHORUS  *Ah, you younger gods, the ancient laws*
*you have ridden down, and snatched them from my grasp!*
*I am bereft of honor, unhappy one! And with grievous wrath*     810
*against this land, alack,*
*venom, venom, in requital for my grief from my heart shall*
        *I discharge,*
*a distillation for the land*
*intolerable; and after that*
*a canker, blasting leaves and children—Ah, Justice!—*          815
*speeding over the ground*
*shall cast upon the land infections that destroy its people.*
*I lament! What can I do?*
*I am mocked! Grievous, I say,*                                  820
*is the fate of the hapless daughters*
*of Night, who mourn, robbed of their honor!*

ATHENE  You are not dishonored; do not with excessive wrath
blight the land of mortals, goddesses that you are!             825
I, for my part, have trust in Zeus, and—why need I speak of
        it?—

----

806  Sacred stones used to be polished with oil.
808  The verbatim repetition of the lyric stanza (from 778f) marks
     the total refusal of the Erinyes, at this stage, even to consider
     ATHENE's offer.
826– The threat is made in the most tactful way possible, but its
829  presence in the text must not be ignored. The possession of

*I alone among the gods know the keys of the house*
*wherein is sealed the lightning.*
*But there is no need of it; let me persuade you,*
*and do not discharge upon this land the words of an idle*
    *tongue,*          830
*so as to cause all things that bear fruit no more to prosper.*
*Lull to repose the bitter force of your black wave of anger,*
*since you shall be honored and revered and dwell with me!*
*As first fruits of this great land*
*you shall have forever sacrifice in thanks for children*      835
*and the accomplishment of marriage, and you shall approve*
    *my words.*

    CHORUS  *That I should suffer this, alack,*
*I with my ancient wisdom, and should dwell in the land,*
*a thing dishonored and polluted!*
*I breathe forth fury and utter rage!*          840

    They utter a loud cry of lamentation.

*What pain comes over my sides, over*
*my brain? Hear, mother*
*Night! For from my ancient honors*          845

---

the thunder enabled Zeus to overcome the Titans, who supported his father Kronos, and later to suppress the formidable rebellion of the Giants. That ATHENE alone among the other gods was allowed by Zeus to borrow it is a familiar story; she used it, for example, to punish the Greek fleet returning from Troy for the violation of Cassandra by the lesser Ajax in her own temple (Euripides, *Troades* 8of).

832  In the original the sound of this line marvelously suits the sense: "*koimā kelainou kȳmatos pīkron menos.*"

834–  Like Demeter, the earth-goddess, the Erinyes did receive of-
836  ferings after the birth of children and after marriages; that chthonic divinities should be prayed to for fertility is not surprising.

842f  The text here is uncertain.

*the irresistible cunning of the gods has reft me, making me
count for nothing.*

ATHENE   I will bear with you in your anger; for you
    are more ancient than I;
and so far you are indeed wiser.
But to me too Zeus has given good understanding.                    850
And if you go to a foreign country,
you shall long for this land: of that I warn you!
For advancing time shall bring greater honor
to these citizens; and you shall have an honored
seat near the house of Erechtheus                                   855
and what you shall receive from men and from processions of
    women
will be greater than anything that other mortals will give you.
But do you not hurl against my country
incentives to shed blood, harmful to the hearts
of young men, maddening them with a fury not of wine;               860
do not pluck out, as it were, the hearts of fighting cocks
and plant in my citizens a spirit of war,
of civil war, making them bold against each other!
Let there be foreign war, which will come easily enough,
in it shall there be a mighty passion for renown;                   865

---

849   Wisdom was traditionally thought to accompany old age.

855   Erechtheus was a legendary king of Athens, who was wor-
    shiped as a hero in the Erechtheum on the Acropolis; the
    present building replaced a much older shrine destroyed by
    the Persians in 480 B.C.

863   The prayer against civil war is significant; at the time of the
    reform of the Areopagus by Ephialtes in 461 B.C., three years
    before the first production of the *Oresteia,* Athens had been
    on the verge of it (see also Appendix).

864–   At the time of the first production Athens was at war with
865    Sparta, and an Athenian force may still have been assisting
    the Egyptian rebels against Persia.

*but I do not approve of battle with the bird within the nest.*
Such is the choice I offer you:
to do good and receive good, and in goodly honor
to have a portion in this land most dear to the gods.

CHORUS  *That I should suffer this, alack,*                    870
*I with my ancient wisdom, and should dwell in the land,*
*a thing dishonored and polluted!*
*I breathe forth fury and utter rage!*

They utter a loud cry of lamentation.

*What pain comes over my sides, over*                          875
*my brain? Hear, mother*
*Night! For from my ancient honors*
*the irresistible cunning of the gods has reft me, making me*
        *count for nothing.*                                   880

ATHENE  I shall not weary of telling you of the good things
        I offer,
that you may never say that by me, who am younger,
and by the mortals who hold this city, you, an ancient goddess,
were driven off dishonored, an exile from this land.
No! If you revere Persuasion's majesty,                        885
the power to charm and soothe that sits upon my tongue,
then you should remain! But if you are unwilling,
you could not justly bring down upon this city
any anger or resentment or harm done to its people.
For it lies open to you to have a holding in this land,        890
of right enjoying an eternal honor.

CHORUS  Queen Athene, what seat do you say shall be mine?

---

885  Persuasion (*Peitho*) is an abstraction often personified in
     Greek poetry; she often figures among the minor divinities
     attendant upon Aphrodite.

892  Now for the first time, the Erinyes show themselves willing
     to consider ATHENE's offer.

ATHENE  One unscathed by any calamity; and do you accept
it!

CHORUS  Suppose I do accept; what honor awaits me?

ATHENE  Honor such that no house can prosper without
you.                                                    895

CHORUS  Will you bring it about that I have such power?

ATHENE  Yes, for him that reveres you I shall make events
to prosper.

CHORUS  And will you promise me this for all time?

ATHENE  Yes; it lies in my power not to promise what I
shall not fulfill.

CHORUS  You seem likely to persuade me, and I am shift-
ing from my anger.                                      900

ATHENE  Then you shall dwell in this land and shall acquire new friends.

CHORUS  Then what fortune do you bid me invoke upon
this land?

ATHENE  Such blessings as may gain no evil victory:
And these shall come from the earth and from the waters of
the sea,
and from the sky, and the blasts of the wind          905
shall pass over the land with sun-warmed breezes:

---

899  ATHENE expresses herself with a kind of wry humor.

900  Now at last the Erinyes yield. Their question at 902 draws
an answer from ATHENE that supplies an easy transition to
the ode of benediction that follows.

903  All the blessings described in this speech and in the ode that
follows are consonant with the fact that the Erinyes, like
other chthonic deities, were implored to grant fertility to
women, crops, and cattle.

*and the increase of the earth and of the herds, teeming with*
*plenty,*
*shall not cease as time passes to prosper for the citizens;*
*and so also shall the seed of mortals be preserved.*
*And may you more incline to make increase the righteous;*
*for like a gardener I cherish*
*and keep far from mourning the race of these just ones.*
*Such things lie in your power; and as for me, in battle's*
*glorious contests I shall not abstain*
*from honoring this city among mankind with victory.* 915

CHORUS *I will accept a share in the house of Pallas;*
*and I will not dishonor a city*
*that the all-powerful Zeus and Ares*
*govern as an outpost of the gods,*
*guardian of the altars of the Greeks*
*and the delight of the immortals.* 920
*For the city I make my prayer,*
*prophesying with kind intent*

---

916 Each stanza of the ode of blessing is separated from the next by marching anapests delivered by ATHENE. The first strophic pair (916-26~938-48) is partly iambic and partly trochaic; these two kinds of meter are very like each other, and are often found together. The second strophic pair (956-67~976-87) is iambo-trochaic mixed with dactyls; the third begins with a dactylic line and continues in the catalectic trochaic dimeters (*lekythia*) that have occurred at several places in the trilogy (see note on *Agam.* 160).

917 Ares is coupled with Zeus, probably because he is the war god and not because the Areopagus is named after him.

919 In about 448 Pericles persuaded the Athenians to invite the other Greek cities to a Panhellenic Congress to restore the temples burned by the Persians in 480 and to establish the freedom of the seas and peace. Pericles wished Athens to be thought of as the "guardian of the altars of the Greeks and the delight of the immortals."

*that in plenty the blessings*
*that make life prosperous*
*may be made to burgeon from the earth* 925
*by the sun's radiant beam.*

ATHENE *This in good will toward my citizens*
*do I bring about. Mighty and hard to please*
*are the divinities I make to settle here.*
*All the affairs of men* 930
*it is their province to manage.*
*And he that encounters their anger*
*does not know from where come the blows that assail his life;*
*for crimes born from those of long ago*
*hale him before them, and in silence destruction,* 935
*loud though he boast,*
*through their wrath and enmity grind him to nothing.*

CHORUS *And may there blow no blast ruinous to trees—*
*it is the grace I give of which I tell—*
*so that no scorching heat that kills the buds of plants*
*passes the boundary of these domains.*
*And with dread ruin of the crops* 940
*let no pestilence come upon them.*
*May Pan make their flocks prosper*
*with twofold issue*
*at the appointed time;* 945
*and may earth's produce*
*making rich the land with lucky finds*
*honor the bounty of the gods!*

---

934  *crimes born . . . long ago:* crimes that men cannot help committing because of the guilt they have inherited from their ancestors—crimes like the sacrifice of Iphigeneia by Agamemnon.

943  Pan had received a state cult at Athens in return for his help during the campaign of Marathon in 490 B.C. He was the god of flocks and herds.

947  The word translated "with lucky finds" is in fact the adjective derived from the name of the god Hermes; he was believed to

ATHENE (addressing the judges) *Do you hear this,*
  *guardians of the land,*
*what things she will ordain?*
*For great is the power of the Lady Erinys* 950
*among the immortals and those below the earth*
*and the fate of men they clearly have power*
*to decide; to some they bring rejoicing*
*and to others a life*
*blinded by tears.* 955

CHORUS *But I prohibit the events that kill*
*men before their time.*
*To lovely maidens,*
*you gods that have the power, grant lives that bring them*
  *husbands;* 960
*among you are the Fates,*
*our sisters by one mother,*
*deities just in apportionment,*
*who have a part in every house,*
*whose might weighs heavily in every season,* 965
*in your righteous visitations*
*in every way most honored among the gods!*

ATHENE *While for my land they eagerly*
*ordain such things*
*I rejoice; and I cherish Persuasion's eye,* 970
*for having guided my tongue and lips*
*when I met their fierce refusal.*

---

be responsible for lucky finds. The discovery of a vein of silver at Laurium, in southeast Attica, supplied the Athenians with the money necessary to build the fleet that saved them at Salamis in 480. It was Themistocles who persuaded them to use this "lucky find" for this purpose.

962 On the parentage of Fates and Erinyes, see note on line 321.

970 The goddess of Persuasion is conceived of as helping ATHENE by literally casting a favorable eye upon her.

But Zeus of the assembly prevailed;
and victory attends our rivalry
in good things forever!                                         975

    CHORUS   But may the voice of faction, who has never had
        enough of evil,
never in this city
resound, I pray;
and may the dust not drink the black blood of the citizens    980
and through passion for revenge
speed on the ruin to the city
wrought by murder in return for murder!
But may each give joy to each,
in a spirit of love toward the common weal,          985
and may they hate with one accord,
for many are the sorrows among mortals that this can cure.

    ATHENE   Have they a mind to find out
the path of benediction?
Then from these fearsome faces
I see great good for these the citizens.                 990
For if, kind in return for kindness,
you do them ever great honor, both land and city
on the straight path of justice
you shall keep, in every way preeminent.            995

---

973    The expression translated as "Zeus of the assembly" is untranslatable. *Agoraios*, meaning "of the marketplace," is a cult-title under which Zeus was worshiped at several places, including Athens; the adjective might also mean "associated with speechmaking," which is the point of its use here.

974–    Hesiod in a famous passage near the beginning of his *Works*
975    *and Days* (11f) says there are two kinds of *eris* ("rivalry," "strife"), one of which is good and the other bad; the former promotes peaceful competition for getting work done, and ATHENE is implying that this sort of *eris* pertains especially to herself and her citizens.

976    Again we find a prayer against civil war.

CHORUS   *Hail, hail in your wealth bestowed by fate,*
*hail, people of the city,*
*whose seat is near to Zeus,*
*dear to the goddess who is dear to you,*
*gaining wisdom as time passes.*                    1000
*On you that sit beneath the wings of Pallas*
*her father looks with kindness.*

ATHENE   *Hail to you also!*

Enter ESCORT of torch-bearers. (Perhaps the jurors
of the Areopagus perform this office.)

*But I must go first to reveal*
*your chambers in the sacred light*                 1005
*given by these who escort you. Go, and as this solemn*
*sacrifice is done, make speed beneath the earth,*
*and keep far away what is baneful,*
*but send what brings advantage,*
*that the city may triumph!*
*Lead the way, sons of Cranaus*                     1010
*that hold the city, for these fellow denizens;*

---

1005   The cave where the Erinyes were worshiped was on a slope
of the Acropolis, some way from the Areopagus. It would be
a mistake to argue that the procession must actually have
moved in the direction of this place (see note on 566).

1005–   Some time before these lines are spoken, an extra chorus of
1006   Athenians carrying torches must have appeared to escort the
Eumenides. *The Suppliants* of Aeschylus also has an extra
chorus that appears only in the final scene, if the generally
accepted view that the handmaidens of the Danaids sing part
of the final lyric scene is right.

1010–   *Cranaus:* pronounce *Krann'-ay-us.* Athens is sometimes called
1011   by poets *Kranaa polis,* "the rocky [or 'the rugged'] city," and
this seems to have caused the invention of a legendary ancestor
called *Kranaos,* "the rugged one."

1011   The word translated as "fellow denizens" is the word regularly used at Athens to denote resident aliens, or *"metics"*;

269

*and may the spirit of the citizens*
*be good in return for good!*

    CHORUS  *Hail, hail once more, for again I say it,*
*all within the city,*                       1015
*gods and mortals!*
*Govern the city of Pallas*
*and reverence me who share your home,*
*and you shall not find fault*
*with your fortune in life!*                     1020

    ATHENE  I thank you for the words spoken in these your
        benedictions,
and I will escort you by the light of blazing torches
to your place below, beneath the earth,
with the attendants who guard my image,
as you deserve.                           1025

        Addressing the ESCORT.

You shall come to the very eye
Of Theseus' land, O honorable band
of children and women and company of aged ladies
        . . . . . .
honor them with robes of crimson dye,
and let the blaze of fire rise up,                1030
that this their sojourn, kindly to the land,
may in future time be made manifest in fortune that brings it
    noble men.

---

        its corresponding noun is the word translated as "share your
        home" at 1018.

1025  Greek and Latin both use the word "eye" metaphorically to
        mean the most precious part of anything.

1027  There is probably more than one line missing here.

1028  At the procession in honor of ATHENE at the festival of the
        Great Panathenaea, the most important festival of the
        Athenian religious year, resident aliens wore crimson cloaks.

Escort  *Go on your way, as is right, mighty ones, jealous*
       *of honor,*
*dread children of Night, under our honest escort.*
*Let your speech be of good omen, people of the land!*       1035
*Beneath earth's primeval caverns,*
*with honors and sacrifices and with much reverence.*
*Let your speech be of good omen, people one and all!*
*Gracious and propitious to the land*       1040
*come hither, venerable ones, rejoicing*
*on your way in the torch the flame devours!*
*Raise a glad cry, echoing our song!*
*There shall be peace forever . . .*
*for the citizens of Pallas; thus have all-seeing Zeus*       1045
*and Fate come to our aid.*
*Raise a glad cry in echo of our song!*

---

Presumably, the Erinyes assumed the cloaks during this scene
in token of their new status.

1033  The extra chorus of the Escort sings two brief strophic pairs,
both in predominantly dactylic measures of a kind that were
thought appropriate to accompany processions because they
conveyed an effect of solemn dignity.

1041  "The Venerable Ones" (*Semnai*), like "The Kindly Ones"
(*Eumenides*), was a common euphemistic way of referring to
the Erinyes.

1044  The text here is corrupt.

# APPENDIX

Only three years before the first production of the *Oresteia*, the Areopagus had been at the center of a fierce political storm that had come near to ending in civil war. At the instigation of the democratic leader Ephialtes, helped by the young Pericles, the Areopagus had been stripped of the special powers that it had held in virtue of its duty to guard the constitution by preventing legislation judged not to be in keeping with its spirit. Violent passions were aroused on both sides, and Ephialtes was soon afterwards assassinated; his murderers went undetected. Several passages in *The Eumenides*, and especially part of the Second Stasimon (517f) and Athene's charge to the Court before the voting (681f), must allude to the special function of the Areopagus in a way that has a bearing on the controversy. Aeschylus is the only author who gives this particular account of its foundation, and he may well have invented it in order to make it part of the subject of his trilogy and hence to give himself the opportunity to comment on what was in 458 a burning issue. But though it is generally agreed that the reform of the Areopagus is relevant to the play, opinions differ widely concerning the poet's attitude toward it. Some think that he wished to praise the recent changes; others that he wished to censure them; others, including the great Hellenist Wilamowitz, have believed that

he alludes to them with a studied ambiguity, being concerned only
to promote the reconciliation of the two conflicting factions.

After his acquittal, Orestes promises that his own city of Argos
will never forget its debt to Athens; this has been generally taken
as an allusion to the alliance with Argos that Athens had contracted
in 461. Ephialtes and Pericles were strongly in favor of this alliance,
which meant that Athens had finally decided to challenge Sparta
for the leadership of Greece by making friends with Sparta's chief
Peloponnesian rival. Most of those who hold that Aeschylus looked
with favor on the Areopagus reforms assume that a poet who
complimented Argos and her alliance must also have sympathized
with the views in domestic politics of those who were responsible
for the Argive connection. But it does not follow that a poet who
makes a polite mention of an ally must necessarily share the attitude in internal matters of those who have promoted the alliance.
Organized political parties in the modern sense did not exist in
ancient Athens, and at this time the case for abandoning the old
friendship with Sparta and contracting one with Argos was strong;
it must have appealed to many Athenians who disagreed with the
domestic policies of its chief advocates but were capable of seeing the
strong arguments in terms of national self-interest that could be
urged in favour of this measure.

Let us now consider the words in which the Erinyes describe
their function in the government of the universe, and which are
later echoed by Athene in her charge to the Areopagus regarding
its function in the government of Athens. The element of terror is
necessary to the well-being of a state; neither anarchy nor despotism
is good; freedom must be tempered by the retention of some institution that has power to punish. As long as the Areopagus is there
to guard the land, waking while others sleep, Athens will have a
bulwark unequalled even by the Scythians and the Spartans, the
two peoples famed beyond others for the excellence of their laws
and for the readiness of their peoples to obey them.

Far from wishing to abolish the prerogatives of the Erinyes,
Athene is anxious to conserve them; so, evidently, does the poet
wish to conserve the functions of the Areopagus. But which of its
functions are in question? After the reforms of Ephialtes, the main
function left to the Areopagus was that of conducting trials for

murder. Those who hold that Aeschylus meant to express his approval of the reforms are constrained to argue that the function to which Athene attaches so much importance is simply that of preventing homicide. This is indeed a highly important function of a civilized state, and one which in the early stages is not achieved without a struggle. When studied carefully, however, Athene's speech seems rather to be concerned with the quality known as *Eunomia*, a word by which the Greeks denoted both the possession of good laws and the willingness of the citizens to observe them. In the universe the Erinyes are not merely the punishers of murder or of a special kind of murder, but the defenders of the universal order, of *Dike*, against any threat of disturbance; in the state of Athens the Areopagus had traditionally been, not merely a court to try murderers, but the protector of the constitution, the authority with power to punish that prevented freedom from turning into anarchy. Definite and conclusive proof is lacking, doubtless because it was not the poet's intention to provide it; one disputed passage that has often been taken to yield it does not do so (690–95; see note). But the concern of Athene with *Eunomia* seems to me to make it likelier than not that Aeschylus looked back with regret on the curtailment of the powers of the dignified institution that he presents with such respect. Not that he meant his play for a political tract aiming to persuade the citizens that the powers of the Areopagus should be restored. Rather, he pronounces a kind of splendid funeral panegyric on the Court in its capacity as guardian of the constitution. Athene solemnly warns her people against civil strife, reminding them that there is no lack of foreign enemies (858f; cf. 976f); the play and trilogy end on a note of peace and reconciliation, as the Erinyes, having assumed their aspect of Eumenides, "The Kindly Ones," bestow every kind of blessing upon the city that has dignified them with new honors.

# BIBLIOGRAPHY

### A.   TEXT WITH COMMENTARY.

No adequate commentary on *The Eumenides* exists in English. A Sidgwick's school edition (Aeschylus, *The Eumenides*, Oxford, 3rd ed., 1902), is useful.

### B.   VERSE TRANSLATIONS.

Richmond Lattimore, in Grene and Lattimore, *The Complete Greek Tragedies*, Chicago, 1953–
Robert Fagles, *Aeschylus: The Oresteia*, New York, 1975 (Penguin, 1977).

### C.   GENERAL

E. R. Dodds, *Morals and Politics in The Oresteia* (*The Ancient Concept of Progress*, Oxford, 1973, ch. III).
Anne Lebeck, *The Oresteia: a study in language and structure*, Washington, D.C., 1971.